Urban Development in India

Indian diaspora has had a complex and multifaceted role in catalyzing, justifying, and promoting a transformed urban landscape in India. Focusing on Kolkata/ Calcutta, this book analyzes the changing landscapes over the past two decades of one of the world's most fascinating and iconic cities. Previously better known due to its post-Independence decline into overcrowded poverty, pollution, and despair, in recent years, it has experienced a revitalization that echoes India's renaissance as a whole in the new millennium.

This book weaves together narratives of migration and diasporas, postmodern developmentalism and neoliberal urbanism, and identity and belonging in the Global South. It examines the rise of middle-class environmental initiatives and Kolkata's attempts to reclaim its earlier global status. It suggests that a form of global gentrification is taking place through which people and place are being fundamentally restructured. Based on a decade's worth of field research and investigation in multiple sites – metropolitan centers connected by long histories of empire, migration, economy, and culture – it employs a multi-method approach and uses ethnographic, semi-structured interviews as well as archival research for much of the empirical data collected.

Addressing urban change and policies, as well as spatial and discursive transformations that are occurring in India, it will be of interest to researchers in the fields of urban geography, urban and regional planning, environmental studies, diaspora studies, and South Asian studies.

Pablo Shiladitya Bose is Assistant Professor in the Department of Geography at the University of Vermont, Burlington, VT. He is an urban geographer and interdisciplinary scholar with interests in urbanization in the Global South, environmental displacement worldwide, and migration and refugee resettlement in North America.

Routledge Series on Urban South Asia
Edited by Henrike Donner
Oxford Brookes University, UK

The series showcases a wide range of disciplines that study processes of urbanization in globalizing South Asian cities and towns. It encompasses monographs as well as edited volumes, which address urban issues including urban lifestyles and subcultures, urban politics and economies, as well as planning regimes and policies in the context of contemporary South Asia.

Urban Development in India

Global Indians in the remaking of Kolkata

Pablo Shiladitya Bose

Routledge
Taylor & Francis Group

LONDON AND NEW YORK

First published 2015 by Routledge

2 Park Square, Milton Park, Abingdon, Oxfordshire OX14 4RN
711 Third Avenue, New York, NY 10017

Routledge is an imprint of the Taylor & Francis Group,
an informa business

First issued in paperback 2018

British Library Cataloguing in Publication Data
A catalogue record for this book is available from the British Library

Library of Congress Cataloging-in-Publication Data
Bose, Pablo S.
  Urban development in India : global Indians in the remaking of Kolkata /
Pablo Shiladitya Bose.
    pages cm. — (Routledge series on urban South Asia)
  Includes bibliographical references and index.
  1. City planning—India—Kolkata. 2. Urbanization—India—Kolkata.
3. East Indian diaspora. I. Title.
  HT169.I52K653 2015
  307.760954—dc23
  2014021432

ISBN: 978-0-415-73597-1 (hbk)
ISBN: 978-1-138-31903-5 (pbk)

Typeset in Times New Roman
by Apex CoVantage, LLC

This book is dedicated to my grandparents, Tripti and Amalendu Bose and Bina and Makhan Lal Roychoudhury.

Contents

Acknowledgements

A book based on research that spans a decade of fieldwork, reflection, and writing is not possible without the support and aid of a great many people. I would like to start by thanking my colleagues past and present at the University of Vermont, especially Glen Elder, Reecia Orzeck, Cheryl Morse, Matt Himley, Clayton Rosati, Meghan Cope, Rashad Shabazz, Susannah McCandless, Paul Martin, and Randall Harp. My work was challenged and shaped in its earliest and ongoing forms through many discussions with graduate school friends and colleagues from York University, particularly Traci Warkentin, Denver Nixon, Stephanie Rutherford, Jenny Kerber, Bruce Erickson, Leah Burns, Lenore Newman, and Bipasha Baruah. I have benefited from much guidance and inspiration from former professors and mentors, including Peter Penz, Liette Gilbert, Ilan Kapoor, Shubhra Gururani, Martin Laba, and Patricia Howard. I am also indebted to the support and encouragement of many others, especially Ananya Roy, John Wood, Bob Anderson, Elizabeth Chacko, Margaret Walton-Roberts, Jen Dickinson, and Sanjukta Mukherjee. The research on which the book is based has been funded at various times by the Social Sciences and Humanities Research Council of Canada, the International Development Research Centre, the Shastri Indo-Canadian Institute, the University of Vermont, and the Center for Global Geographic Education of the Association of American Geographers.

The fieldwork itself would not have been possible without considerable assistance from Susanta Ghosh, Anjan Ghosh, Manas Ray, and Partha Chatterjee at the Centre for Studies in Social Sciences, Calcutta, as well as from Indranil Chakraborty, Mohit Ray, Arijit Bannerjee, Ranabir Samaddar, and Asish Ghosh. Much of my thinking and reflecting on transnational linkages and processes has emerged out of many fruitful discussions with Jonah Steinberg, as well as by his own groundbreaking studies on street children in India and the Roma throughout Europe. I would also like to thank my research assistants, who have been instrumental in collecting background information and organizing my data, especially Elizabeth Wolfe, Tony Hollop, and Sameera Ibrahim. My editors with Routledge – Dorothea Schaefter, Jillian Morrison, and especially Rebecca Lawrence, as well as Henrike Donner, the series editor – have been of great help and even greater patience as this project has inched towards completion.

My observations of the transformations in contemporary Kolkata and India have been significantly enriched by the questions posed and opinions offered by friends and family – especially the extended Bose and Roychoudhury families in Kolkata, Bombay, and Delhi. I am also deeply grateful to the many informants who provided their time.

I received perhaps the greatest insight into my inquiries during the many times I spent during my first two fieldwork trips speaking with my grandmother about the changes taking place in the city she had lived in for so many decades. The final book that emerges out of this research enormously misses her perspective on the Kolkata that has continued to take shape since her passing.

My family in North America has also been central to the completion of this book. I have received much encouragement from the Laramee clan, even when they have not been quite sure what I have been working on. Various cats – Peanut, Mika, and Mishka – have helpfully positioned themselves on various keyboards during the writing process.

I thank my sister Sarika Bose for her constant love and support during this project. My mother, Mandakranta Bose, has been an inspiration and role model in her incredible capacity to take on a wealth of different kinds of research and initiatives. Finally, this book would have never come to its final form without the critical commentary, sage advice, and careful editing suggestions made by my father, Tirthankar Bose.

For opening up new possibilities of inquiry and a desire to put limits on seemingly boundless research questions, I thank my sweet daughter, Lily. And for putting up with so many absences; lending a thoughtful, insightful, and critical ear to the analysis; and giving me unwavering love, support, and the time needed to finish writing, I thank the lovely Alisha Laramee.

Abbreviations

EKW	East Kolkata Wetlands
EKWMA	East Kolkata Wetlands Management Authority
GoWB	Government of West Bengal
KEIP	Kolkata Environmental Improvement Project
KMC	Kolkata Municipal Corporation
KMDA	Kolkata Metropolitan Development Authority
NRI	Non-resident Indian
PIO	Person of Indian origin

1 Introduction

Calcutta[1] is a dying city. Kolkata is a city reborn. Kolkata is a fading city. Calcutta's time has come again. Calcutta is a provincial backwater. Kolkata is a global city on the rise. These are only a handful of the many descriptions I have heard over the years of the city in which I was born, in which I have lived only occasionally since my family left when I was a child, and to which I returned as an adult for a decade's worth of research into its most recent transformations. The city, it seems, is one that engenders strong opinions.

It is also a city with a negative reputation that is hard to shake. In an earlier era, it was one of the iconic centers of the British Raj. But a century of slow decline accelerated by post-Independence turmoil has created an image of a blighted urban landscape. Kolkata is most often associated across the globe with poverty, pollution, and unyielding despair – a city characterized by slums, brothels, and charity missions (Hutnyk, 1996). Kolkata is much more than this, of course – a city that remains vibrant, colourful, full of mystery and possibility, a touchstone for cultural traditions and practices, for intellectual inquiry, and a base for political movements both radical and reactionary. Despite my critical and sometimes jaundiced appraisal of its current evolutions, it is a city that I embrace and love.

This is a sentiment shared with many – though certainly not all – in the Indian Bengali diaspora, and it is that sense of attachment to an ancestral homeland, region, and place that is at the heart of this book. While some may choose to view the city through a nostalgic lens that valorizes its past glories, today's Kolkata is awash in new construction and energy, full of projects that celebrate contemporary global connections, international lifestyles, and opportunities. This new age has left many both in India and abroad eager to focus on an apparent revitalization of the city's fortunes, to emphasize an upward trajectory that echoes India's 'rising' star and renaissance in the new millennium. The last two decades have witnessed momentous changes in the city and the state of West Bengal, of which it is the capital, not least of which has been the end of decades of democratically elected Marxist-led governments. Despite the decline of leftist political parties, the development models they embraced of late have continued under their successors. Indeed, an almost two-decade-long form of neoliberal urbanism in Kolkata has led to a surge of investments in infrastructure, speculative land-grabbing, and – most importantly for the purposes of this book – the explosive growth of housing projects and facilities like malls with a self-described 'global' appeal. These changes, argue many of their most ardent proponents, are part and parcel of Kolkata's re-emergence on the global stage (*The Telegraph*, 2011).

The desire to remake itself as 'world class' is not a uniquely Kolkata conceit, of course. The race to achieve such distinction is a seemingly ubiquitous concern in many metropolitan regions. Yet it is not always clear how a city can regain its place in the race for fame and achieve prominence. It could be argued that there are a finite number of corporate headquarters, universities, stock exchanges, factories, convention centers, monumental buildings, and all else that supposedly make up a global city to be parcelled out across the globe. But despite its recent strides in attracting corporate businesses and brands, Kolkata remains secondary even in India when it comes to the global circuits of labour, capital, and finance that flow through cities like Mumbai, Bangalore, and Delhi – or Ahmedabad, Cochin, and Amritsar, for that matter. In this book, I am interested primarily, therefore, in the reason why – given the relatively smaller number of emigrants and return migrants compared to other Indian cases – the idea of Global India and Global Indians has played such a significant role in the recent transformations of Kolkata, as I argue it has. What might global connections mean to those promoting new projects in housing, conservation, and urban infrastructure development? What is spurring the growth in new developments, and at whose behest? For whom is the city being remade, and at what cost? *Urban Development in India* examines these questions by weaving together narratives of migration and diasporas, postmodern developmentalism and neoliberal urbanism, and identity and belonging in the Global South. The book is based on a decade's worth of ethnographic field research and investigation in multiple sites – primarily Kolkata but also a number of other 'global cities,' including Mumbai, Delhi, Toronto, Vancouver, New York, and London, metropolitan centers connected by long histories of empire, migration, economy, and culture. This study suggests that we must pay as much attention to the discursive power of global identities in the reshaping of such sites as we pay to the material and political economy of urban restructuring on the ground.

Key arguments

The central contention of this book is that it is the *idea* rather than the actual presence of Global Indians that is crucial to our understanding of what is taking place in Kolkata – and many other places in the world today. This is not to suggest that there are no diasporic Bengalis actually purchasing apartments in the new townships in the Wetlands in the east of the city or the former industrial areas in the west. It does not mean that Bengalis and other Kolkatans living elsewhere do not return to work in branch offices of international firms or that non-resident Indians (NRIs)[2] do not stroll beside locals in the malls, hotels, multiplexes, and restaurants that increasingly appear across the city. Such figures are present, and they are important. But to some degree their actual physical appearance and numbers are secondary to the significance of the ideas they embody – an affirmation of cosmopolitan values, the trappings of affluent lifestyles, and 'global' hybrid identities. A Kolkata that can be a welcome home to such bodies can potentially provide access for the city and its residents through specific occupational and consumption patterns to that kind of a globalized Indian lifestyle.

One could therefore be led to believe that the new developments in Kolkata are built with these imagined global bodies and their preferences in mind – luxurious, spacious, and modern new apartments to live in, free of the clutter, dust, dirt, and grime so often associated with the old city, conveniently accessible by subway or serviced by the new flyovers and highways that pass by the more congested parts of the metropolis to reach the newly renovated airport and beyond. According to the planners, developers, and politicians who promote such projects to diasporic Indians and local professionals, the new gated developments promise not only convenience of access but also all the amenities that can apparently support a global lifestyle. These include 'international-style' schooling to help produce "the next Bill Gates or David Beckham" (South City International School [SCIS], 2012), golf courses for networking, parks and ecotourism adventures for relaxation and to reconnect with the environment of the motherland, and shopping malls filled with familiar brands (both domestic and international). As my research suggests, while the presence of Indians living abroad validates the projects, it is the imagery of the Global Indian – a monolithic set of concepts explored in depth in Chapter 2 – that is crucial for mobilizing key actors and supporting material transformations in the city.

Urban Development in India suggests that the power of such ideas lies in their ability to catalyze, justify, and promote a transformed urban landscape through a complex and multifaceted set of processes, one befitting a 'world class' city and its denizens. For urban planners and politicians, an emigrant community and its desire to return to its roots can symbolize the metropolis' place in the network of global cities. For diasporas, the ability to return through physical, economic, political, or cultural presence is a form of recognition – that one can reconnect materially with one's homeland not as a tourist or occasional visitor but as a full (if transnational and transitional) participant in the lived city. For local communities, the challenge is sometimes a more complicated one – living in the ruins of Kolkata's tarnished legacy is not particularly desirable; a city with an ascendant reputation and material improvements is an understandably attractive alternative to the prevalent experience of living in a city where many things simply do not work (or at least not very well).

But many residents ask: at what cost is the city changing, who will bear the brunt of the transformations, and who will benefit from these changes? Many remain inconvenienced, for example, by increased traffic brought to a locality by new high-rise towers. Others find their access to local water bodies restricted as new users utilize land to placate the needs of new audiences. Yet others may find themselves disenfranchised and displaced in the new city – which raises serious questions about the intended beneficiaries of urban restructuring. In this book, I argue that what we are witnessing today in Kolkata is a form of global gentrification through which places and social relations are fundamentally restructured. At the same time, this study shows that the process is neither monolithic nor inevitable and highlights the ways in which local communities are able to adapt, resist, and transform the changes that they are part of.

The predicament of Kolkata, expressed most obviously as a struggle over space, is how to articulate a set of ideas and futures for the city. There are several important related issues at stake here: identity and globalization; nation and representation; social justice and rural-urban and peri-urban links; and the struggle over the meanings of 'home' and 'development.' In exploring these issues, I focus (through my conceptual discussion and case studies) on the involvement of diasporic communities in processes of development in putative or imagined homelands and the resulting consequences of such involvement. What might diasporic involvement (or invocations) mean for the actual transformations of the city?

Why Kolkata?

One might well ask whether Kolkata is the best example for such an inquiry. Bengal, while the point of origin of many migrants, does not have the reputation for out-migration as many other regions of India do, let alone the world, though the city has long been a launching-off point for many journeys abroad (Carter and Torabully, 2002). Compared with other metropolitan areas, it barely registers at the lower end of the list of the many rankings one finds today of world cities, whether by economy, culture, infrastructure, or many other measures outside of population (Liu and Taylor, 2011). And yet the processes at work in so-called alpha cities – from the heights achieved by New York and London, through the second tier (Hong Kong, Beijing, Tokyo, Paris, etc.) down to the third (São Paolo, Vienna, Madrid) are apparent in Kolkata – urban restructuring and gentrification, privatization of city services, attempts to attract global capital, investments in monumental events and buildings, and speculative housing developments, among others. The presence of a multicultural population is also often hailed as a marker of the global city. Indeed, the urban landscape of immigrant gateway cities like New York, Toronto, and Sydney has long been marked by ethnic enclaves like Chinatowns and Little Italys or the newer 'ethnoburbs' (Li, 2009) on the outskirts of Washington and Vancouver. In many cities of the Global South, a more recent phenomenon has been the emergence of gated communities and international-style townships meant to cater specifically to diasporas. We see examples of this in cities from Istanbul to Tegucigalpa, from Dubai to Manila, from Mexico City to Kingston, and many others. Postcolonial labour migrations have moved significant populations to metropolises, especially in the industrialized world, while remittances, investments, ideas, and bodies have moved in the other direction and in continual circuits of exchange.

The desire to attract diasporas 'back home' is thus a recurrent theme in many postcolonial cities. There are many examples that one might examine in this context – metropolises such as Hong Kong, Manila, Bangkok, New Delhi, Mumbai, and Singapore all have significant populations that have both emigrated and immigrated and also are important points of diasporic departure, arrival, and circulation. Many such urban centers have become particularly significant in the postcolonial era and especially during the recent period of increased economic and cultural integration. As Sassen (2001: 347–348) points out, global cities are strategic sites where transnational processes materialize in national territories and where international dynamics run through national, regional, and local institutional arrangements. In the process, global cities must "endogenize" or "syncretize" key processes and conditions that define the global economy (Sassen, 2001: 347).

One may well argue that Kolkata has had far less success than many other postcolonial cities in achieving global recognition or materializing these connections for a host of reasons that become clear in Chapter 5. But its desire to do so has become increasingly apparent, from wooing multinational corporations to set up offices in information technology (IT)–oriented townships, attracting foreign investment in the private sector, and joining with international partners for major initiatives like the Kolkata Environmental Improvement Project discussed at length in this book. In addition to such moves, this book argues, the idea of diasporic return also plays an important role in the city's rebirth, as evidenced, for example, in West Bengal Chief Minister Mamata Banerjee's announcement during the North American Bengali Conference in 2012 that she was setting up an NRI office to attract increased foreign investment (Sen Gupta, 2012). Much of this investment would be directed at Kolkata and its immediate surroundings, which becomes, therefore, an important site in which to examine the dynamics of diasporas in imagining globalized cities. In Kolkata, we have a secondary city desperate to regain its former standing, which it is attempting to do by drawing on discourses of migration, transnationalism, and return to catalyze its transformation and to imagine its renewal. The ensuing struggle to redefine identity, citizenship, and belonging in the city is what drew me to Kolkata in my own study of globalization and urbanization in the contemporary moment.

Situating myself

The research on which this book is based began as my dissertation fieldwork for an interdisciplinary PhD in the Environmental Studies Program at York University in Toronto, Canada. With support from the International Development Research Center, the Shastri Indo-Canadian Foundation, and the Social Sciences and Humanities Research Council of Canada, I embarked in 2004 on a year-long study – initially meant to examine diasporas and their ongoing connections to Gujarat and Kerala and to focus in particular on public infrastructure projects and rural development. I began with several initial weeks of fieldwork in several major Indian cities – notably Mumbai and Delhi – conducting interviews with civil servants, elected officials, businesspeople, and bankers (among others) to explore how both the state and private sector were trying to develop policies and mechanisms to better understand and essentially capture the seemingly 'untapped' developmental potential of diasporas. My time in these urban landscapes and visits to see family in Kolkata triggered a shift in my focus, however, as I realized that something equally significant was happening in the world of the Indian cities and to the cityscape itself. Globalization in its many forms was helping to reshape these sites, and the figure of the Global Indian was being mobilized in both principle and practice to help catalyze and legitimize these changes. Thus, I changed my study site and case to look at recent urban transformations in Kolkata in order to try to understand what 'global' might mean for a secondary postcolonial city striving to regain its past glory, whether and how Global Indians were implicated in this process, and what the resulting changes meant for Kolkatans themselves.

In the 10 years since my original fieldwork, I have returned to this field site twice for extended periods – in 2007 and again in 2012 – and continued an active research project on the region. This lengthy period of engagement has allowed me to step back and examine the multilayered process as a whole, as I have followed the reimagining of the city in the planning, building, and materialized phases. This has allowed me to study the evolution in the design and articulation of the new cityscape and its relationship with older institutions and cultural norms and witness a range of ongoing struggles of local residents over citizenship. Each of these visits has been shaped by political events related to the themes and sites of my research. Significantly, 2004 brought a change in government at the national level, with the defeat of the Hindu Nationalist–led coalition, whose "India Shining" campaign and explicit appeals to NRIs and global positioning fell flat at the polls. In 2007, my research was overshadowed by ongoing controversies surrounding the appropriation of land by the state government of West Bengal designated for the creation of export processing zones in the villages of Nandigram and Singur and the violence that followed (Sarkar and Chowdury, 2009). In 2012, West Bengal and Kolkata grappled with the transition from a Marxist-led coalition government, which had been in power for decades, to the new government formed under populist Trinamool Congress leader Mamata Banerjee, whose ascendance has been partly attributed to the aforementioned controversies over economic restructuring and land (Donner, 2011).

My immersion in the field sites throughout these periods has reinforced my interest in this case on both a personal and professional level. As an urban geographer and a migration scholar, I am fascinated by the intersections between diaspora, globalization, and the city. To someone with roots in Kolkata, what is happening to the place I sometimes call home is of equal interest. And as a diasporic individual myself, I embody some of the processes I was studying. The question of belonging and identity therefore has been a constant theme throughout the process of this research.

This is not to suggest that my background gives me an inherently unique insight into this topic or that my identity determines my analysis. As Nagar argues regarding the use of declarative statements about authorship and identity as a way of establishing bona fides:

> [this] demand needs to be challenged and resisted because uncovering ourselves in these terms contradicts our purpose of problematizing the dominant meanings attributed to pre-defined social categories – that is, social

categories that are not just essentialist or overly coherent, but a view of categories as existing prior to and isolated from specific interactions, rather than as created, enacted, transformed *in* and *through* those interactions.

(Nagar, 2002: 183)

I do not flash a diasporic identity as a way of legitimizing my analysis; I am employing it as a point of departure to explain particular perspectives. My fluency in Bengali and local idioms; my connections to a social network based around a middle-class, upper-caste family with deep roots in the city; and my levels of comfort as young, male, and mobile all allowed me to move in and out of a range of different spaces and interact with a multitude of respondents, from bureaucrats, bankers, educators, politicians, social workers, and journalists to informal labourers, construction workers, and farmers, among others.

My identity as a first-generation NRI also helps to explain my investment in exploring the topic of what is happening to Kolkata. I have never pretended to be a dispassionate observer of the different phenomena I study, and I agree with Scheyvens and Storey, who suggest that a participatory or interventionist orientation to fieldwork requires a "move beyond positivist assumptions about the neutral role of the researcher to more nuanced understandings of ways in which one's positionality, relationships and personality affect the research process" (2003: 8). My desire to understand the relationship between diasporas and development originated from a concern about the growing support that a number of parochial (at best) and regressive (at worst) movements active in India continue to receive from overseas Indian communities. On a different level, I was also curious to understand how material support – remittances sent back home to families, neighbours, communities, friends, and larger networks – might alter – perhaps radically – the social, ideological, and material characteristics of a particular place. This book is then an attempt to employ the question asked by a transnational solidarity network, the Association for India's Development – namely: "What kinds of developments in India are the Indians in the US (and other countries) making possible?" (Association for India's Development [AID], 2004). It turns out that in the context of Kolkata, as this book suggests, the answer is a complicated one.

Research methods

The approach that frames the research in *Urban Development in India* is both interdisciplinary and qualitative. It draws on economics and sociology to understand patterns of migration and transnational practices that connect diasporas with places of origin. I use the lenses of cultural studies and anthropology to explore the construction of global identities both informally and by the state and build on traditions in urban studies and geography to analyze the formation of global urban landscapes across the globe. Lastly, and significantly, I draw on political ecology to understand conflicts over environments and urban space in the Global South.

The empirical fieldwork on which this study of transformations in Kolkata is based consists of three primary sets of data – archival research, semi-structured interviews, and participant observation during site visits. The documentary analysis of archival material includes planning documents, maps and land records, reports from regulatory bodies, and technical studies and consultants' reports. Much of this research was conducted at the archives of the Kolkata Metropolitan Development Authority, at the offices of the Kolkata Environmental Improvement Project (KEIP), in the Indian Official Documents section of the National Library of India in Kolkata, as well as in its newspapers and periodicals collections, and at the offices of several state and private financial institutions. My particular focus was the long period from the 1950s to the 2000s of intense planning and preparation that preceded the development of the city's peri-urban fringes, especially the Wetlands, and the pursuit of the less obvious objective of recapturing Kolkata's past standing.

The over 100 semi-structured interviews conducted over a 10-year period fall into two categories. Those in the first group were conducted with key informants, including planners, politicians, developers, promoters, social activists, consular staff, civil servants, journalists, financial officials, construction workers, displaced canal dwellers, rag-pickers, agricultural workers, fishers, and academics, all of whom have direct and often expert knowledge of the transformations taking place in Kolkata. Among those I interviewed (as set out in greater detail in the following chapters) comprise the leadership of the East Kolkata Wetlands Management Authority; the KEIP; officials in the Ministry of External Affairs, NRI Branch (now the Ministry of Overseas Indian Affairs); and the Kolkata Metropolitan Corporation. A majority of key informants such as these asked to remain anonymous in publications of research results and are thus identified only by their organizations and occupations in this book.

I conducted a second set of interviews with a number of owners – resident and non-resident – of the housing projects that I have been studying. While I selected most of the first group because of their expertise, I located the respondents in my second set of interviews through snowball sampling methods, beginning by approaching residents' associations for various buildings. Those who chose not to be explicitly identified – some of the key informants along with all of the homeowners in the second set of interviews – are referred to by pseudonyms, as is common in the presentation of ethnographic and qualitative research (Dunn, 2010). Interviews were organized around a set of questions common to both groups, tailored for the specific context of either the informant's occupation/ position or the housing development of which he or she was a member. The semi-structured format allowed me to follow various lines of questioning that were raised within individual interviews as they emerged. Interviews with all respondents were analyzed and integrated into this book primarily to illustrate and illuminate specific issues regarding urban development in Kolkata – i.e. how individual organizations operate, details of notable events and processes, or reasons for purchasing a particular property.

Finally, all three of the fieldwork periods drawn on in this book included extensive site visits to multiple locations in and around Kolkata. These include proposed, in-progress, completed, and inhabited housing projects and townships (such as the newly completed Rajarhat); model units showcased by developers; and malls, schools, multiplexes, amusement parks, and other amenities associated with these projects. I also visited parks, ponds, and canals slated for improvement by the KEIP and farms, fisheries (both cooperative and private), villages, waste recycling sites, and landfills in the East Kolkata Wetlands. I was also able to spend significant amounts of time in other sites in India examining similar processes – global connections and the building of diaspora-focused housing, especially in Gurgaon, a township near New Delhi that is one of India's leading financial and industrial centers and home to many business process outsourcing (BPO) and IT-related firms. Another site where I spent considerable time was Bangalore, a South Indian city with a global reputation for much the same reasons but of additional interest because of connections to the Persian Gulf through different patterns of migration and return.

My site visits included the collection of promotional and advertising materials related to the various developments, visual documentation by way of over 1,500 photographs and 50 short video clips, and extensive field notes based on my impressions of each site. I developed portfolios for each of the sites by combining each of these forms of research, using documentary sources, interviews with informants, and field notes and images to create a narrative and history for each development site.

Outline of the book

Urban Development in India opens with three conceptual chapters to help establish the framework used to analyze the cases. Chapter 2, "Theorizing diaspora," contextualizes the attachments between homelands and émigrés, beginning with a brief overview of the increasing global recognition of overseas communities and continuing with an exploration of the relationship between India and its variously constituted peoples abroad. Once dismissed and distrusted as unpatriotic for abandoning their motherland and for seeking greener pastures abroad, the NRI and those of Indian origin have become darlings of politicians and public discourse. This chapter explores the emergence and reification of the figure of the Global Indian and problematizes the often myopic, monolithic, and ahistorical renderings of migration journeys from the subcontinent. It focuses in particular on the ways in which the Global Indian has been produced politically via policies regarding overseas citizenship and rights, as well as in terms of its representation through celebratory festivals and the media.

Chapter 3, "Transnational practices," focuses on the ways that diasporas might demonstrate their commitments to former homelands. I begin by exploring the relationship between migrants and transnationalism. I look closely at the long-distance nationalism expressed by political involvements, such as support for separatist and independence movements and for electoral parties. I also examine the economic arena of finance, remittances, investments, and philanthropy. I use the case of India's own entanglements with remittances to India in particular to illustrate some of the complexities and nuances that transnational practices might entail. In this context, the contradictory and pivotal role overseas Indians played in both sustaining and weakening the Indian economy prior to 1991's economic crisis is of particular interest. The chapter also examines some of the key initiatives launched by various governments to try to mobilize the overseas community (and their coffers) for development projects at home. Finally, I explore in detail the example of Kerala, an Indian state that is often discussed globally as a model of a remittance-based economy for the benefits that Gulf money has brought to the region and the vulnerabilities to external conditions that such a reliance and interconnection can create.

Since so much attention in this book is paid to the attempts by Kolkata to regain 'global' status, Chapter 4, "Building a global city," is devoted to understanding the aspiration for Kolkata to become such a city. This includes defining the concept of the 'world city' as it emerged in the 1980s among urban and Marxist geographers in particular. I also explore the critique that world city theory has engendered, particularly as advanced by postcolonial urban scholars who have promoted the concept of the 'ordinary city' as an antidote to what they see as an obsessive focus on structure. In addition to the theoretical framework of the global city, in this chapter I also review some of the major processes by which such a new city is built. To that end, I explore the concept first of gentrification and next its expansion on a world stage through the idea of global gentrification. I am especially interested in the notion of a 'global gentrifier class' and whether this might be an accurate way of describing the catalytic and transformative role of diasporas in my case studies. I shift in the final part of this chapter to a discussion of the potential for Kolkata to be seen as a diaspora city: if it is indeed to become a global player once again through mobilizing the bodies and life spaces of diasporas, can Kolkata actually engender strong sentiments in its overseas Indian communities?

Chapter 5, "The context of Kolkata," turns our attention to the city at hand. The rise and fall of Calcutta has been described by some urban scholars as a paradigmatic case of urban decay. Its initial founding and its flourishing during the era of the British Raj were intimately tied to colonial designs and desires. Somewhat paradoxically, it also became the heart of both an intense regional movement and a nascent anti-colonial uprising. This chapter describes both this early history and especially the impact of the post-Independence period on the city and its struggle to retain coherence and relevance in the face of ongoing upheavals. The other sections of this chapter are devoted to the most recent decade in Kolkata's evolution, in particular its renaissance during India's general growth during the post-liberalization era.

The final three chapters of *Urban Development in India* present specific cases through which we can observe 'globality' remaking various parts of Kolkata. Chapter 6, "The East Kolkata Wetlands," focuses on the East Kolkata Wetlands, the last vestiges of once-extensive wetlands that stretched across what represents the few remaining green spaces near the metropolis. The chapter details the Wetlands' social and ecological significance for the city and the contested nature of their current development and/or protection. It reviews the history of reclamation and urbanization in the area, with a focus on the building of IT- and global industry–focused townships. The chapter also closely examines the growth of illegal construction in conservation areas and the clash between environmental groups, developers, local politicians, and state regulators (among others) over the present and future of the Wetlands.

Chapter 7, "The Kolkata Environmental Improvement Project," continues to explore the struggle over the right to define and demarcate different spaces of Kolkata by focusing on a $400 million effort to update Kolkata's sewage and drainage infrastructure and other environmental projects throughout the city. The chapter opens with a discussion of environmental concerns as a driving force behind urban renewal and the ideology of developmentalism. I use the lens of bourgeois environmentalism to consider the winners and losers of such a process. I explore the structure and purpose of the initiative, with a focus on three particular components. The first is the renovation and rehabilitation of urban parks and water bodies for educational and leisure purposes. The second is the clearing of canals, the resulting displacement of informal settlements, and the building of compensatory social housing for those displaced by the process. The final example is the proposed conversion of a large section of the previously discussed East Kolkata Wetlands into a site for ecotourism and environmental education. As this chapter shows, the project's many facets are marked by an insistence on 'international environmental standards' and appeals to the sensibilities of NRIs.

The last of the case study chapters, Chapter 8, "New housing developments: global living in Kolkata," maps the 'international' style and appeal meant to symbolize the global connections at the heart of this book – namely, large international housing projects. The chapter catalogues the range of projects envisioned to give a sense of just how much of a transformation is taking place in Kolkata right now. I then go on to discuss the particular appeal to the Global Indian in the selling and advertising of such projects. The three cases discussed have courted different kinds of controversy in their time and have all achieved different levels of success. The first is the Kolkata West International Township built on the western edge of the city in former industrial lands, funded in part by a consortium of NRIs and Indonesian capital. The second is the Vedic Village gated complex of spas and luxury eco-bungalows built deep into the heart of the Wetlands and meant to combine the 'best of east and west.' The last is the highly successful South City project of apartment towers dominating the skyline of the southern residential neighbourhoods, along with an enormous mall and other amenities. This chapter explores the ways in which these three projects epitomize the desire to 'go global' and to entice diasporas and locals alike with an international aesthetic by populating the living space with multinational brands, franchises, and amenities. Each case has had its own share of controversies and opposition; this chapter also details some of the responses by local communities to the building of these projects on their doorstep. It is through these conceptual arguments and the analysis of field research that *Urban Development in India* examines a critical period in India's investment in a global scheme of living valorized both within India and abroad.

Notes

1 While used interchangeably here, in general I use Calcutta to refer to the city prior to its current transformations – approximately beginning in 1997 – and Kolkata to refer to its newest incarnation. The actual official name change occurred in 2001.
2 The term 'NRI' (as is explored in greater detail in the following chapter) is used by the Indian government to describe an Indian citizen living abroad. It is often used colloquially within India and abroad, however, to describe what I am calling 'Global Indians' – persons of either Indian citizenship or ancestry residing outside of India.

References

Association for India's Development (AID) (2004). "Association for India's Development projects: rights and social justice, your voice counts." Retrieved January 10, 2004, from http://www.aidindia.org/hq/misc/vcounts/voice_counts.shtml.

Carter, M. and K. Torabully (2002). *Coolitude: an anthology of the Indian labour diaspora*. London, Anthem.

Donner, H. (2011). "Locating activist spaces: the neighbourhood as a source and site of urban activism in 1970s Calcutta." *Cultural Dynamics* 23(1): 21–40.

Dunn, K. (2010). Interviewing. *Qualitative Research Methods in Human Geography*. I. Hays. Oxford, Oxford University Press.

Hutnyk, J. (1996). *The rumour of Calcutta: tourism, charity and the poverty of representation*. London, Zed Books.

Li, W. (2009). *Ethnoburb: the new ethnic community in urban America*. Honolulu, University of Hawai'i Press.

Liu, X. and P.J. Taylor (2011). "Research note – a robustness assessment of global city network connectivity rankings." *Urban Geography* 32(8): 1227–1237.

Nagar, R. (2002). "Footloose researchers, 'traveling' theories, and the politics of transnational feminist praxis." *Gender, Place and Culture* 9(2): 179–186.

Sarkar, T. and S. Chowdhury (2009). "The meaning of Nandigram: Corporate land invasion, people's power, and the Left in India." *Focaal* 2009(54): 73–88.

Sassen, S. (2001). *The global city: New York, London, Tokyo*. Princeton, NJ, Princeton University Press.

Scheyvens, R. and D. Storey, Eds. (2003). *Development fieldwork: a practical guide*. Thousand Oaks, CA, Sage Publications.

Sen Gupta, T. (2012). "Mamata Banerjee to launch NRI cell in West Bengal to woo foreign investment." *The Economic Times*. Retrieved March 15, 2014, from http://articles.economictimes.indiatimes.com/2012–07–10/news/32618403_1_nri-cell-amit-mitra-finance-ministry.

South City International School (SCIS) (2012). "South City International School." Retrieved March 8, 2014, from http://scis.co.in.

The Telegraph (2011). "Wheel deal with eye on London." *The Telegraph* Online. Retrieved March 16, 2014, from http://www.telegraphindia.com/1110601/jsp/calcutta/story_14056417.jsp.

2 Theorizing diaspora

The figure of the Global Indian is central to the transformations of Kolkata explored in this book. But such a term can be taken to mean many things – those Indians living in India who adopt cosmopolitan lifestyles and attitudes, for example, or those who engage in any of a number of transnational practices. What I imply by 'Global Indian' is something quite different, however; my focus is on the identity formations associated primarily with Indians abroad, whether non-resident citizens of India or people of Indian ancestry living outside of India. This chapter examines the ways in which the idea of 'Global Indians' has developed, using in particular the concept of *diaspora* to explore the complicated and often contradictory ways in which belonging and borders intersect in the politics and beliefs of migrant bodies. I begin by defining what I mean by diaspora, a term often synonymous with transnationalism, but one that has its own particular origins and debates regarding its usage. With that definition made clear, I next review some of the patterns of migration that have led Indians abroad historically and in the contemporary period, going on to describe in particular detail some of the difficulties in identifying a Global Indian population. Despite such challenges, the Indian state and the culture industries (both within the subcontinent and abroad) have devoted significant energy to detailing, discussing, representing, and wooing Indians abroad, a process that involves both cultural and political work – often overlapping in style and substance. In this chapter, I look at a few examples of each – an annual celebration of overseas Indians hosted by the Central Government of India and an initiative to extend overseas citizenship to Global Indians as a way to cement the ties between the diaspora and India, as well as the increasing significance of Global Indians as social icons in both domestic and diasporic film and literature.

Defining and debating diasporas

Diasporas have – especially in the postcolonial era – drawn the attention of diverse groups. Politicians, economists, scholars, novelists, community activists, security services, and many others have become increasingly interested in the ties that migrants now and in the past have maintained with their countries of origin. Diasporas confound tidy notions of linear migration, of nationalism, borders, and citizenship, exhibiting as they do attachments to distant lands, different cultures, or distinct identities. The concept of diaspora has at its core the idea of dispersal, whether voluntary or coerced. While the earliest uses of the term were in reference to the colonization efforts of Greek city–states, diaspora has come to be predominantly associated with Jewish exile from the Middle East, the transatlantic slave trade of Africans, and the forced displacement of Armenians and Palestinians due to genocide and the loss of a homeland (Cohen, 1997). It is that sense of loss and yearning for a return to an ancestral or perhaps imagined home that is often a central part of the identity of many groups who find themselves living 'abroad.'

Terms such as transnational, émigré, immigrant, and expatriate have also been used synonymously, despite the fact that they may describe very different forms of movement (Gilmartin, 2008). For many migration scholars, the conflation is a troubling one. Ong (2003) argues that equating contemporary mobilities associated with globalization with forms of permanent exile trivializes the political implications of the latter. In this view, it is the lack of voluntariness in movement that should be seen as *the* defining characteristic of diaspora, if the word is to have analytic importance in its meaning. Others caution that such a reading of the concept may be too narrow and rigid or may rely on weighing one cause of dispersal against another, resulting in what Walsh (2003) argues would amount to a ranking of systems of oppressions. This might lead in turn to a distinction between 'true' diasporas – caused by slavery, genocide, or anti-Semitism – versus what she calls "diaspora lite" (Walsh, 2003: 5) – those forcibly relocated by economic privation or a changing cultural landscape. Not only are such determinations open to considerable interpretation, but they also imply the creation of potentially troubling hierarchies between migrant identities. Walsh therefore suggests that both political and intellectual rankings in understanding diasporas should be resisted.

My own use of the term 'diaspora' in this book recognizes that while there are often very different reasons for leaving, communities that might be identified as diasporic in nature share some common and identifiable traits. In particular, they express a belief in an original homeland – whether an imaginary, ancestral, or more contemporary one – from which they have been exiled or from which they have left voluntarily and to which they often wish to return or at least remain connected to. Regardless of the reasons for leaving, these communities retain a distinct identity – expressed through the retention of language and cultural traditions, including food, literature, and music; social structures of family and kinship; and an ongoing political concern for their homeland – while living in a new home. In many ways, the existence of diasporas undermines the assimilationist view of immigration and acculturation processes in multicultural societies of the Global North. Ho (2008) suggests that the transnational practices of diasporas challenge traditional understandings of citizenship itself. The existence of diasporas also suggests that "persistent ethnicity" remains a key feature for those who migrate to the US, Canada, Australia, and similar countries (Portes and Rumbaut, 2006). Far from stripping away the baggage and background of their places of origin, the migration process and immersion into a new dominant culture can simultaneously reinforce roots in an old home and the forging of ties to a new one. Hall (1994: 396) offers an influential definition of the diasporic experience as one that should be understood

> [not] by essence and purity, but by the recognition of a necessary heterogeneity and diversity; by a conception of "identity" that lives with and through, not despite, difference; by hybridity. Diaspora identities are those which are constantly producing and reproducing themselves anew, through transformation and difference.

Gilroy (2000: 23) builds on this definition by arguing that

> the idea of diaspora offers a ready alternative to the stern discipline of primordial kinship and rooted belonging. It rejects the popular image of natural nations spontaneously endowed with self-consciousness, tidily composed of uniform families: those interchangeable collections of ordered bodies that express and reproduce absolutely distinctive cultures as well as perfectly formed heterosexual pairings. As an alternative to the metaphysics of "race," nation, and bounded culture coded into the body, diaspora is a concept that problematizes the cultural and historical mechanics of belonging. It disrupts the fundamental power of territory to determine identity by breaking the simple sequence of explanatory links between place, location, and consciousness.

For cultural critics like Gilroy and Hall, diaspora is a useful concept in opening up the question of identity beyond the particularities and atavisms of static, essentialized Selves, brought into clear definition by stark definition to the cultural practices and mores of ambiguous Others. Instead, diaspora can be a starting rather than an endpoint, a node of intersection between physical, cultural, and economic spaces. I follow Mavroudi's (2007) lead in using diaspora in this book as a way of moving beyond the dichotomy between bounded and unbounded definitions of transnational identity.

Out-migration and the difficulties of identifying an Indian diaspora

If diaspora is the central concept in understanding global lives in this book, is there a particularly Indian diaspora that one can identify as a catalyst and actor in the dynamics under study? If so, how has it been constituted? Where is it located? Unlike the spread of Chinese labour and trading communities across the globe historically, movement out of the Indian subcontinent has been uneven. Indeed, for many years, cultural and religious prohibition meant that leaving the physical space of early India was limited. As early as the classical and medieval periods, we can see migration in the form of trading communities in East Africa and Central Asia, Roma journeys out into Europe, Buddhist missionaries in China and Indonesia, and Hindu kingdoms all throughout Southeast Asia, but in far smaller numbers than the Chinese equivalents (Sahoo, Baas, and Faist, 2012). In the modern era, scholars have identified the following major flows when considering movement out of India and the subcontinent more generally (Jain, 2011; Brown, 2006; Landy, Maharaj, and Mainet-Valleix, 2004):

- merchants and traders to East Africa or Southeast Asia prior to the sixteenth century;
- traders, farmers, and labourers to neighbouring countries (such as Sri Lanka or Nepal) from the pre-colonial era through the modern period;
- indentured labourers during the colonial period to various corners of the British Empire, such as the Caribbean, Fiji, Mauritius, and South Africa;
- contract labour (through the kangani and maistry systems) to Burma, Malaysia, and Sri Lanka via familial or village middlemen;
- emigrants, especially Sikhs from Punjab, settling in the Pacific Northwest of North America during the late nineteenth and early twentieth centuries for work, primarily in the agricultural and resource sectors;
- skilled and unskilled workers filling labour shortages in countries such as the United Kingdom following the Second World War;
- contract workers, especially from western Indian states such as Kerala to the Gulf countries following Independence;
- secondary or 'double' migrations of populations of Indian descent, such as the forced expulsions from East Africa in the 1970s and conflict-induced displacements from Sri Lanka and Fiji in the 1980s and 1990s;
- the migration of technical and knowledge workers from the mid-1960s onwards to the Global North, especially North America;
- an increase in migration from India to the US (both skilled and unskilled labour) from the 1990s onwards.

The actual presence of populations in some form connected to the Indian subcontinent – as well as the difficulties in making such determinations – can be found in a report by a High-Level Committee that was tasked with making such an assessment by the Bharatiya Janata Party (BJP)–led government in the early 2000s. The committee estimated the numbers of the overseas Indian population worldwide as given in Table 2.1.

Such numbers and patterns have produced a highly diverse and complex range of communities that can claim – or can be claimed to be – Indian in origin, ethnicity, or identity. While large populations exist in the Global North, in countries like Canada, the US, Australia, and the United Kingdom, they project a perhaps outsized influence and image relative to the even greater numbers in India's neighbouring countries. The potential economic and political significance of the Indian diaspora has meant that who they are and what they do is of increasing importance to the Indian governments at the federal, state, and local levels. But who is and who is not part of this imagined set of groupings? Depending on one's perspective and definition, the Indian diaspora could be estimated at anywhere between 18 and 40 million people worldwide (Singhvi, 2001). The wide discrepancy in figures

Table 2.1 Selected countries' diasporic Indian populations

Country	Persons of Indian Origin (PIOs)	Non-Resident Indians (NRIs) (Indian Citizens)	Stateless	Total
Australia	160,000	30,000	–	190,000
Bahrain	–	130,000	–	13,000
Canada	700,000	150,000	1,000	851,000
Fiji	336,579	250	–	336,829
Guyana	395,250	100	–	395,350
Kenya	85,000	15,000	2,500	102,500
Kuwait	1,000	294,000	–	295,000
Malaysia	1,600,000	15,000	50,000	1,665,000
Mauritius	704,640	11,116	–	715,756
Myanmar	2,500,000	2,000	400,000	2,902,000
Netherlands	200,000	15,000	2,000	217,000
Oman	1,000	311,000	–	312,000
Qatar	1,000	130,000	–	131,000
Reunion Islands	220,000	55	–	220,055
Saudi Arabia	–	1,500,000	–	1,500,000
Singapore	217,000	90,000	–	307,000
South Africa	–	–	–	1,000,000
Suriname	150,306	150	–	150,456
Trinidad and Tobago	500,000	600	–	500,600
United Arab Emirates	50,000	900,000	–	950,000
United Kingdom	–	–	–	1,200,000
US	–	–	–	1,678,765
Yemen	100,000	900	–	100,900

Source: Singhvi, 2001: xlvii

has much to do with how one defines membership; the numbers include Indian citizens living outside the country, those who have emigrated directly/recently from India but no longer retain citizenship, and those who have Indian or mixed-Indian heritage.

Yet many to whom the Indian government might grant (or wish to grant) familial status do not themselves necessarily claim membership in the Indian diaspora. For example, there are some descendants of indentured labourers in the Caribbean or trading classes who migrated to East Africa and were then forcibly expelled and who resettled in North America. Some of these groups identify more with their more recent 'homes' than a primordial one. An ethnographic account by Mani and Varadarajan (2008) of the first *Pravasi Bharatiya Diwas* (PBD) or Overseas Indian Day held in New Delhi in 2003 recounts the resistance of some attendees – especially South African and Fijian – to their interpellation as Indian. They further report that other attendees criticized attempts to gather the diverse participants into one large 'family' tent in ways that ignored or attempted to subsume both historical and contemporary divisions along racial, class, gender, or caste lines by appealing to a mythical Indian identity.

Similarly, in their examination of the potential for building economic relationships between India and South Africans of Indian descent (a currently negligible set of flows), Landy, Maharaj, and Mainet-Valleix (2004) note that while there are identifiable and visible Indian identity formations among the latter, these are highly fragmented and differentiated by geographic, caste, religious, and class distinctions. A singular Indian identity has been difficult to forge or maintain, though "neo-Indian Creole" formations have emerged (Landy, Maharaj, and Mainet-Valleix, 2004: 206). India remains a key referent for South Africans who trace their origins to the subcontinent but do so mainly by conceiving India as an idealized space, not as one that they engage with materially and actively.

Compounding such complexities is the manner in which the Indian state launched its first attempts to embrace and entice its diaspora in the new millennium to engage (primarily economically) with the old country. In the global citizenship schemes discussed in the next section, South Africans of Indian descent were conspicuous by their absence, as Dickinson and Bailey (2007) point out in their study of the politics of dual citizenship, the tactics of transnational governance, and the geographies of inclusion and exclusion. In her later and ongoing study of the South African case, Dickinson (2012) suggests that as a way of rectifying the oversight and the inability to mobilize an effective diasporic linkage to this site, there has been a conscious attempt to rewrite colonial histories by the Indian government, binding the two closer through a shared history of anti-colonial struggle – albeit one that requires considerable amnesia about other parts of the relationship. This is not to imply that there are no ties between Indians of South African origin and India. As Dickinson argues,

> The links that governments foster with their overseas populations entail more than managing material flows of people, money, skills and ideas: it involves a performative staging of the temporalities that tie (or indeed, untie) people in diasporas both to national entities and to each other. Just because diasporic affiliations and practices may not articulate exactly with government diaspora agendas does not mean that their particular histories and identities are made invisible or subsumed. Rather, we need to be aware that the government's narration of how their multiple diasporic communities "belong" to a homeland is an ongoing process of inclusion and exclusion that shifts according to multiple external and internal conditioning forces.
>
> (Dickinson, 2012: 620)

Moreover, being counted as part of the diaspora may not always be a choice and might have possible negative consequences. Ong (2003) illustrates such a situation with the case of ethnic Chinese communities in Indonesia who, while welcoming support from the global Chinese diaspora against the attacks and scapegoating it faced from the Indonesian military and media during the East Asian financial crisis, did not necessarily consider themselves to be ethnic Chinese or possessing hyphenated identities but rather saw themselves as Thai, Malaysian, Indonesian, etc., first and foremost. Being identified primarily through their Chinese identity only reified their position as eternal outsiders and contributed to ongoing accusations of disloyalty and national 'impurity' along ethnic/racial lines (Ong, 2003: 95–97).

Being precise when speaking of the Indian diaspora may therefore be difficult. How does one enumerate membership? By census data? If so, does nationality become the determining factor? Yet diasporas are not synonymous with the nation state, and using census data is a poor way of aligning the various parts of the diasporic identity – region, language, ethnicity, and culture being only a few of these – with diasporic membership. Some overseas communities certainly identify with a particular nation state, but many do not, preferring a primary affiliation with a family, kin-group, region, hometown, or even neighbourhood. Counting an Indian diaspora by using census figures, as the High-Level Committee has done, might be possible, but how would one find and measure a Punjabi, Gujarati, or Bengali diaspora? What might we miss about the social structures, networks, and affiliations of particular communities by aggregating them under the broad umbrella of national identities? As Prashad argues at a broader level, the tendency to conflate national and broader regional origins has had the effect – in the US at least – of rendering invisible the migration experiences and especially the prejudices and hardships endured:

> India is present today in the body of the Indians and others from the South Asian subcontinent, who now number 1.4 million in the United States. But these people are not all "Indians." Many are from Pakistan, Bangladesh, India, Sri Lanka, Bhutan, the Maldives, Africa, England, Canada, Fiji, or the Caribbean, and many are born and bred within the United States. The stain of ancestry and the hegemony of the word "India" remains with us as we seek to make our own way through the morass of the contemporary world.
> (Prashad, 2000: 2)

A singular focus for observers of Global Indians both at home and abroad creates a myopia, whether it is of past voyages of indenture (Carter and Torabully, 2002), internal migration of temporary agricultural workers (Rogaly, 2009), or the exploitation of migrant labour in the Gulf countries (Buckley, 2012). Perhaps one of the enduring aspects of the dominant mythology of the Global Indian is its exclusionary nature. In her study of the production of middle-class Indian subjectivities in Dubai, Vora (2008) argues that labour diasporas in the Gulf tend to be absent or invisible in much of the discussion of emigration from India. Her examination of discrimination, racism, and the adoption of certain modes of consumer culture by professional (though not elite) Indian migrants reveals a complicated and often contradictory sense of attachment to place. Vora's respondents are irrevocably alien in largely closed Gulf societies, yet find that their experiences have little resonance or familiarity within the larger diasporic narratives replayed both in India and abroad, which predominantly recount the stories of software engineers, doctors, lawyers, academics, and entrepreneurs.

Prashad (2000) and like-minded critics caution that a narrow focus on elite diasporas can have serious political implications within host countries. Indians have become an integral element in the 'model minority' theory that lauds the socioeconomic successes of certain Asian groups (primarily Indian and Chinese) to the detriment of other marginalized populations (especially African-American and Hispanic groups in the US). The model minority thesis has been embraced not only by conservative groups in the US to argue against affirmative action and minority rights but also by many within the Indian (and other Asian) diasporas as well (Shah, 2014). Indeed, Prashad argues that the recruitment of Indian diasporas in the condemnation of other minorities has been used as a "perpetual solution to what is seen as the crisis of black America . . . a weapon in the war against black America" (2000: 6). For many who subscribe to the 'model minority' perspective, the apparently seamless integration of middle-class Indian professionals into North American and European societies is proof not only of their adaptability but also, more importantly, of the failures of certain other minorities to achieve the same success. People of Indian origin are, in this reading, characterized as hardworking, entrepreneurial, intelligent, and/or willing and able to be educated; in other words, the antithesis of those 'troublesome' immigrants and minorities who have long been depicted as lazy, grasping, and needy (Prashad, 2000: 3–6). Their apparent over-representation within the fields of education, science, and technology, especially the information technology (IT) industry, is often referenced by their use of specialized immigration mechanisms such as the H1-B program in the US (Sahoo, Sangha, and Kelly, 2010). The growth of the information economy in India and the increasing influence of Indian diasporas and NRIs within centers such as Silicon Valley have helped to produce what Radhakrishnan (2011) describes as a small but significant transnational class of professionals who actively engage in creating notions of a cosmopolitan and interconnected India. Their identity is primarily one of affluence and links Silicon Valley and Bangalore through social networks.

The perception of Indian diasporas abroad is not, of course, static or perhaps even stable. Racist stereotypes of Indians as cab drivers and corner-store clerks remain highly visible, especially in popular culture. And following the September 11, 2001, terrorist attacks in New York City, the discourse of racialized securitization has often overwhelmed celebratory chords of globalization, and diasporic Indians often find themselves lumped into the category of 'threatening' dark-skinned Others, not only in the US but also in many other countries. Attacks – both verbal and physical – on Sikhs and South Asians in general have increased. People of South Asian origin find themselves swept up in supposedly random security raids by police or under suspicion when taking flying lessons or buying garden fertilizer. Even for brown-skinned high-tech millionaires, doctors, lawyers, and other professionals, navigating airport and border security becomes an exercise in frustration and fear. Bhatia and Ram (2009) reveal a wide range of such anxieties in their interviews with middle-class professionals living in the US and their concerns about being misidentified as terrorists.

If one steps back from the narrow view of the Indian diaspora – and keeping in mind that not all would agree to be labeled as such – there are some broad patterns of migration, settlement, and identification that one can discern. They have followed, for the most part, colonial connections – first to the former or affiliated territories of the British Empire, later to other areas of the postcolonial and globalizing world. The US, UK, Australia, and Canada all have large NRI/ person of Indian origin (PIO) populations but are closely matched in size by Myanmar and Malaysia combined. Caribbean and African countries also continue to house large numbers of the Indian diaspora as well. The countries of the Persian Gulf have among the most restrictive standards globally in terms of allowing naturalization and citizenship. However, while these settlement patterns might suggest a truly 'global' reach for the Indian diaspora – situated in multiple locations, leaving from diverse trajectories, working in different occupations, and assuming a range of identities – I discuss in the following pages the ways in which particular narratives of the Global Indian have come to dominate political initiatives and cultural representations alike.

Producing Global Indians politically

That Indian governments at all levels today wish to woo diasporic Indians is clear. This is a marked and, some might suggest, a profound change. In the post-Independence era, Nehru intimated that emigrants' loyalties should be first and foremost to their countries of settlement, not to those of departure. Edwards (2008), in her discussion of the genealogy of Global Indians, describes 1950–1980 as a period of limited engagement by India with its diasporas, considering the latter irrelevant at best and disloyal at worst. By the late 1970s and early 1980s, with the Indian economy spiralling out of control, Global Indians – especially NRIs, their remittances, and their bank deposits – became increasingly important for keeping their country afloat. When, as a result of a series of crises by the late 1980s, the Indian economy finally crashed and Global Indians pulled their deposits, NRIs became a target for much domestic blame and ire (Nayyar, 1994). A quarter-century later, however, Global Indians and NRIs have been considerably reha-bilitated. What has transpired during this time to change the perception and position of Global Indians so much? In the final sections of this chapter, I will explore how this development has unfolded as a political and cultural process.

The rehabilitation of Global Indians from 'those who left' to 'those whose return we desire' has been a long and slow process. A first step in the modern era, says Edwards (2008), was the gradual transformation of the category of 'overseas Indian' into that of 'non-resident Indian.' In this process, the depiction of Indians overseas changed from those who left for work, education, family reunification, or other motives in the colonial and post-Independence period, never to return, to those retaining significant and sustainable ties to their country of origin. The increasing economic success of some segments of the Indian diaspora – affluent Gujaratis in New Jersey or London, for example – brought their wealth and influence to the attention of the central government. On a global scale, India's historic lack of engagement with its diaspora also stood in stark contrast to China's extended networks with overseas populations. This became ever more apparent as the newly 'business-friendly' China of the late 1990s rapidly extended its reach into new markets and regions (Zhu, 2007).

As early as the late 1970s, the Indian central government's policies towards its diasporas began to change and become less restrictive. In part, this reflected its dependence on diasporic capital in foreign currency, as detailed in the next chapter. But increasingly, the cultural and political significance of the Indian diaspora – engaging with ancestral or imagined homelands through travel, remittances, political support, or any of a number of other forms – began to intensify the relationship. While the Indian state has undertaken a number of reforms and adopted a range of policies designed to embrace the Global Indian diaspora, I will focus on just one important illustrative example in this chapter: the annual PBD or Overseas Indian Day initiated by the coalition government led by the Hindu Nationalist BJP and held in New Delhi in January 2003. Mani and Varadarajan (2008) describe the PBD as a combination of nationalist re-imaginings of diasporic networks, an opportunity for sales and marketing pitches, and an extravagance of cultural displays and representations. It is, in their view, the perfect intersection of nationalism, neoliberalism, and diaspora; the PBD illustrates the "new historical, political and cultural relationship between the Indian state and diasporic populations in the early twenty-first century" (Mani and Varadarajan, 2008: 45).

In his opening speech to the conference, then–Prime Minister Vajpayee made clear that the linkage between émigrés and development was both recognized by and made a priority for the Central Government of India. He thanked members of the Indian diasporic community for their contributions to intellectual, financial, cultural, and political developments throughout the world. He also suggested that members of the Indian diaspora played an important role as ambassadors of goodwill for the Indian state. He reassured his audience that India had a positive investment climate and was firmly entrenched on a path towards modernization and equitable development but emphasized that it was not only the wealth of the diaspora that was so attractive to the Indian state. Vajpayee repeatedly exhorted émigrés to return to India – in spirit if not in body:

> I have always been conscious of the need for India to be sensitive to the hopes, aspirations and concerns of its vast diaspora. We invite you, not only to share our vision of India in the new millennium, but also to help us shape its contours. We do not want only your investment. We also want your ideas. We do not want your riches, we want the richness of your experience. We can gain from the breadth of vision that your global exposure has given you.
>
> (Vajpayee, 2003)

Vajpayee also mentioned several rewards for the Indian diaspora's support for the Indian state over a period of tumultuous economic and political change.

Two years earlier, the Government of India had created an NRI and PIO division within its Ministry of External Affairs. The Indian central government also established a High-Level Commission on Indian Diaspora, whose policy recommendations as released in January 2003 proposed the extension of dual citizenship rights to NRI and PIO individuals – though initially only to those residing in the US, Canada, the European Union, Singapore, Australia, and New Zealand, excluding diasporas in Africa, the Middle East, and the Caribbean (Lakhilal, 2003). After much protest and criticism of these exclusions, the Manmohan Singh coalition government elected in 2004 amended the Citizenship Act of 1955 and the Citizenship Rules of 1956 in order to offer diasporic Indians "Overseas Citizenship of India" (OCI), as long as their country of residence allowed dual citizenship. Such citizenship would afford holders a lifelong multiple-entry visa and exemptions from having to register with the government during a long-term stay in India. However, the OCI does not cover diasporic individuals who left the country before 1950 and further denies holders voting rights, public employment benefits, and standing for election. The question of voting rights for overseas Indians has become increasingly contentious – in 2011, the two programs (OCI and PIO) were merged into one, and the Singh government at the time proposed a law enabling diasporic Indians to vote in the general elections. While not a particularly successful initiative – only some 11,000 out of over 10 million individuals registered with the NRI Ministry were also registered to vote – prior to the 2014 election, the Indian Supreme Court sided with the Indian Election Commission's position that it was simply too difficult logistically to extend voting privileges to the overseas community (NDTV, 2014).

Despite the difficulties inherent in the question of citizenship – both in terms of voting and in its wider sense – it is clear that attracting the interest (and resources) of members of the diaspora is an important government policy regardless of the party in power. The significance of such a strategy is also evident in the views offered by one of the chief architects and members of the High-Level Committee on Diaspora and a driving force behind the establishment of the PBD, J.C. Sharma. I interviewed Sharma at length in 2004 when he was the Member Secretary (Policies, Consular Services and Diaspora) in the Union Ministry for External Affairs. When asked about the success of the Indian diaspora, he responded that

> [the] biggest strength that they have is their heritage, coming from one of the world's most pluralistic societies. It is a central Indian trait, an extraordinary ability to harmonize differences in languages, cultures, cuisine. This exposure to a pluralistic society and living with differences has aided Indians in fitting into an alien environment. They have a shorter adjustment period than other immigrants. Many receiving or "home" countries' dominant groups attempt to zealously protect their own identity and culture, but still Indians everywhere are embraced. It is this extraordinary ability to adapt that is noticeable in all Indian migrants, whether they come from a village or a

town. Many Indians speak two or three languages; in Europe they do not do this. An Indian may speak one language at home, another at work, watch programs on television in another but a German only speaks German and watches German programs. This adaptability is coupled with a traditional value and emphasis placed on education. This is part of the Hindu ethos, a social respect for learning; within Indian households, whether in the diaspora or elsewhere, it is a quick decision to send the son to college. The priority in middle-class families has always been education. The route adopted by Indians for upward social mobility in other countries is education and skill development. Entrepreneurship is also an Indian trait, as well as seizing opportunities when they presented themselves. The Indian diaspora carried these traditions with them to their new countries but they also retained a social safety net in their communities.

(Sharma, 2004)

This response, like the narrow image reproduced in the cultural texts to be discussed shortly, is quite telling in what is considered an 'ideal' representation of the Indian diaspora. Looking at the code words – Hindu, middle class, son, entrepreneurship, education, adaptability – again we see that it is a specific range of migration identities and experiences that is mythologized and idealized as emblematic of the entire Indian diaspora. When asked why the Indian diaspora is such a priority for the Government of India, Sharma stated that

[it] is a confluence of factors. The NRI profile became very high in the 1990s. At the same time the profile of India was growing very high as well. Especially in 1998 when the nuclear tests happened. Our destinies are interlinked. The overseas Indians are an excellent resource for us. If today India is shining, then the diaspora is shining too. We say to the diaspora that you have as much to gain from us as we do from you; it is a mutually beneficial relationship.

(Sharma, 2004)

The question remains: mutually beneficial to whom? To all members of the diaspora? To those who would claim membership or to those who would have it thrust upon them? The government's attempts to capitalize on this resource are quite clearly defined. As early as 1998, the Indian government began outlining its intention to prioritize connections with diasporas in a series of documents titled Policies, Incentives and Opportunities through its embassies, consulates, and high commissions in select countries – the UK, Canada, Australia, and the US initially (Sharma, 2004). By 1999, the Indian government began to offer the NRI/PIO card scheme. This was announced as "a passport to visa-free travel to India" along with "other attractive privileges" (Bose, 2007). Eligible were those who, at any time, had held an Indian passport; had parents or grandparents born or resided in India (as defined by the Government of India Act 1935); or were spouses of citizens of

India or a PIO, as defined by the aforementioned criteria. The scheme covered up to four generations in defining who might be of Indian origin. The benefits of the PIO card included a waiver on visas necessary for entering or studying in India. The card cost roughly US $500 and was valid for up to 15 years.

The Congress-led government that ruled from 2004 to 2014 saw no need to break with the tradition of its BJP predecessors with regard to the diaspora and moved to further bureaucratize affairs by appointing a Cabinet-level minister to the position of Minister of Overseas Indian Affairs. The Ministry's mission is to support "development through coalitions in a world without borders . . . [and] connect the Indian Diaspora community with its motherland" (Ministry of Overseas Indian Affairs [MOIA], 2014). It is organized into four units: Diaspora, Financial, Emigration, and Management Services and is focused on developing networks among Global Indians; promoting trade and investment; and fostering educational, cultural, and scientific links between the Ministry and India. The different central governments have also made attempts to offer forms of overseas citizenship to Global Indians over the past decade. When this was first announced, it only included a select few countries – Canada, the US, the UK, Australia, New Zealand, and Singapore among them – which led to considerable protest among those who were left off the list. Overseas citizenship, it should be noted, is not the same as dual citizenship; that is, it does not confer political or voting rights. Rather, its original intent was to

> remove for those who have taken foreign passports, the obstacle in travel to and from India, permit investment in business ventures and foster a greater sense of belonging. This provision is an incentive for people to relate themselves with India, to make investments, to make technology transfer and such like things.
>
> (MOIA, 2014)

To be eligible, one has to meet basic national citizenship requirements, belong to a territory that became part of India after 1947, and have never been a citizen of Pakistan or Bangladesh. The main benefits are that holders can avoid visa and entry processes, make investments in certain economic sectors domestically, and have parity with NRIs in issues such as adoption of children; domestic airfares; and entrance fees to museums, national monuments, and parks. The Indian state – whether led by Hindu Nationalist or center right parties – has thus made a strong investment in its connections to the diaspora. Not only has the government continued to develop initiatives such as the OCI but the PBD also remains a lavish and well-attended affair held every year on January 9. It has met 12 times since its inception, mainly in New Delhi (2003–2004, 2007–2008, 2010–2011, and 2014), but has also ventured out of the capital region to be hosted in Mumbai (2005), Hyderabad (2006), Chennai (2009), Jaipur (2012), and Kochi (2013). There are no plans as yet to host a PBD in Kolkata.

Imagining Global Indians culturally

Finally, while central and local governments might covet the wealth and resources of Global Indians, including NRIs and PIOs, it is also clear from cultural representations of the Indian diaspora that not all are created equal. There are rules, apparently, for good and bad diasporic behaviour:

> There are good NRIs and there are bad NRIs. Good NRIs send their savings back to India, give money to their poorer relations, set up schools, colleges and hospitals in towns and villages where they grew up. Bad NRIs involve themselves in Indian politics without knowing very much about the issues at stake. Living abroad exaggerates their desire to reaffirm their identity with their parent community in India. They identify themselves with the more extremist sections to which they send money and organise meetings for leaders of those groups in countries of their domicile.
>
> (Singh, 2002)

Furthermore, NRIs (and by implication PIOs) are disavowed for a variety of reasons – those who marry for a dowry and then abandon their bride, those who swindle a business partner in India, those who fail to maintain their Indian roots in the face of temptations from overseas. Others are ignored, as we have seen in the definition of the Global Indian, and yet others are mostly invisible, at least to the mainstream gaze. Who, then, are the 'good' NRIs? How are they defined, and where are they located?

The prominence and position of those Indian immigrants who represent the 'model minority' seem quite clear. And while it is true that many new immigrants from India to countries in the Global North struggle socially and economically to adjust to their new surroundings, it is becoming equally apparent that significant sections of the Indian diaspora across the globe are highly successful and prosperous in their new homes. Indian IT engineers rank second in number only to Chinese immigrants in Silicon Valley and make up a sizable proportion of today's high-tech millionaires across the globe (Saxenian, 1999). Some have estimated the combined gross assets of the Indian diaspora at around US $300 billion (roughly equivalent to India's gross domestic product [GDP]), with a combined net worth of between US $40 and $60 billion (Singhvi, 2001: 417). The Gujarati diaspora alone, which makes up less than 0.01 percent of the population of the US, is estimated to control over 5 percent of that country's wealth (Singhvi, 2001: 169–177). Nor have these successful émigrés been keeping their good fortune to themselves. As previously noted, India outpaced China, the Philippines, Mexico, and Nigeria as the country receiving the largest volume of remittances in the world, totalling over US $71 billion in 2013, up from approximately US $16 billion in 2003 (World Bank, 2014).

The success of the Global Indian imagery is also reflected in a wide variety of cultural texts, within India, within the diaspora, and among interested observers in 'new' countries as well. The embrace of transnational Indian 'chic' by significant parts of the entertainment industry of the West is evidenced by big-budget theatrical productions such as Andrew Lloyd Webber's musical *Bombay Dreams*; hit songs such as Cornershop's "Brimful of Asha"; and the wide readership enjoyed by an array of diasporic South Asian writers, including Salman Rushdie, Amitav Ghosh, Bharati Mukherjee, Kiran Desai, and Jhumpa Lahiri (among many others) – all of whom have written about the subcontinent and the diasporic experience. While the wealth of diaspora-related literature presents a far greater range of possibilities, the Global Indian represented in much of popular culture is the transnational professional rather than a figure who might be more marginalized or engaged in a financially and socially precarious occupation like that of a writer.

Specific visions are reinforced by many of the stories that the 'successful' Indian diaspora tell about themselves. While earlier films like Gurinder Chadha's *Bhaji on the Beach* (1993), Mira Nair's *Mississippi Masala* (1991), and Damien O'Donnell's *East is East* (1999) focused on the difficulties of integration and issues of racism and marginality (albeit often in a humorous fashion), many of the more successful films made by diasporic Indian filmmakers are far more celebratory of the transnational lifestyle and existence of 'the' diaspora. This is exemplified by Chadha's *Bend It Like Beckham* (2002), Deepa Mehta's *Bollywood/Hollywood* (2002) and *Bride and Prejudice* (2004), and Nair's *Monsoon Wedding* (2001). In each of these films, diasporic characters play significant, often central roles – the aspiring female soccer star pursuing her dreams in the Global North; the successful software engineer living in a lavish house in Toronto; the multi-millionaire from London visiting rural Punjab for a family wedding; the Houston-based engineer who goes to Delhi for an arranged marriage.

Other forms of diasporic media also reinforce this limited view of the 'Indian abroad.' While older UK-based television programs such as *Goodness Gracious Me*, *Life Is Not All Ha Ha Hee Hee*, and *The Kumars at No. 42* have dealt with the experiences of South Asian immigrants to the West during the 1960s and 1970s, more recent television programs dealing with diasporas have presented a narrower perspective of their lives. The tremendous growth and availability of specialty satellite channels has greatly increased the range of programming that is accessible to diasporic Indians. Not only are Indian-made programs now common in many cities in North America and Europe with large diasporic Indian populations, there has also been a considerable increase in the production of programs made by diasporic players themselves, specifically geared towards the NRI market. Soap operas are particularly concerned with these topics – for example, *Mausam*, which self-consciously marketed itself as an international Indian soap opera and was shown first in the diaspora and then in India (Dunn, 1995). Set in New Jersey, the show features a father who is a lawyer, a mother who is a doctor, and the stories of a family and community torn between Indian and American identities, though positioned within the narrow confines of the 'model minority' and *desi* myths.

Soap operas and television programs made in India pick up on similar themes. During my field research, I was fascinated by the number of storylines revolving around NRI characters or diasporic themes, especially conflicts between 'traditional' and 'modern' lifestyles. "Desi soaps" (Mankekar, 1999) often featured the struggle of returning diasporic success stories to reconcile their Indian heritage with their new American, Canadian, or British identities. They also reaffirmed the notion that going abroad meant success in the software industry, financial services sector, or an equally lucrative, professional career.

While television and literature have had a considerable influence on the imagination (and imagining) of the Global Indian diaspora, film remains the most widely consumed and available medium on the subcontinent. Here, too, the diasporic Indian has emerged as an important figure. Bhatawadekar (2011: 247) argues that for domestic cinema,

> while attracting a wide international audience, Bollywood specifically aims to address the lifestyle and cultural concerns of the Indian diaspora in the West. Bollywood's global orientation signifies not only the industry marketing itself to Western audiences, but also the orientation of global culture itself: the increasing worldwide interest in all things Eastern (and specifically Indian) has dramatically boosted the international consumption of "Bollywood," which, in addition to widely legitimizing it as a music, dance, and cinematic genre, has also placed the industry to represent how India looks, thinks and behaves.

Similarly, Desai (2004: 40–41) remarks that

> Indian film industries have "discovered" the diasporas (as lucrative markets). More recent export of films has occurred between India and its newer diasporas in Britain, North America, Australia, the Gulf states, and New Zealand. British Asians with greater disposable income have been significant in asserting the primacy of diasporic markets and spectators. This interest is accompanied by the shifting of the political economy of India which has generated an investment in representing diasporas in different ways. The deterritorialized nonresident Indians became imagined as crucial to the Indian economy and nation-state in filmic national narratives such as *Dilwale Dulhaniye Le Jayenge*. Since then, the deterritorialized Indian has been imagined as internal and integral to the Indian nation-state. Consequently, filmic representations as well as state policies have shifted to reflect this discourse.

More recently, some films have begun to destabilize the more triumphal readings of the Global Indian. Bhatawadekar (2011: 247) argues that films such as *Delhi 6* "dismantle three particular trends in Bollywood's global model, namely its upper-class affluent (Hindu) milieu, family-centered narratives, and [the] portrayal of the transnational Indian."

But despite such subversive readings, the dominant imagining of Global Indians continues to be celebratory and recirculated as such within many arenas of public discourse in India and in the diaspora, notably in the mainstream news media. For example, *India Today*, a prominent English-language magazine with a wide circulation both within India and abroad, featured special issues in 2003 and 2004 devoted to the diaspora and now includes a "Global Indian Report" in each publication. *India Today*'s editorial made it clear who they considered to be part of the Indian diaspora were and why they should be celebrated:

> There are 1.7 million Indian-Americans in the US, 1.5 million British-Indians in the UK. Across the world, in 108 other nations, there are almost 17 million people of Indian origin. Call it the great Indian diaspora, or call it the quiet Indian takeover, there are probably very few foreign fields which have never been Indian.
>
> Last year, *India Today*, which shares a sense of adventure with these intrepid Indians, saluted their achievements in a special Global Indian issue. This year, we celebrate the second generation, or overseas-born Indians (OBIs), who may not call India their home but who are nevertheless more than the sum of the fragments of their parents' lives. Born in the two great migrations of the 1960s and 1980s to largely educated professionals, these navigators of the New and Old Worlds are slowly rising to great prominence in their homelands, often in areas their parents would not have dreamed possible.
>
> (Bamzai, 2004: 3)

This statement is interesting not only for what it says but also for what it leaves out. There are, in this interpretation, only "two great migrations" which have spawned the Indian diaspora. Such a reckoning leaves many out of the picture – descendants of indentured labour, of traders and of labourers who established themselves in farming, and those who continue to labour today as taxi drivers, domestic workers, and janitors and work in many other non-professional occupations in North America, Europe, and especially the Gulf states – in other words, all those others previously detailed as part of successive waves of Indian emigration. These people have not disappeared, as the current statistics on the distribution of the diasporic populations illustrate, but in terms of the myth of the Global Indian diaspora, they may as well not exist.

If one were to look at popular culture and the glut of publications devoted to hybrid identities now popular within the subcontinent and abroad, it would seem that the only diasporic individuals deemed successful are IT workers and other highly trained people in the professions, academia, industry, and business, including high-achieving students destined for such occupations. Consider the categories within which *India Today* groups its OBIs: the politicians, the trail-blazers, the professionals, the hybrids, and the entertainers. Those profiled include recording artists, advertising executives, doctors, software engineers, Hollywood actors, stock analysts, scriptwriters, venture capitalists, and US senators. Such success stories are not only celebrated, they are venerated, sometimes in ways that are difficult to imagine. This leads, at times, to a strange circumstance in which Global Indians and local ones are unable to recognize one another. Ray (2001), for example, describes the curious case in which diasporic Indians who fled Fiji following a military coup and settled in Australia encountered serious culture clashes with more recent immigrants from India who had settled in several Australian cities. To the Indo-Fijians (who did, in this case, identify with an Indian ethnic heritage), those who had migrated directly from India were not, paradoxically, 'Indian enough'; that is, they did not represent the India that the diaspora had seen both portrayed in Bollywood films and in other forms of global media, nor did they reflect the creolized Indian culture the Indo-Fijians had created, which they saw as being more authentic than that of more recent migrants. This is not an uncommon case, for many scholars have noted the tendency of immigrants to ossify culture, especially in situations of oppression and marginalization (Prashad, 2000). In such situations, it is not unusual to hold tightly to static notions of social behaviour, forms, and roles, including those concerning class, sexuality, gender, and religion. But, in this particular case, co-ethnic or origin-based solidarities dissolved in the face of imagined and idealized identities.

It is evident that the diasporic Indian has moved from the margins of a presumed Indian identity to its center and that this shift is changing India. In the next chapter, I explore the ways in which scrutinizing various forms of transnationalism can help us to understand the actual material and ideological transformations that global diasporas can create in their homelands.

References

Bamzai, K. (2004). "AB but no longer CD: overseas-born Indians no longer cringe at their hyphenated identity." *India Today (International Online Edition)*. Retrieved November 25, 2014, from http://indiatoday.intoday.in/story/overseas-born-indians-no-longer-cringe-at-their-hyphenated-identity/1/196854.html.

Bhatawadekar, S. (2011). "Locating the diaspora: Delhi 6 and its challenge to Bollywood's image of the transnational Indian." *South Asian Popular Culture* 9(3): 247–258.

Bhatia, S. and A. Ram (2009). "Theorizing identity in transnational and diaspora cultures: a critical approach to acculturation." *International Journal of Intercultural Relations* 33: 140–149.

Bose, P. S. (2007). "Dreaming of diasporas: urban developments and transnational identities in contemporary Kolkata." *TOPIA: Canadian Journal of Cultural Studies* 17(Spring): 111–130.

Brown, J. M. (2006). *Global South Asians: introducing the modern diaspora*. Cambridge, Cambridge University Press.

Buckley, M. (2012). "From Kerala to Dubai and back again: construction migrants and the global economic crisis." *Geoforum* 43(2): 250–259.

Carter, M. and K. Torabully (2002). *Coolitude: an anthology of the Indian labour diaspora*. London, Anthem.

Cohen, R. (1997). *Global diasporas: an introduction*. London, Routledge.

Dickinson, J. (2012). "Decolonising the diaspora: neo-colonial performances of Indian history in East Africa." *Transactions of the Institute of British Geographers* 37(4): 609–623.

Dickinson, J. and A. J. Bailey (2007). "(Re)membering diaspora: uneven geographies of Indian dual citizenship." *Political Geography* **26**(7): 757–774.

Dunn, A. (1995). "As the world and soap operas turn; blondes, brain tumors and buckets of tears on Hindi TV." *New York Times*. Retrieved November 25, 2014, from http://www.nytimes.com/1995/09/26/nyregion/world-soap-operas-turn-blondes-brain-tumors-buckets-tears-hindi-tv.html.

Edwards, K. (2008). "For a geohistorical cosmopolitanism: postcolonial state strategies, cosmopolitan communities, and the production of the 'British', 'Overseas', 'Non-Resident', and 'Global' Indian." *Environment and Planning D: Society and Space* **26**: 444–463.

Gilmartin, M. (2008). "Migration, identity and belonging." *Geography Compass* **2**(6): 1837–1852.

Gilroy, P. (2000). *Against race: imagining political culture beyond the color line.* Cambridge, MA, Belknap Press of Harvard University Press.

Hall, S. (1994). Cultural identity and diaspora. *Colonial Discourse and Postcolonial Theory: A Reader.* P. Williams and L. Chrisman. New York, Columbia University Press: 392–403.

Ho, E. L.-E. (2008). "Citizenship, migration and transnationalism: a review and critical interventions." *Geography Compass* **2**(5): 1286–1300.

Jain, R. K. (2011). "Anthropology and diaspora studies: an Indian perspective." *Asian Anthropology* **10**(1): 45–60.

Lakhilal, P. (2003). "Dual citizenship greeted with mixed feelings." *India Tribune.* Retrieved May 11, 2009, from http://www.globalpolicy.org/nations/citizen/2003/01/18india.htm.

Landy, F., B. Maharaj and H. Mainet-Valleix (2004). "Are people of Indian origin (PIO) 'Indian'? A case study of South Africa." *Geoforum* **35**(2): 203–215.

Mani, B. and L. Varadarajan (2008). "'The largest gathering of the global Indian family': neoliberalism, nationalism, and diaspora at Pravasi Bharatiya Divas." *Diaspora: A Journal of Transnational Studies* **14**(1): 45–74.

Mankekar, P. (1999). *Screening culture, viewing politics: an ethnography of television, womanhood, and nation in postcolonial India.* Durham, NC, Duke University Press.

Mavroudi, E. (2007). "Diaspora as process: (de)constructing boundaries." *Geography Compass* **1**(3): 467–479.

Ministry of Overseas Indian Affairs (MOIA) (2014). "Ministry of Overseas Indian Affairs." Retrieved March 29, 2014, from http://moia.gov.in/services.aspx?mainid=6.

Nayyar, D. (1994). *Migration, remittances, and capital flows: the Indian experience.* New York, Oxford University Press.

NDTV. (2014). "Registered NRI voters overseas will have to wait for future elections." Retrieved August 26, 2014, from http://www.ndtv.com/elections/article/election-2014/registered-nri-voters-overseas-will-have-to-wait-for-future-elections-507477.

Ong, A. (2003). "Cyberpublics and diaspora politics among transnational Chinese." *Interventions* **5**(1): 82–100.

Portes, A. and R. Rumbaut (2006). *Immigrant America: a portrait.* Berkeley, University of California Press.

Prashad, V. (2000). *The karma of brown folk.* Minneapolis, University of Minnesota Press.

Radhakrishnan, S. (2011). *Appropriately Indian: gender and culture in a new transnational class.* Durham, NC, Duke University Press.

Ray, M. (2001). Bollywood down under: Fiji Indian cultural history and popular assertion. *Floating Lives: The Media and Asian Diasporas.* S. Cunningham and J. Sinclair. Lanham, MD, Rowman & Littlefield: 149–179.

Rogaly, B. (2009). "Spaces of work and everyday life: labour geographies and the agency of unorganised temporary migrant workers." *Geography Compass* **3**(6): 1975–1987.

Sahoo, A. K., M. Baas and T. Faist (2012). *Indian diaspora and transnationalism*. New Delhi, Rawat.

Sahoo, A. K., D. Sangha and M. Kelly (2010). "From 'temporary migrants' to 'permanent residents': Indian H1-B visa holders in the United States." *Asian Ethnicity* **11**(3): 293–309.

Saxenian, A. (1999). *Silicon Valley's new immigrant entrepreneurs*. San Francisco, Public Policy Institute of California.

Shah, S. (2014). Asian American. *Race, Class and Gender in the United States*. P. S. Rothenberg and K. S. Mayhew. New York, Worth: 245–247.

Sharma, J. (2004). Member Secretary, High Level Committee on Diaspora. P. S. Bose. Ministry of External Affairs, New Delhi.

Singh, K. (2002). "NRIs, good and bad." *Hindustan Times*. Retrieved May 16, 2006, from http://www.hindustantimes.com/news/181_90809,00120002.htm.

Singhvi, L. M. (2001). Report of the High Level Committee on the Indian Diaspora. New Delhi, Government of India, Ministry of External Affairs, Non-Resident Indian and Persons of Indian Origin Division.

Vajpayee, A. B. (2003). "Address to the First Indian Diaspora Conference." Retrieved July 12, 2006, from http://www.indianembassy.org/pm/vajpayee/pm_jan_09_03.htm.

Vora, N. (2008). "Producing diasporas and globalization: Indian middle-class migrants in Dubai." *Anthropological Quarterly* **81**(2): 377–406.

Walsh, R. (2003). "Global diasporas: introduction." *Interventions* **5**(1): 1–11.

World Bank. (2014). "Migration & remittances data." Retrieved May 29, 2014, from http://econ.worldbank.org/WBSITE/EXTERNAL/EXTDEC/EXTDECPROSPECTS/0,,contentMDK:22759429~pagePK:64165401~piPK:64165026~theSitePK:476883,00.html.

Zhu, Z. (2007). "Two diasporas: overseas Chinese and non-resident Indians in their homelands' political economy." *Journal of Chinese Political Science* **12**(3): 281–296.

3 Transnational practices

The fact that diasporas continue to engage with their homelands – ancestral, recent, or imagined – is not a revelation. But there are a number of reasons why the interest among scholars, policymakers, and community members in the connections built and maintained between immigrant groups and their former homes has intensified in recent years. These reasons include geopolitical and security concerns, questions of identity in multicultural societies and the related integration of immigrants into new host communities, and the economic impact of remittances (Demmers, 2002; Levitt, 2001; Mohan, 2006). The possibility that diasporas might help to build or rebuild their home countries has spawned a flurry of activity by international institutions, national governments, and local authorities alike to try and capture this potential (De Haas, 2010; Hugo, 2012). In this context, diasporas are increasingly viewed in the international community and by national governments as important contributors to their homeland economies.

The fact that remittances – money sent back by workers to their home countries – rank second only to oil exports globally and far outpace both foreign direct investment (FDI) and aid to developing countries makes it clear why the migration development nexus has become such an integral growth strategy in places as far apart as Haiti, Lesotho, and Tajikistan, among many others (World Bank, 2014). Some scholars, however, have questioned the long-term viability of such strategies, given the vulnerability of migrant income to external pressures – natural disasters, economic downturns, and political conflicts, to name but a few (Fix *et al.*, 2009). Others have suggested that the scramble for diasporic resources by various actors leaves the actual nature of development and the roles played by diasporas relatively underscrutinized (Mohan, 2006; Raghuram, 2009). As the US-based transnational solidarity network Association for India's Development (2004) has asked, "What kinds of developments in India are Indians in the US (and other countries) making possible?"

This chapter explores such questions by focusing on several forms of diasporic transnational practices – cultural, political, and economic. I begin by briefly discussing the affinities between diasporas and homelands. I then explore the idea of what Anderson (2006) has called "long distance nationalism" – the ideological and political commitment of groups overseas to various matters in their ancestral, putative, or imagined homes. Lastly, I focus on the developmental impact of the Global Indian so that the bulk of this chapter is devoted to examining the economic and developmental potential of diasporic involvement, using India's engagement with non-resident Indians (NRIs) as a case study. I review, therefore, the increasing significance of diasporic capital vis-à-vis other forms of external flows, such as foreign aid and FDI. To that end, I look at the various ways in which states have increasingly begun to try and actively 'capture' such flows. Finally, I illustrate the potential and challenges of a remittance-based economy by examining in closer detail a more prominent case of diasporic involvement in India – that of the western state of Kerala, whose experience could provide important lessons for Kolkata's own attempts to entice its diaspora to invest in its redevelopment.

Migrants and transnationalism

Studies of migration and transnationalism have long suggested that contemporary immigrants maintain transnational connections to their countries of origin and beyond. There are many reasons for keeping such connections active. In some cases, migration may be temporary – for example, in cases of seasonal (or cyclical) labour and short-term contracts. Migrants may have relatives, property, and/or business ties in their homeland, or they may have an ongoing interest in the politics of their place of origin. Those who leave may also express a desire to return, whether soon or in the future. For these and many other reasons, transnational engagements are the rule rather than the exception of diasporic involvements in former homelands. Basch, Glick-Schiller, and Szanton-Blanc (1994: 6) describe migrant transnationalism as "the process by which transmigrants, through their daily activities, forge and sustain multi-stranded social, economic, and political relations that link together their societies of origin and settlement, and through which they create transnational social fields that cross national borders."

These daily activities, however, are not only about connections between 'sending' and 'receiving' countries – as many scholars have noted, migration is far more complex than the linear narrative we are familiar with. Instead, we see that diasporas imagine themselves and their links to various places through a diverse set of practices, including literary and artistic productions. It is in a wide assortment of cultural texts that we clearly see an expression of longing, of connections, of visions of long-remembered homes, traditions, habits, and patterns. One need only turn to the wealth of fiction, poetry, films, music, dance, and festivals that mark diasporic life to see evidence of this fact. The importance of collectivities can be judged from the evidence of diasporic identities in cultural, hometown, and mutual aid associations founded by émigrés, as well as in religious charities, professional and trade groups, political organizations, sports clubs, and a range of other formations.

These identities are especially apparent in global cities that are destination points for many immigrants – many large urban centers that have significant diasporic populations have seen a rise in minority community–specific media and social institutions: 'ethnic-language' newspapers, magazines, television channels and programs, music, electronic publications, and media; the establishment of language schools, sports clubs, ethnic festivals, and holiday celebrations; and the commodification of ethnic enclaves such as Little Indias and Chinatowns. Such expressions of diasporic identity are not, of course, without challenge – from the outside, some view these celebrations with suspicion and as evidence of disloyalty or the inability of immigrants to integrate with new host communities, while many within various diasporas chafe against monolithic and often narrow readings of who can be part of the group and what behaviours and beliefs are acceptable within it (Prashad, 2000; Dasgupta, 2006).

The focus of this book is not, however, on transnational practices *in* the diaspora, but rather the ways in which diasporas reach back to their origins and migrants remain active in their former homes. Examples of such activities are not necessarily distinct from one another but can overlap in form and purpose. For example, providing in-kind assistance can have political motivations, remittances may be used specifically for investment purposes, and philanthropy is a highly political form of investment. The latter itself may be one of the most prominent forms of diasporic involvement in the world today, as seen through the mobilization of overseas communities following natural disasters and civil strife in former homelands and the establishment of numerous charitable foundations and gift-giving enterprises by diasporic individuals:

> Diaspora communities have long evidenced a strong obligation to help others through the giving of time, goods, talents, skills and money . . . [diaspora] philanthropy is not a new phenomenon. Both the migration of people from their country of origin and the tradition of "giving back" are centuries old. But in an era of accelerated globalization, the relationship between diaspora philanthropy and the economic and social development of many countries is increasingly relevant. . . .
>
> (Geithner, Chen, and Johnson, 2004: xv–xvi)

The following sections look at two important elements and mechanisms in this tradition of giving back to homelands that are implicated in diasporic involvement, whether philanthropically motivated or otherwise – for instance, driven by the purpose of forging political or economic ties.

Political involvement

Diasporas have long been entangled in ideological projects to reshape, resurrect, defend, or even enlarge homelands, ancestral or putative. Nationalist struggles and sectarian strife have lengthy histories of overseas assistance from departed sons and daughters. Fundraising for the Irish Republican cause in Boston, political support for early twentieth-century Indian nationalism among the Ghadr Party in California, Palestinian and Jewish demonstrations on behalf of respective positions in Middle East conflicts, or Tamil and Sikh agitation in Canada for separatist movements in South Asia are but a few examples. This involvement can take the form of moral support and encouragement, it can manifest itself through material assistance in money and materials, and it can even take the form of physical presence in armed struggles, as in the case of Canadians of Serbian and Croatian origin who took part in the civil war in the Balkans (Satzewich and Wong, 2003: 273).

Another example more directly related to the idea of identity assertion and development as a political project is the case of the strong support demonstrated by large segments of overseas Indian communities for the resurgent Hindu right that has dominated much of Indian politics since the 1990s (Menon and Nigam, 2007). One of the myriad entities that comprise the *Sangh Parivar* or 'family' of organizations that collectively espouse the ideology of *Hindutva* – an aggressive form of right-wing Hindu Nationalism – is the *Vishwa Hindu Parishad* (VHP or World Hindu Council). The VHP plays an important role alongside the official political wing of the *Hindutva* movement, which is the Bharatiya Janata Party (BJP), the 'cultural' organ known as the *Rashtriya Swayamsevak Sangh* (RSS), trade unions, professional associations, and women's organizations, among many others. Active in fundraising and nationalist calls directed at raising patriotic fervor, especially among Indians living abroad or diasporic Indian communities, the VHP has been tremendously successful at fundraising for the *Hindutva* cause in places ranging from the United Kingdom to the US to Australia. During and after the 2002 pogroms against Muslims in Gujarat, VHP officials abroad were also particularly active in their defense of the violence and sought to minimize evidence that state authorities were complicit in the murders and brutalization of the Muslim community in Gujarat (Sundar, 2004).

This self-assertion co-opts development as one of its goals. In some Indian regions where the *Hindutva* movement has proved particularly strong (such as Gujarat, Uttar Pradesh, and other parts of the so-called Hindi Belt), the VHP's success in recruiting overseas support has had far-reaching consequences. Corbridge and Simpson (2006) describe, for example, the ways in which the diaspora has aided Hindutva groups to reshape Gujarat – especially after earthquakes and communal riots – increasingly along religious and caste lines. Some argue that the Gujarati diaspora in the US in particular has an important enough influence – or at least resources – that many local politicians will make fundraising trips to places like Gujarat to fund their campaigns (Nanda and Bhatt, 2002). Controversy has simmered over the activities and intentions of the India Development and Relief Fund (IDRF), a US-based, tax-exempt fundraising initiative meant to concentrate on the "interaction and convergence of development and relief work, particularly in relation to the needs and welfare of the poor" (India Development and Relief Fund, 2006). To its supporters, the IDRF is an invaluable source of funds and psychological aid for development efforts in education, housing, and sanitation (among others), as well as in reconstruction and rehabilitation needs following natural disasters such as earthquakes and floods. But critics of the IDRF have pointed out that the bulk of the funds raised have gone to RSS-affiliated organizations and have been directed at promulgating

Hindutva beliefs under the guise of relief and development activities, especially in marginalized and tribal areas. Dismayed by the clear linkages between diasporic fundraising and the growth of right-wing politics in India, critics of the IDRF launched a very public and successful "Campaign to Stop Funding Hate" to highlight these problematic connections (Mathur, 2013). More recently, the successful campaign by the BJP led by Narendra Modi in 2014 has received significant support from NRIs (*Times of India*, 2014).

Economic involvement

While political connections between diasporas and homelands have been recognized for some time, the importance of remittances in the global economy is a more recently acknowledged trend. A growing body of literature has noted the growth of remittances in both absolute terms and as relative to the receiving countries' gross domestic products (GDPs) (Batzlen, 2000; Gammeltoft, 2002; de la Garza and Lowell, 2002; Nayyar, 1994). They are today one of the largest flows of money in the world, reaching nearly US \$550 billion in 2013, with US \$414 billion of that figure going from workers to the developing world (World Bank, 2013). All trends point to an increase in such numbers, with the two world regions that currently see the largest interchange of workers and remittances being Latin America/the US and the Persian Gulf/South Asia.

Part of the increase is due to more attention paid to data collection and the increased surveillance of the transnational practices of diasporic individuals due to security concerns. Yet the figures are still impressive – perhaps more so since real remittance rates are almost always severely undercounted due to the tendency by many migrants to rely on informal, non-banking channels to move their money. While some foreign workers may transmit money through banks, money-transfer services (such as Western Union), or other official sources, the majority of remittances are transferred in ways that are not easily detectable. This may include simply carrying cash back home in a suitcase or using unofficial money brokers and lenders. The majority of funds go to families and friends, though many national governments are actively trying to convince their overseas workers to put their remittances towards more productive uses in things like development projects and businesses (Levitt and De La Hesa, 2003; Ley, 2004).

Whatever their precise quantities, remittances are significant and have become an economic necessity for many nations. Ratha (2003: 157–158) points out that remittances far outstrip traditional sources of financial flow to many less developed countries, such as foreign aid. Unlike foreign aid, remittances are also not 'tied' to the self-interest of donor nations or to the loan conditionalities of multinational institutions such as the International Monetary Fund (IMF). Yet remittances are hardly a new phenomenon. One could argue that diasporas have always played a significant role in 'developing' their homelands, whether ancestral or putative. Social networks, kinship ties, and ongoing cultural and political affiliations with organizations and individuals 'back home' have kept money, materials, and moral support flowing across continents, oceans, and even time.

Those who have left home have often tried to send resources to assist their families in maintaining their lives or in building newer and better ones. Whether helping a parent to improve a house or purchase a larger plot of land, sending money to build a village hospital or a neighbourhood school, or enabling distant relatives to live a more affluent lifestyle relative to their neighbours, diasporic capital has a long history beyond the nation–state itself.

Why, then, have instruments such as remittances and diasporic investment caught the recent attention of so many national governments, international financial institutions, private banks, and transnational corporations? Why are development agencies increasingly recognizing the importance of diasporas and incorporating their potential into visions for the future (Kuznetsov, 2006; Özden and Schiff, 2006; Ratha, 2003)? Part of this new urgency to examine an age-old process is that this 'diasporic capital' might become essential in filling gaps in a global economic development assistance system. As foreign aid is in decline or comes with unpalatable strings attached, this 'development funding gap' is expected to be filled by diasporic capital. Thus, it is not simply diasporic transnational practices but specifically the connection between diasporas and development that is key to understanding the interest that so many national governments have in capitalizing on the resources of their citizens overseas.

Private FDI, of course, remains a lure for governments across the world; however, unlike transnational trade and open markets – heralded by many as the obvious alternative to traditional development assistance – diasporic funds are seen by those who urge national governments to seek them as being more altruistic and sustainable resources than those available in the international marketplace – at least, they are intended to complement the latter. Dade and Unheim (2007), for example, explore the potential impact of diasporas on private sector development, looking at ways in which the former might act as facilitators for the latter. Some overseas groups, such as the Chinese diaspora, have been especially successful in this regard. In fact, as evidence from several parts of the world suggests, labour migrants may today be putting their money into investment schemes, government bonds and funds, and development projects at the national, regional, local, and even neighbourhood levels (Ratha, 2011; Orozco, 2010).

But diasporas are more than just the sum of their remittances. Conway and Potter (2007), for example, see Caribbean return migrants as agents of change who deeply affect the landscapes of their homelands by their activities and attitudes. Where once the narrative of return referenced retirees, they argue that today a number of different types of diasporas are returning at different stages of life and with markedly dissimilar life trajectories and goals. These journeys, they suggest, should not be viewed as linear but circular, employing various strategies for living between two worlds. Conway and Potter's (2007) work argues against the notion of brain drain alone – the influential narrative in migration literature that describes the siphoning off of intellectual and professional talent from the Global South by industrialized nations. Many have decried this process through which highly skilled and educated workers leave less developed countries for more industrialized and richer ones. Currently, one in ten tertiary educated adults born in the developing world resides in the developed world, and a further 30 to 50 percent of the South's scientists live and work in the North (Beine, Docquier, and Rapoport, 2003). While many of these workers may well contribute the very remittances that help keep their 'home' countries economically afloat, what does it mean to a broader sense of development to have so much of the human capital leave these nations? However, like Conway and Potter (2007), Tung (2008) argues that the migration patterns of elites may be vastly oversimplified in the literature. In Tung's (2008) study of Chinese and Indian transnational elites, she uses the term "brain circulation" to describe the manner in which some diasporic professionals make their stay abroad temporary. In her view, their time overseas may in fact benefit the 'sending' country considerably by providing experience and expertise that migrants would in theory be able to use to improve their homeland.

Not all see remittances and diasporic capital as an unalloyed boon, however. Pozo and Amuedo-Dorantes (2002: 2–5), for example, suggest that workers' remittances in fact have a negative impact on receiving countries' economies in the form of a real exchange rate appreciation, artificially inflating the value of domestic currencies and decreasing productive capacities. Moreover, Bailey (2013) reminds us that remittances are subject to 'external' political and economic contexts beyond migration and development alone. He examines the effects of the global recession of 2007–2008 on migration and remittance patterns in Europe and notes the intersection between discourses on neoliberalism, labour, securitization, and sovereignty that constrain, discipline, and regulate migrant behaviour and patterns of movement. Dependence upon remittances and other forms of diasporic capital to provide a stable economic support appears to be fraught with risk. Far from insulating economies against 'external shocks,' there is mounting evidence, including the Indian case discussed in the following, that, in some situations, diasporic capital flows can indeed exacerbate crisis situations.

Finally, as many scholars point out, a focus on diasporas and development often leaves out the complexity and diversity between different forms of migration patterns and migrant groups themselves. Diener (2008), for example, reminds us of the number of groups who claim diasporic identities in Central Asia not based on the nation–state but on pre-existing, tribal, or non-state histories. To whom and to which land do they owe allegiance? Rubinov (2014), in his study of the impact of remittances on development in Kyrgyzstan (one of the most remittance-dependent countries in the world), suggests that far from leading to the types of macroeconomic change envisioned by multilateral institutions and national governments, money sent by Kyrgyz workers in Russia back home are primarily used to supplement daily household needs and to finance festivals, elaborate marriages, and other cultural rituals.

Page and Mercer (2012) argue that the traditional view of remittances has been dominated by economic thought, which treats migrants primarily through the lens of rational choice theory as decision-makers and option-choosers. Instead, they suggest, our scrutiny of transnational practices needs to be a far more nuanced understanding of how and why migrants act the way they do. In their view, most perspectives provided by the state and multilateral actors on remittances are profoundly patronizing and portray migrants as wasteful and in need of appropriate guidance. Drawing on examples from Africa, they suggest that a focus on migrant remittances as a community of practice in which participants are socialized in the use of remittances is a more productive approach. Levitt and Waters' (2002) seminal studies of migrant connections between sites in the Dominican Republic and Boston (2001), immigrant religious practices and connections with the homeland (2007), and the changing lives of the second generation have helped to lay the foundation of much of the recent work on transnationalism (Khagram and Levitt, 2008). In a recent article, Levitt and Lamba-Nieves (2011) revisit the idea of social as opposed to economic remittances, where they argue that we need to reconceptualize diasporas and development as a much larger field in which ideas travel in many forms, emphasizing that multiple types of impacts of remittances exist that we should consider. The Indian case outlined in the next section illustrates the importance of such a larger view more fully.

The Indian case

Let me turn briefly to the example of India's experience as a way of illustrating some of the benefits and challenges of incorporating diasporic capital into national development strategies. In the late 1990s, a controversial dam-building project in the western Indian state of Gujarat became stalled in light of increasing environmental and social protests regarding its impacts and purpose. International donors and multilateral institutions such as the World Bank were unwilling to support the initiative, so the state government began to turn to the wealthy Gujarati diaspora for funds. As the then–State Minister for Major Irrigation Jay Narayan Vyas said:

> Traditionally investment in the bond market is done after looking at the security, liquidity, safety and returns. We will add Emotional Property to tap funds from NRIs. We would appeal to their emotions and ask them to lend for development in the motherland.
>
> (Vyas, quoted in Amin, 2000)

Such appeals may have been novelties at the state level, but on the national scale they expanded on an established tradition of seeking diasporic funds to help fund development projects and sustain the Indian economy. How had this pattern emerged and evolved? The economic strategy on which India's postcolonial political autonomy and economic prosperity was founded had proven to be a rather dismal failure by the early 1970s. Even a decade earlier – scarcely into the first few economic plans – India had begun running massive payment deficits. By 1967, the Indian rupee had been devalued by 20 percent, but the deficits continued. The collapse of the Bretton Woods economic system in 1971 created a further crisis and resulted in the spiralling devaluation of the rupee. In

1972, the Indian currency remained pegged to the British pound sterling even as the latter's exchange rate was floated, resulting in a parallel depreciation for both currencies. By 1975, the rupee's ties to the pound had disappeared, and its exchange rate was placed on a controlled, floating basis that was linked to a "basket of currencies" of India's main trading partners (Seshadri, 1993).

It is within this scenario of economic crisis that we first see the emergence of a global Indian diaspora as an important economic actor in Indian politics and the economy. As the Indian government sought to staunch the bleeding of its domestic economy, it turned to the resources of successful Indian émigrés. As discussed previously, the decades since the end of the Second World War and India's Independence had led to a steady stream of migration towards industrialized nations such as the US, Britain, Canada, and the oil-rich Persian Gulf. At the same time, older diasporic Indian communities – many the descendants of indentured labourers – had deep roots in East Africa, the West Indies, and Southeast Asia.

And the money did flow, not only in the form of remittances but also in the form of foreign currency deposits. The state-controlled Reserve Bank of India initiated two programs in the late 1970s to attract funds in foreign currency from overseas Indian communities. The first was to create Foreign Currency Non-Resident Accounts, which insured the depositor against exchange rate fluctuations by providing a fixed rate. The second scheme was called the Non-Resident (External) Rupee Account, which offered a higher interest rate without the guarantee of a fixed exchange rate. By 1982, these initiatives were further refined to make it even more attractive for NRIs to deposit their money in Indian banks and to invest in and buy real estate in India, including offering assured repatriation of funds and a further 2 percent extra interest on foreign currency deposits held in India.

The success of this strategy to woo NRI money was considerable, if ultimately only a temporary solution. Throughout the 1980s, NRI money helped to stabilize India's national economy, but 'leakages' in the trade account and elsewhere helped to substantially offset these gains. Indeed, as Krishnamurty (1994) argues, to a large extent the support provided by NRI funds merely put off the economic reforms that sooner or later needed to be undertaken by the Indian state. Krishnamurty (1994) also points out that diasporic capital has a complex and often contradictory effect on the receiving country's economy. Deposit flows, he suggests, come out of savings and wealth, while remittances come out of income. There are two different trajectories and class implications for these types of diasporic assistance – and possibly two different outcomes. Krishnamurty (1994: 19) goes so far as to suggest that "remittances bring down the measured deficit while deposits help to finance it." Remittances in an earlier era in India, therefore, were primarily used to stabilize the national economy as a whole, whereas today they are intended to fund specific projects and catalyze urban restructuring and the construction of infrastructure.

The differences between the nature of these forms of diasporic capital – and the risks of informally relying on the flow from remittances for financial stability – became stark when the growing economic crisis finally reached meltdown status in 1991. Inflationary pressures, coupled with overvalued exchange rates and rising fiscal deficits, had severely affected the Indian economy. It could not, however, recover from the series of external shocks, the most severe of which was the 1991 Gulf War. Not only did the Indian state have to take responsibility (at considerable expense) for repatriating hundreds of thousands of workers threatened by war, but the flow of foreign exchange from the Gulf dried up, while the sudden spike in oil prices further crippled the economy. India's credit rating plummeted as commercial lenders shied away. Furthermore, the second part of the diasporic capital equation – foreign currency deposits – abruptly evaporated. Nearly US $1 billion in NRI deposits exited the country in 1991. Capital flight in general was precipitous, often citing severe exchange restrictions as the motivation but also following the general trend of unease regarding the Indian economy. By the end of June 1991, foreign currency reserves were down to US $975 million (barely enough to cover 2 weeks of imports), and India was forced to pledge part of its gold reserves as collateral in order to access the international overnight market and avoid a loan default. Export and industrial growth were both negative, and inflation soared above 16 percent. India's GDP growth for 1992 was projected at less than 1 percent. Accordingly, the rupee was devalued by 20 percent in July 1991, with a promise of partial convertibility by March 1992 and full convertibility by March 1993.

In the face of such an overwhelming crisis, India was forced to turn to the IMF and World Bank, who insisted on a series of economic reforms as part of the condition for receiving assistance. On April 13, 1992, India accepted the Multilateral Investment Guarantee Agency Protocol (Krishnamurty, 1994). Among the package of liberalization reforms that the Indian government was forced to adopt were the following policies (all previously tightly controlled by the state): in addition to the devaluation of the rupee, the government had to permit majority ownership by foreign investors (up to 100 percent in some sectors) and automatic approval of foreign equity proposals up to 51 percent in 34 high-priority industries.

As with other nations that have adopted World Bank/IMF structural adjustment policies, India's move towards trade liberalization has been a mixed blessing. Its economic health, measured in terms of industrial production and export earnings, has seen a marked improvement. The redistribution of positive net economic gains within the country is another story but is outside the scope of this chapter. What is pertinent to this discussion is the renewed emphasis that the Indian government has placed on attracting diasporic capital to its shores in the form of remittances, FDI, and foreign currency deposits. That diasporic capital has come to India is unquestionable. India has had among the highest global increases in remittance inflows over the past 5 years, from US $13 billion in 2001 to more than US $71 billion in 2013 (World Bank, 2014). But these figures stand in stark contrast to its experience with FDI, which is as important a flow as remittances are in diasporic economic involvement.

Investments constitute a category that overlaps with the two previously discussed categories but also has some unique characteristics present in the many forms of diasporic investments. They can include the aforementioned currency deposit accounts. They can also consist of property ownership in the private sector or in residential real estate, as illustrated by the case study of Kolkata offered later in this book, and they can take the form of business ventures or partnerships. These, unlike remittances, are difficult to distinguish as being diasporic because they are recorded in national accounting figures under FDI.

So far, India's success in attracting FDI has been limited, in large part because of its 'closed' or 'command' economy. Since India fully adopted liberalization as an economic strategy in 1991, it has actively and aggressively courted foreign investors. In 2004, India's FDI inflows totalled US $5.335 billion, rising from an annual average of US $452 million between 1985 and 1995 (United Nations Conference on Trade and Development, 2005b). In contrast, China's FDI inflows in 2004 comprised an astounding US $60.630 billion dollars, with their 1985–1995 average standing at US $11.715 billion (United Nations Conference on Trade and Development, 2005a). This is an extremely sore point in India, and many politicians, scholars, and political pundits devote much time and effort to discussing the disparity. Some argue that the success of the Chinese has been a result of their extensive connections to high-earning diasporas across the globe and that India lags behind because of its inability to engage its own (Prashad, 2005). Others caution against engaging in endless comparisons and competitions between the emerging Asian powers and suggest that the statistics themselves need to be viewed more critically (Nagraj, 2005).

Whatever the reasons for the differences, it does appear that India has been less successful at mobilizing diasporic investments than some of its neighbours, a failure that it has more recently sought to rectify at both national and regional levels. As recent FDI inflows demonstrate, private sector investment is growing, albeit slowly. Outsourcing operations, while not synonymous with direct investment, have been a considerable success, especially in the IT and financial services sectors located in and around cities like Hyderabad, Bangalore, Gurgaon and, to a degree, Kolkata. And investments and loans have been made available on a smaller scale to diasporic individuals. These loans are secured against foreign currency deposits and hence involve the inflow of foreign exchange. The State Bank of India (SBI), a semi-privatized bank whose majority shareholder is the Reserve Bank of India (RBI) (the central bank), currently accounts for 20 percent of India's banking sector and 22 percent of NRI-related banking. It offers several programs designed to meet the needs of diasporic individuals interested in investing and/or participating in development within India. Examples include SBI's "Pravasi Plus Loan Products": healthcare loans, financing for the purchase of combine harvesters and tractors, small business loans, auto loans, and personal loans. Similar loan programs are offered by many other banks; however, SBI's officials in charge of NRI services noted to me in 2004 that the amounts generated through these programs are not sizable because they are not particularly attractive from an investment/return point of view.

Returning to the issue of foreign investment more generally, while India has been unable to attract the same level of FDI as China and its other competitors, it has been more successful in encouraging diasporic investments in both property and public sector bonds. Changes to NRI and PIO investment possibilities have opened up a great deal of potential. But the most visible success in India's quest for diasporic investment has arguably been public sector bond issues. At the regional level, for example, Gujarat and Kerala – states with considerably different political traditions and development trajectories – have identified investment by their expatriate communities as being an integral part of their current strategies of growth, seeking funds from diasporic communities located in North America and the UK through instruments such as bonds and direct private investment. Gujarat, which claims the title of "The Business State of India," initiated its own regional program designed to recognize diasporic individuals from that state through the Gujarat State Non-Resident Gujaratis Foundation. Membership in this organization includes perks such as a "Gujarat Card" – somewhat similar to the Indian Central Government's "Person of Indian Origin Card" – which entitles the bearer to "special consideration by the Government of Gujarat" (Government of Gujarat, 2004). Kerala, which declared 2003–2004 to be "The Year of Investment," has similarly embarked upon an aggressive search for NRI-assisted regional development through programs such as the Global Investor Meet, which boasts of having raised several millions of dollars from the state's émigrés for regional projects (Government of Kerala, 2004).

Nationally, the central government reached out to overseas Indians through three separate bond and savings schemes between 1991 and 2000. Each followed a particular political or economic event that placed the Indian state in a precarious financial position. In 1992, the government issued India Development Bonds following the debt crisis described previously. In 1998 and 2000, the government launched the Resurgent India Bonds and the India Millennium Development Bonds, respectively; the former was a direct appeal for diasporic assistance following global sanctions on India due to nuclear weapons testing. I interviewed two senior bank officers who were in charge of managing these bond issues for their perspective on these initiatives. Much of the following information is drawn from those interviews and archival research.

Each offering was targeted towards infrastructure financing in India, though in actual terms, less than one-third of the funds were directed in this manner, with the rest entering general revenues. All three were offered globally, except for the India Millennium Development Bonds, which could not be sold in the US due to newly revised securities and exchange regulations. In total, there were over 100,000 subscribers to the three bonds. The India Development Bonds matured in 1997, raising US $2 billion (no original target amount was set on issuance). Offered in three currencies (US dollar, British pound sterling, and German deutsche mark), this bond provided an annual rate of return of 8 percent. Resurgent India Bonds matured in October 2003, with an objective to raise US $2.3 billion (they actually raised US $4.23 billion). This bond was denominated in the same three currencies: US dollar (7.75 percent annually), British pound sterling (8.00 percent annually), and German deutsche mark (6.25 percent annually). The India Millennium Bond aimed to raise US $3 billion but passed that mark with a subscription rate totalling US $5.5 billion. According to the bank officers I interviewed, the bulk of investment came from the Persian Gulf states, with a substantial portion from the US and Canada.

One of these officers, who views NRIs as an excellent "low-cost resource for the Indian government," pointed out the difference she saw between types of diasporic investors. Those from the Gulf, she suggested, because they are restricted from owning property or investments in their country of work, are really migrant workers – they send the vast majority of their earnings back as remittances or as investments against their return to India, while those from "the West" are more interested in India as an investment destination or in aiding the development of India. Furthermore, this officer also suggested that, with the exception of well-educated Gulf migrants, investors from "the West" are generally more knowledgeable and expect transparency. Her view of the success of the offerings was that they had attractive rates of return, were a stable and secure investment instrument and, most interestingly, that all three bond issues offered confidentiality in the transactions. She pointed out that some clients wanted to ensure that they would not be subject to surveillance by their 'host' nation; others did not want written records of their communications. These were services that the SBI was able to provide – though such flexibility is unlikely in the era of the endless War on Terror. The officials I interviewed did not foresee the Indian government floating similar bond issues in the near future after the RBI capped interest rates (rates of return are not much more than 0.5 percent over regular bank deposits) and because India had built up substantial reserves in the time since the India Development Bonds were first offered. Nevertheless, she felt that they performed a significant function:

> These bonds were important resources for both the central government and SBI. They allowed the central government to quickly accumulate foreign currency deposits and they also generated revenue for SBI in terms of commissions from conversions.

Others I interviewed – for example, another banker specializing in NRI funds – questioned just how strong the "emotional ties" mentioned by investors in some studies might be. He suggested that this might be more a political/patriotic statement, but one that is not really borne out by facts. In his opinion, the success of the bond issues had to do with the rates of return, not the fact that they were for India's development. If sentimental attachment was the key determinant, then the government should have been able to raise other monies at many other times. From a longer-term perspective, he suggested that the bond issues were "suicidal" – that though they raised funds and provided needed foreign currency immediately, the rates of return were so high that India had to pay back through the nose.

The case of Kerala

Kerala is one of the best-known examples of a remittance economy in the world today. A densely populated state in the southwestern part of India with a high literacy rate and a low rate of population growth, Kerala is a persuasive example of both the potential and the pitfalls of reliance on diasporic capital to sustain a local economy. The state has a long history of labour migration and has a strong reputation for achieving many human development goals, including high levels of education, health, and civic engagement, as well as urbanization. Many communities in Kerala have had considerable experience of both sending emigrants abroad and experiencing the effects of return migration (or maintaining transnational ties) first-hand. At the same time, Kerala has found itself at different moments vulnerable to the effects of global trends, such as political conflicts and economic downturns. It is an excellent case study, therefore, through which we may see how migration and development may be linked, how this process has changed over time, and to predict what some of its changing circumstances might mean for other regions that adopt similar strategies.

The flow of migrants out of Kerala broadly follows the patterns outlined in the previous chapter's discussion of Indian diasporas. In its modern history, post-Independence Kerala has seen many Keralites emigrate to other parts of India and to regional neighbours such as Singapore and Malaysia, primarily for semi-skilled work. Between 1960 and 1975, a number of professionals began to join these out-migrants, including a growing number of nurses. A wave of mass migrations began in 1975 to the Persian Gulf (and, to a lesser extent, to North America and Europe) from South Asia generally and from Kerala in particular. Following the interruption of the First Gulf War, labour migration from Kerala resumed in at least three distinct streams: semi-skilled and unskilled labour to the Persian Gulf; professionals (including engineers, doctors, IT experts, and academics) to various parts of the world; and family-related chain migration to places previously settled via out-migration.

While many other South Asian migrant communities exist in the Persian Gulf, non-resident Keralites (NRKs) represent one of the most significant, with one out of every four Indians in the region hailing from Kerala. Over 2 million people from Kerala work in the region, particularly in countries such as the United Arab Emirates (UAE), Saudi Arabia, Kuwait, and Oman. The migrants work in a variety of occupations ranging from construction to high-skill professional services. These migrants are 'guest workers' who are expected to return to Kerala after the completion of their contracts, which typically last 2 to 5 years. Unlike countries such as the US and Canada, the Gulf countries offer little scope either for family migration and unification or for permanent residency and citizenship. Some studies suggest that remittance-related migration has been the single most dynamic factor in Kerala's post-Independence development and that it has contributed more to poverty alleviation than any other factor, including agrarian reforms, trade union activities, and social welfare legislation (Zachariah and Irudayarajan, 2008). Migration to the Gulf – while on a steep decline in recent years – continues to see nearly 3 million Keralites overseas, with the majority in the Gulf. The proportion of Kerala households with an NRK each in them has remained more or less at the same level as in 2007; in 2003, it was 25.8 percent (Zachariah and Irudayarajan, 2008). The background of the emigrants is affected by religion – a larger proportion of Muslim households see emigration compared to Hindu and Christian ones.

NRKs, like many other South Asian migrant communities in the Gulf, maintain close contacts with family in India, including frequent home visits. They also remain knowledgeable about political developments and socioeconomic changes in the subcontinent and have been active in providing not only remittances but also financial assistance during natural disasters and political upheaval. In Kerala, remittances are often popularly called 'Gulf money' and have been described by the state government as "the most dynamic contribution to the economy of the State," while labour migrants are described as "very high contributors" to that economy. Indeed, Kerala is highly dependent on remittances to help support a much more affluent lifestyle than many other Indian states – the total remittances sent home by foreign workers in 2011 was some four times the state's entire domestic product (Zachariah and Irudayarajan, 2012). Other forms of the economic impact of NRKs include financial savings, real estate and business investments, and new home construction, in addition to the creation of business networks and the development of financial expertise (Zachariah and Irudayarajan, 2008). Therefore, it is little wonder that the Kerala government at the state level has established a ministry for NRKs and has invested in upgraded international airports in cities such as Thiruvananthapuram and Kochi.

In Kerala, the political impact of labour migrants overseas has also been felt in party politics but more crucially in regional development as a whole. Indeed, the 'Kerala model of development' – focused on achieving high levels of growth in quality of life indicators (such as literacy, infant mortality rates, and civic engagement) and addressing issues of land reform – has been considerably dependent on the influx of remittances over the past half-century. These inflows have also kept unemployment relatively low within the state and decreased poverty while augmenting the industrialization and consumer culture of Kerala (Pani and Jafar, 2010; Singh, 2011). However, Kerala's heavy reliance on remittances makes it vulnerable to economic and political shocks that could result in job cuts and resulting losses of revenues. The vulnerability of Kerala's economy to such shocks has been documented. In 1990, Iraq invaded and annexed Kuwait; soon after, the First Gulf War broke out. Thousands of guest workers based in Kuwait, including those from Kerala, fled the country and returned home. This unexpected influx of returning migrants was a dual problem for Kerala, which was suddenly deprived of remittances from its citizens in Kuwait and also had to take care of the returnees, who did not know if and when they would be able to return to their jobs in the Gulf country. The First Gulf War ended in 1991, and many of the migrants returned to the Gulf countries, but during the period of the war, the Kerala economy was adversely affected.

In 2008, the global economic recession accelerated the pace of the return migration from labour receiving countries. Migrant flows to these countries have fallen since the beginning of the global financial crisis, which has also affected the Gulf region unfavourably. Abandonment of large-scale construction and infrastructural projects and the economic crisis in the oil industry have pushed low-paid migrant workers, particularly those in the Gulf countries, to return to India temporarily or permanently. The unskilled migrants are vulnerable to unscrupulous middlemen who promise them good jobs in the Middle East in exchange of large fees but sometimes do not deliver on that promise. Some employers in the Gulf countries are also known not to pay migrant workers the wages that they are owed. As employers of low-skilled workers usually hold on to migrants' passports until they return to their home country, this also places migrant labourers in a vulnerable position. Economists predict that as the Middle Eastern labour market becomes saturated, the flows of labour migrants from Kerala and hence remittances will decline and the state's economy will suffer. Although optimists argue that the Gulf has survived past crises like the Iraq–Kuwait War and that the migration of labour from Kerala has kept up, a remittance-based economy may be unsustainable for Kerala in the long run.

Kerala thus epitomizes the changing modalities of diasporic transnationalism that has brought radical changes in theorizing diasporas. Much more so than Gujarat, the other Indian state that has adopted and pursued migrant Gujaratis as economic and – increasingly – political partners, Kerala continues to depend on its diasporic population as the fulcrum of its economic policy and everyday reality. The diaspora no longer consists of remittance senders alone but comprises active decision-makers in their homeland, as much economically as politically and culturally.

Diasporic action and the forces that drive it are thus essential subjects of scholarly analysis and interpretation leading to the understanding of the relationship between diasporas and their homelands, actual or imagined as the case may be. That relationship becomes a focus in the economic impact of diasporas on their home countries, one that is a sum of both diasporic initiatives and government invitations. As noted in the previous discussion and illustrated particularly by the role of migrants in Kerala, the transnationality of diasporas introduces a fluidity bordering on imponderability in the calculus of the interaction between diasporas and homeland governments. While economics by itself cannot capture the range of that interaction, and certainly not its quality or the values that both underlie it and are generated by it, the economic contribution of diasporas to their homelands does form a measurable groundwork for understanding how, whether, and to what extent diasporas intervene in the development of their homelands.

References

Anderson, B. R. (2006). *Imagined communities: reflections on the origin and spread of nationalism*. London, Verso.

Association for India's Development (2004). "AID projects: rights and social justice, your voice counts." Retrieved January 10, 2004, from http://www.aidindia.org/hq/misc/vcounts/voicecounts.shtml.

Bailey, A. J. (2013). "Migration, recession and an emerging transnational biopolitics across Europe." *Geoforum* **44**: 202–210.

Batzlen, C. (2000). *Migration and economic development: remittances and investments in South Asia, a case study*. New York, P. Lang.

Beine, M., F. Docquier and H. Rapoport (2003). "Brain drain and LDC's growth: winners and losers." *IZA Discussion Paper Series No. 819*. Bonn, Germany, Institute for the Study of Labor.

Conway, D. and R. B. Potter (2007). "Caribbean transnational return migrants as agents of change." *Geography Compass* **1**(1): 25–45.

Corbridge, S. and E. Simpson (2006). Militant cartographies and traumatic spaces: Ayodhya, Bhuj and the contested spaces of Hindutva. *Colonial and Post-Colonial Geographies of India*. S. Raju, M. S. Kumar and S. Corbridge. New Delhi, Sage: 70–84.

Dade, C. and P. Unheim (2007). "Diasporas and private sector development: impacts and opportunities." Ottawa, FOCAL: Canadian Foundation for the Americas.

Das Gupta, M. (2006). *Unruly immigrants: rights, activism, and transnational South Asian politics in the United States*. Durham NC, Duke University Press.

De Haas, H. (2010). "Migration and development: a theoretical perspective." *International Migration Review* **44**(1): 227–264.

de la Garza, R. and Lowell, B. L., Eds. (2002). *Sending money home: Hispanic remittances and community development*. New York, Rowman & Littlefield.

Demmers, J. (2002). "Diaspora and conflict: locality, long-distance nationalism, and delocalisation of conflict dynamics." *The Public – Javnost* **9**(1): 85–96.

Diener, A. C. (2008). "Diasporic and transnational social practices in Central Asia." *Geography Compass* **2**(3): 956–978.

Fix, M., D. G. Papademetriou, J. Batalova, A. Terrazas, S. Yi-Ying Lin and M. Mittelstadt (2009). "Migration and the global recession." Washington, DC, Migration Policy Institute.

Gammeltoft, P. (2002). "Remittances and other financial flows to developing countries." *International Migration* **40**(5): 181–211.

Geithner, P., C. Chen and P. Johnson, Eds. (2004). *Diaspora philanthropy and equitable development in China and India*. Cambridge, MA, Global Equity Initiative, Harvard University.

Hugo, G. (2012). "Migration and development in low-income countries: a role for destination country policy?" *Migration and Development* **1**(1): 24–49.

India Development and Relief Fund (2006). "Home page." Retrieved November 26, 2014, from http://www.idrf.org/.

Khagram, S. and P. Levitt (2008). *The transnational studies reader: intersections and innovations*. New York, Routledge.

Krishnamurty, V. (1994). *Study of investment preferences of expatriates from India*. New Delhi, National Council of Applied Economic Research.

Kuznetsov, Y., Ed. (2006). *Diaspora networks and the international migration of skills: how countries can draw on their talent abroad*. Washington, DC, World Bank.

Levitt, P. (2001). *The transnational villagers*. Berkeley, University of California Press.

Levitt, P. and R. De La Hesa (2003). "Transnational migration and the redefinition of the state: variations and explanations." *International Migration Review* **26**(4): 587–611.

Levitt, P. and D. Lamba-Nieves (2011). "Social remittances revisited." *Journal of Ethnic and Migration Studies* **37**(1): 1–22.

Levitt, P. and M. C. Waters (2002). *The changing face of home: the transnational lives of the second generation*. New York, Russell Sage Foundation.

Ley, D. (2004). "Transnational spaces and everyday lives." *Transactions of the Institute of British Geographers* **29**(2): 151–164.

Mathur, C. (2013). The Indian state, the diasporic Hindu Right and the "desire named development." *Enacting Globalization: Multidisciplinary Perspectives on International Integration*. L. Brennan. New York, Palgrave Macmillan: 13–19.

Menon, N. and A. Nigam (2007). *Power and contestation: India since 1989*. London, Zed Books.

Mohan, G. (2006). "Embedded cosmopolitanism and the politics of obligation: the Ghanaian diaspora and development." *Environment and Planning A* **38**(5): 867–883.

Nagraj, R. (2005). Industrial growth in China and India: a preliminary comparison. *Workshop on Indian Economy: Policy and Performance 1980–2000.* Vancouver, BC, Canada, Center for India and South Asia Research, University of British Columbia, June 23–24, 2005.

Nanda, T. K. and S. Bhatt (2002). "The NRIs reaction to the Gujarat State Election." *Rediff Online.* Retrieved November 26, 2014, from http://www.rediff.com/election/2002/dec/11spec.htm.

Nayyar, D. (1994). *Migration, remittances and capital flows: the Indian experience.* Oxford, Oxford University Press.

Orozco, M. (2010). "Worker remittances in an international scope." Washington, DC, Inter-American Development Bank.

Özden, C. and M. Schiff, Eds. (2006). *International migration, remittances, and the brain drain.* New York, Palgrave MacMillan.

Page, B. and C. Mercer (2012). "Why do people do stuff? Reconceptualizing remittance behaviour in diaspora-development research and policy." *Progress in Development Studies* **12**(1): 1–18.

Pani, N. and Jafar, K. (2010). "Mass education-led growth and non-agrarian villages: long-term results of the Kerala model." *Oxford Development Studies* **38**(1): 25–42.

Prashad, S. (2005). "Can the Indian diaspora help India overtake China?" Retrieved November 26, 2014, from http:www.gopio.net/India_China_0703.doc.

Prashad, V. (2000). *The karma of brown folk.* Minneapolis, University of Minnesota Press.

Raghuram, P. (2009). "Which migration, what development? Unsettling the edifice of migration and development." *Population, Space and Place* **15**(2): 103–117.

Ratha, D. (2003). "Workers' remittances: an important and stable source of external development finance." *Global Development Finance: Striving for Stability in Developmental Finance.* Washington, DC, World Bank: 157–175.

Ratha, D. (2011). *Leveraging migration for Africa: remittances, skills, and investments.* Washington, DC, World Bank.

Rubinov, I. (2014). "Migrant assemblages: building postsocialist households with Kyrgyz remittances." *Anthropological Quarterly* **87**(1): 183–216.

Satzewich, V. and L. Wong (2003). Immigration, ethnicity and race: the transformation of transnationalism, localism and identities. *Changing Canada: Political Economy as Transformation.* W. Clement and L. Vosko. Montreal and Kingston, McGill-Queen's University Press: 364–384.

Seshadri, R. K. (1993). *From crisis to convertability: the external value of the rupee.* Bombay, Orient Longman.

Singh, P. (2011). "Wellness and welfare: a longitudinal analysis of social development in Kerala, India." *World Development* **39**(2): 282–293.

Sundar, N. (2004). "Teaching to hate: RSS' pedagogical programme." *Economic and Political Weekly* **39**(16): 1605–1612.

Times of India (2014). "US-based NRIs land in India to campaign for Modi." Retrieved August 27, 2014, from http://timesofindia.indiatimes.com/nri/us-canada-news/US-based-NRIs-land-in-India-to-campaign-for-Modi/articleshow/33818982.cms.

Tung, R. L. (2008). "Brain circulation, diaspora, and international competitiveness." *European Management Journal* **26**(5): 298–304.

Vyas, J. quoted in Amin, A. (2000). "Bid to tap NRI funds for Narmada project." *India Abroad.* Retrieved November 26, 2014, from http://www.highbeam.com/doc/1P1-79278973.html.

World Bank (2013). "Developing countries to receive over $410 billion in remittances in 2013 says World Bank." Retrieved November 26, 2014, from http://www.worldbank.org/en/news/press-release/2013/10/02/developing-countries-remittances-2013-world-bank.

World Bank (2014). "Migration and remittances data." Retrieved May 12, 2014, from http://web.worldbank.org/WBSITE/EXTERNAL/TOPICS/0,,contentMDK:21924020~pagePK:5105988~piPK:360975~theSitePK:214971,00.html.

Zachariah, K. C. and S. R. Irudayarajan (2008). *Kerala migration survey report 2007.* Thiruvananthapuram, Center for Development Studies.

Zachariah, K. C. and S. R. Irudayarajan (2012). *Kerala migration survey report 2011.* Thiruvananthapuram, Center for Development Studies.

4   Building a global city

Kolkata is certainly not unusual in hosting projects that market 'global lifestyles' and supposedly 'international' spaces. Cities across the globe – for example, Chinese mega-cities like Beijing, Shanghai, Hong Kong, and Guangzhou – are increasingly surrounded by suburban development projects, including villas and apartment towers sold to wealthy residents and overseas expats who demand an 'international style' (King, 2004; Ma and Wu, 2013). Gated condominiums that offer a high standard of living – with amenities that are considered 'world class' and a familiar modernist layout, design, and feel – are increasingly common across the world, from the Middle East (Glasze and Alkhayyal, 2002) to the Caribbean (Mycoo, 2006), from Istanbul (Genis, 2007) to Puerto Rico (Sanchez, 2009). Baecker (2013) suggests that even in post-conflict situations, the presence of the diaspora is an important motivation for urban planners to re-invent their cities – he argues that in Beirut, there has been explicit attention paid to connecting the rebuilt city center with global networks in business and marketing in order to entice the bodies and resources of the Lebanese diaspora to come home. Perera's (2011) study of new apartment towers and townships in Colombo, Sri Lanka, being built after the end of the decades-long civil war are similarly designed to attract wealthy locals and diasporic Sri Lankans to reinvest in the country.

Given such trends, we need to ask what the opportunities offered to residents of such spaces are really like and why an 'international style' might feature so centrally in their representation. Furthermore, we need to explore what the impact of such spaces is on local communities and on diasporas more generally. How do these new developments define 'world class,' and why is such a designation so sought after by civic leaders all across the globe? How might such ideas affect the way in which a city is developed, and how might they transform the lives of those who already live in it? Such questions will be explored in much greater detail in the chapters that follow, but here I will focus on some of the concepts that are central to the processes that are so rapidly changing Kolkata today. How has the opportunity to "live the way the world does," as one development in Kolkata boasts (South City, 2014), gained such currency not only with prospective real estate owners but also with civic leaders, politicians, and planners as well? What has convinced so many of the latter that the building of these housing projects will be a key marker for regaining global recognition for the city?

This chapter takes up these questions in several parts. I begin by examining the concept of the world or global city – how it has been defined by scholars, what the idea describes, and how it has been contested. In particular, I explore the notion of the 'ordinary city' in the critique of the world city thesis and the related idea that urban informality might tell us as much about global formations as the more visible manifestations of urban power do. The next section of the chapter focuses on one of the processes through which the city is and has been actively remade: gentrification and the displacement of current residents in service to the ideal of a 'renewed' urban landscape. I also briefly examine the idea that the gentrification process – once used primarily to describe urban change in postindustrial cities of the Global North – has become a global phenomenon affecting multiple sites and whether this is being catalyzed by the presence of "global gentrifiers" (Bridge, 2007). In this exploration, I take up the forms of neoliberal urbanism and revanchist politics that currently dominate much of city building across the globe today. Finally, since this book is primarily interested in the attempt to re-invent Kolkata as a (once-again) global city, I close the chapter by looking at what potential allure Kolkata as a specific urban site has for the diaspora.

World cities and global cities

What is it that marks a city as global? And why does it seem that so many urban agglomerations today are vying for the designation? Considerable scholarship has been devoted to the question of cities; their planning; and their economic, social, and political impacts in recent years. Particularly influential have been accounts of world city formation offered by scholars such as Friedmann (1986), Friedmann and Wolff (1982), and Sassen (2001). Sassen asserts that while some believed that the end of the twentieth century would signal a decline in the importance of cities due to the emergence and consolidation of globalization, the reverse is in fact true: "the power of transnational capital must be produced spatially, in physical as well as temporal sites of global control" (2012: 1). She states that

> [the] last two decades have seen transformations in the composition of the world economy, accompanied by the shift to services and finance, that have renewed the importance of major cities as sites for certain types of activities and functions. In the current phase of the world economy, it is precisely the combination of the global dispersal of economic activities and global integration – under conditions of continued concentration of economic ownership and control – that has contributed to a strategic role for certain major cities. These I call global cities.
>
> (Sassen, 2012: 4)

The intersections between politics, finance, and management are, in such a view, increasingly concentrated in central cities – particularly those which grow ever larger in size and stature to become mega-cities, global cities, and world-class cities. These do not function independently but are rather linked with others like them in networks of communication, transport, and capital. Such sites are simultaneously competitors and collaborators in the world systems of economic, political, and cultural flows. That command and control functions are centered in cities is not surprising, urbanization being one of the defining characteristics of modernity. Moreover, with the urban population of the Earth having surpassed that of the rural within the past decade (Seto, Güneralp, and Hutyra, 2012), the world in which we live continues to move more towards the city than to the country.

This is not to suggest that the majority of the world will now inhabit gated enclaves and luxury towers. Indeed, the opposite is true – the majority of urban growth is in informal developments and slums. Davis (2006) points out that much of the world's poor are being pushed and pulled into insecure housing in a "planet of slums," as his book of the same name calls them. Interestingly, Davis' only mention of Kolkata in his discussion of the "future history of the Third World's post-industrial megacities" takes the form of passing references to its pavement dwellers, rag-pickers, and those who live on mounds of garbage. Many Kolkatans would no doubt be mortified by such a representation of their city. It is the global city that Kolkata aspires to become, not a city of slums, as it has long been described.

Yet what exactly are the features that might constitute a global city? If a focus on the nodes of economic and political control and the networks of travel and trade define a global city, then surely a global city would contain the institutions and infrastructure that enable these connections. These might include the presence of international or international governance institutions like the World Bank, United Nations, European Union, or North Atlantic Treaty Organization (NATO). They might house the headquarters of Fortune 500 companies, international financial institutions, stock exchanges, and transnational law firms. A downtown business district and a sophisticated communications infrastructure – including international media – are also often important markers of the global city, as well as an advanced transportation system, including an airport that acts as a hub, and perhaps a light-rail transit system. Cultural institutions and a cultural 'scene' are also crucial elements: art galleries, theatres, playhouses, and bookstores. Educational institutions are similarly important, especially large universities, colleges, and research centers. Sports teams and sporting events – such as 'major-league franchises' and the Olympics – are also much-sought-after markers of global prominence. Indeed, as Gold and Gold (2008) argue, winning the opportunity to become an Olympic city – despite the seemingly ruinous financial and social cost of doing so – has become a key signifier of world-class status. So, too, are the spectacular structures that often represent the city on the international stage, such as the Eiffel Tower, the Statue of Liberty, or Big Ben. Small wonder, then, that emerging global cities are invested with their own monuments, whether the Petronas Towers in Kuala Lumpur, Burj Khalifa in Dubai, or the Bayterek in Astana. All such features are an important part of the marketing strategies that cities across the world increasingly employ to sell themselves to global investors, to convince companies to set up shop (Kavratzis, 2007), and to increase tourism (Gillen, 2010).

And while a large population is not necessary in order to gain the label of global city – there are reasons why Dhaka, Mexico City, or indeed Kolkata are generally not at the top of one's mind when one thinks of global cities, despite the sheer numbers of their inhabitants – having a diverse population is helpful. Ethnic neighbourhoods with shops and restaurants, often host to parades and celebrations, are increasingly commodified and marketed by global cities as evidence of cosmopolitan tolerance and the acceptance of difference. Such enclaves are not only to be found in former ethnic ghettoes – Chinatowns, Little Italys, and Little Indias – but also in what Li (2009) calls the "ethnoburb": suburban ethnic communities on the outskirts of global cities. King describes such an example in the case of diasporic Indians based in the suburbs of Washington, DC, where the "highly visible collective identity of these communities is primarily evident in the public landscape of malls, shops, temples, cinemas, wedding houses, festivals and the Asian-American subjects themselves" (2004: 105).

Such urban forms and variations are common in many of those cities deemed to have achieved global city status. Traditionally topping most global city lists are London, New York, and Tokyo (Sassen, 2001). More recently, we have witnessed a rise of certain Asian mega-cities such as Hong Kong, Singapore, Shanghai, and Beijing, which have been described (or describe themselves) as global (Bastida and Huan, 2014; Goh, 2014; Wang *et al.*, 2011). Dubai, before the worldwide economic meltdown in the mid-2000s, was explicitly attempting to transform itself from a desert trading post to the most fantastical and extravagant global city one might imagine (Vora, 2011; Buckley, 2012). Many other cities undergoing an urban transformation have expressed the goal of building themselves into a world-class city – from São Paolo to Seoul, Berlin to Budapest, Sydney to Stockholm, and Toronto to Taipei (Brenner and Keil, 2006). Indeed, it would likely be harder to find a city that is *not* engaging in a project of becoming global than to find one that is.

The ranking of cities by some researchers is perhaps the most common representation of world cities or global cities in the mass media and, while it may come off to some as a crude and decontextualized popularity contest, such scaling remains of significance to many others. Trying to ascertain which city occupies what position also reifies the idea that world cities are and should be competing with one another for primacy, an aspiration embraced by many urban players. But it is a view accepted by few researchers, most of them having pointed out, on the contrary, the disastrous consequences of such strategies. A key challenge is that while the idea of studying world/global city formation became a compelling one in the 1980s, by the mid-1990s, as Derudder (2008) points out, the lack of actual empirical evidence to substantiate the world city hypothesis and the agenda for research failed to persuade many that the neo-Marxist perspective developed by Friedmann (1986) and others was relevant. The Globalization and World Cities (GaWC) group and network set out to rectify this lack of evidence of the actual command and control functions of world cities. Over the past two decades, researchers associated with this network have focused on developing methodological approaches and gathering empirical evidence of the world city. This has included studies of the presence of global service firms (Beaverstock *et al.*, 2000; Taylor, 2001), multinational corporations (Rozenblat and Pumain, 2007), media and telecommunications (Zook, 2008), and transport (Smith and Timberlake, 2002; Derudder and Witlox, 2005). Yet the challenge to world cities and global cities research has come not only from those who seek to advance the project by finding better and more convincing evidence of the phenomenon but also from those who suggest that the focus itself may be misplaced.

Ordinary cities

Some scholars argue that world cities research has been dominated by structuralist readings of urban space such that the agency of those who inhabit and experience it are absent from the analysis. Ley's (2004) study of cosmopolitan professionals and the transnational business class as represented by Chinese-origin 'astronaut families' in Vancouver demonstrates the grounded nature of globality. He argues that a focus on the actual experiences and everyday lives of residents in global cities can yield empirical details that a disembodied view of flows, structures, and processes may not. Ley is critical in particular of what he calls "globe-talk" – in his view, world cities research that is focused primarily on economic functions simply reinforces the discourse of those who push the agenda of becoming world class and leaves urban processes seemingly monolithic, inaccessible, and inevitable:

> The abrogation of agency leaves a spectre of inevitability to urbanism in a global age. The absence of agents liberates teleological aspects of globalization discourse that see a city's destiny as fixed, sometimes even unavoidable, before the global space of flows, an interpretation that has been internalized all too often by policymakers and politicians in their pursuit of the place marketing of business elites.
>
> (Ley, 2004: 154)

Other critics of world cities research suggest that there is too much time and energy spent primarily on cities of the Global North (Roy and Ong, 2011; Simone, 2010; McCann, 2004; McFarlane, 2008). Roy (2009) advocates the need for "dislocating" the Euro-American center of theoretical production that dominates much of the scholarship on urban lives and futures. Moreover, she argues that

> [it] is not enough simply to study the cities of the global South as interesting, anomalous, different and esoteric empirical cases. Such forms of benign difference-making keep alive the neo-Orientalist tendencies that interpret Third World cities as the heart of darkness, the Other.
>
> (Roy, 2009: 2)

The work of Robinson (2002, 2011) has similarly suggested that urban theory needs to "break free of the categorizing imperative" as a way of decolonizing the approach to both studying and engaging politically with the city. She offers as an alternative the idea of the "ordinary city," building on the work of Amin and Graham (1997), among others, as a different conceptual framework with which to explore diverse urban forms and practices, rather than simply reifying the trajectory and momentum of the global city discourse and world city analysis. Indeed, as Çinar and Bender (2007: xiv) have argued, "the very practice of daily urban life emerges as the means through which the collective imagination that conjures up a city takes place." It is therefore necessary to examine more closely the cracks and fissures in seemingly fixed social formations and spatial relations; the challenge, contestation, and co-optation that take place between groups and discourses; and the daily negotiations and reorientations that constitute the making and remaking of cities at different scales and at different times.

Multiple variations of this theme of studying 'ordinary cities' have emerged. Some scholars have rejected the literal enormity of global cities by focusing on smaller-sized sites for examining processes that affect all of them (Jayne *et al.*, 2010; Bell and Jayne, 2009). For others, this process has implied looking at different practices – for example, urban sexualities and the city beyond the megapolis – looking at Chengdu; suburban Australia; or Burlington, Vermont, rather than at New York or London (Brown, 2008; Andrucki and Elder, 2007). McFarlane (2010) suggests a return to a more comparative urban geography, one that bridges the North–South divide rather than reproducing a binary between world cities and those unworthy of making the cut. Simone's work offers such a comparative lens in productive and provocative ways through his examination of four postcolonial cities in Africa (2004) and his portrait of urban informality in Djakarta (2010). Rather than simply reifying particular notions of the contemporary urban landscape as being characterized by individual resilience, community adaptation, and triumph on the one hand or despondence, decay, and hopelessness on the other, Simone argues persuasively that we need instead to look at the persistence, dynamism, and contradictions of cities – especially in the Global South – as works in progress.

Some of the key proponents of world city and global city research have responded forcefully to their critics, arguing that the original research agenda has been misunderstood or misrepresented in the intervening years. Smith, for example, suggests that

> [postcolonial] and ordinary cities advocates have misunderstood the neo-Marxist work of authors such as Friedmann, Sassen, Beaverstock et al. and Taylor inasmuch as they have imagined them to have invented a supplicant urban world – containing the majority of the world's cities – which is notable for its absences, rather than having over several decades of research into the urban geography of command and control actually found one.
>
> (Smith, 2013: 2301)

From Smith's viewpoint, those who advocate an ordinary cities research agenda have therefore conflated the study of global cities by researchers with the production of global cities by developmental forces.

Gentrification and displacement

Whether urban researchers favor a focus on ordinary cities or on global ones, they see many of the same processes transforming the urban landscape in both types. One of the most prominent of these is displacement in the context of gentrification. Displacement in the urban context is, as Hartmann suggests, "an old, old story" (2002: 109). But where earlier histories of enclosure, industrialization, and colonialism focused on processes of transformation from rural to urban lives or the privatization of commonly held spaces, many twentieth-century theories of urban displacement have centered on the appropriation and redefining of already-existing properties as a form of development. Building upon Glass's (1964) coining of the phrase 'gentrification' to describe the "invasion" and "upgrading" of working-class districts by new upper- and middle-class denizens, a substantial body of work has studied the phenomenon across many – mainly Western – cities. Much like international development projects that build dams, railroads, ports, and other forms of infrastructure that often displace populations from homes and livelihoods (Vandergeest, Idahosa, and Bose, 2007), processes of gentrification are usually presented in the media and political discourse as a common good (though primarily on a civic rather than a national scale). Specific urban sites – inner cities, factory districts, low-income neighbourhoods – are seen as being in a state of organic and inevitable decay and in desperate need of 'renewal,' 'refurbishing,' or 'revitalization.' Such euphemisms obscure the economic and political processes that have resulted in the degradation of public infrastructure, the lack of affordable housing, and the deindustrialization of manufacturing sectors in many regions. It is important to recognize, as Hartmann reminds us, that

> [displacement] at heart is a political process, having to do with operant values and power in the society. Forced displacement occurs when one group of potential users of a piece of property has the motivation and power to force others out of that property, usually because the former desires to put the property to what the planners and economists term a "higher and better use."
>
> (Hartmann, 2002: 109)

Processes of gentrification, including the forced and imposed displacement upon which it relies, are often represented in conceptualized terms as a 'cleaning up' of the city, a removal of 'urban blight' and the unseemly decay it signifies. Instrumental in this process is the deployment of those who, if one subscribes to the logic of urban renewal, might make newly refurbished spaces fit to live in once again – or might encourage developers to reshape neighbourhoods to suit a new aesthetic. Many studies of gentrification have, for example, pointed to the role of artists, students, and certain immigrant groups – such as the model minorities mentioned previously – as a bleeding edge in the process (Zukin, 1996; Ley, 1996; Gibson, 2004). As Ley remarks,

> the artist's very presence, the deployment of a critical aesthetic disposition on the streets of old neighbourhoods, has become a principal tool for goading on gentrification, thereby lining with gold the pockets of buyers and sellers in the inner-city property market.
>
> (Ley, 2003: 2544)

Others have noted that many of these early residents of newly gentrified spaces are themselves subject to further displacement as neighbourhoods become more chic and attractive to middle-class consumers (Zukin, 1995).

Gentrification, as a process that has been ongoing through much of the latter half of the twentieth century, has not, of course, gone unchallenged. Low-income residents, anti-racism organizations, immigrant coalitions, citizen's rights groups, anti-poverty activists, squatters, the homeless, and many others have resisted the dislocations forced by urban planners and private developers alike. Such conflicts have been so pronounced that Smith (1996) goes so far as to ask: "[Is] gentrification a dirty word?" The Right to the City movement, with its roots in the writings of Lefebvre (1996 [1967]) has emerged as an important articulation against neoliberal urbanism by linking the reshaping of cities and their impact on communities to a global discourse of human rights. Such an attempt has resonated with many – in New York City, for example, the Right to the City Alliance (2014) brings together some 45 different social justice groups fighting gentrification. But as Marcuse points out, the concept needs definition to be effective: "Whose right is it about, what right is it, and to what city?" (Marcuse, 2009: 185). Purcell argues that the idea is valuable not as a panacea to cure what ails the urban condition but rather as a way to create a new approach to the crisis of neoliberal restructuring, one that focuses on what he calls "an urban politics of the inhabitant" (Purcell, 2002: 99). Harvey, who formulated the idea of "accumulation by dispossession," argues that displacement lies at the core of urbanization under capitalism (Harvey, 2003, 2008). He has also emerged as a strong proponent of the Right to the City concept. For him,

> the right to the city is far more than the individual liberty to access urban resources: it is a right to change ourselves by changing the city. It is, moreover, a common rather than an individual right since this transformation inevitably depends upon the exercise of a collective power to reshape the processes of urbanization. The freedom to make and remake our cities and ourselves is, I want to argue, one of the most precious yet most neglected of our human rights.
>
> (Harvey, 2008: 23)

Yet despite the many struggles against neoliberal restructuring both within and outside the academy, the process of 'urban renewal' has continued and indeed intensified. It has become an ideological project as much as any technocratic initiative in urban planning, in many cases extended to what Smith calls the instance of "the new urban revanchism," a vengeful and vicious attack upon the most marginalized and the targets of displacement (1996: 44–47). Smith and many other scholars, as well as social and environmental justice activists, have long been deeply critical of gentrification (Wolch, Byrne, and Newell, 2014; Eckerd, 2011). Among many civic leaders and even some researchers, it has been described in much more celebratory terms, especially in such examples as Florida's (2012) work on the 'creative class' and the emphasis on a form of cosmopolitanism that accepts difference (at least in terms of sexuality and a generalized form of multiculturalism). Slater (2006) decries such a turn and the surprising absence of ethnographies of the displaced themselves – whether working class or racialized – from discussions of gentrification, shifting the focus instead onto the gentrifiers themselves.

Gentrification has also taken on increasingly diverse forms – discrete and enclosed gated communities not only on the suburban fringes of the city but also within established neighbourhoods are today as likely to be a marker of urban change as a rebuilt neighbourhood where artists, students, and hipsters push out older residents. As Le Goix and Webster (2008) point out, such defensive and privately governed enclaves are not so much an innovation but rather the resurrection of much older traditions. The explosive growth of gated communities in the US in recent decades often marks them as North American in form and style, but Le Goix and Webster (2008) suggest that while their appearance and ubiquity are global, they are underpinned by diverse local manifestations:

> Gated communities became, for some, both symbols and symptoms of a line that is being crossed from voice-based citizenship to exit-based citizenship; from politically organized to market-organized civic society. While the discourse on gated urbanism seemed to spread from American sources, the phenomenon itself had its own local history in every continent and country: in China, South-East Asia and Australia, Europe, Eastern Europe, South Africa and the Arab world. Gating may thus be interpreted as a global trend. It is undoubtedly influenced in many ways by US models but it is developed according to local political, legal and architectural traditions.
>
> (Le Goix and Webster, 2008: 1189)

Global gentrification

The presence of gated communities in so many parts of the world and the changes they are creating in the worldwide urban landscape have given credence to the idea of a trend towards global gentrification. A number of studies have shown gentrification – whether through gated communities, urban renewal projects, the building of entire townships, or some other form – to be expanding across multiple geographic locations (Harris, 2008; Lees, 2012; Lopez-Morales, 2011; Shin, 2009). These suggest that there are considerable variations in style, including the development of vacant lands, "designer neighborhoods," and "off-the-peg new-build developments, often beside water or in other landmark locations in the city" (Atkinson and Bridge, 2005: 4). Indeed, Smith has argued that gentrification in its present incarnation has evolved into what he calls a "global urban strategy," a new form of neoliberal urban policy (Smith, 2002: 427). Similarly, Atkinson and Bridge suggest that

> [the] current nature and extent of gentrification raises questions not just about its interrelations with globalisation but also its manifestation as a form of new urban colonialism. The geographical spread of gentrification over the last twenty years has been reminiscent of earlier waves of colonial and mercantile expansion, itself predicated on gaps in economic development at the national scale. It has moved into new countries and cities of the global "south" but has also now cascaded down the urban hierarchies of regions within the urban north where it has been established for much longer. In short, gentrification appears to have migrated centrifugally from the metropoles of North America, Western Europe and Australasia. This has happened at the same time as market reform, greater market permeability and population migration have promoted internal changes in the economies of countries not previously associated with gentrification.
>
> (Atkinson and Bridge, 2005: 2)

The centrality of global gentrification for the expansion of neoliberal policies broadly (Peck and Tickell, 2002) and for neoliberal urbanism in particular cannot be understated. Smith argues that as the Keynesian project of liberal, limited intervention in public policy eroded throughout the 1970s and 1980s in the North American context (and at the same time that command economies were under assault in the Global South), gentrification was "embraced by productive capital":

> As cities became global, so did some of their defining features. The emerging globalization of gentrification, like that of cities themselves, represents the victory of certain economic and social interests over others, a reassertion of (neoliberal) economic assumptions over the trajectory of gentrification.
>
> (Smith, 2002: 446)

In the case of India, the planning of global cities has gone hand in hand with the expansion of neoliberal policies and gentrification strategies. As detailed in the previous chapter, the years following the Indian state's acceptance of an emergency International Monetary Fund (IMF) loan in 1991 and (necessarily) concomitant opening up of its command economy have generally been viewed in the popular imagination as a successful and much-needed break from the stagnation of the 'Hindu rate of growth.' But as Banerjee-Guha (2006) points out in her examination of the construction of Mumbai as a global site, growing inter- and intra-city disparity during this period raises serious questions as to just who benefits and who loses from increasing integration into global economic and cultural chains. She focuses on planning policies to show that while the

current context is qualitatively different from the past, it is one more of inten-
sification than rupture:

> During the initial post-independence years, the gap between the declared
> planning objective and the obtained reality started showing up in the process
> of urban development in Mumbai. . . . In the post-liberalization years in the
> 1990s till this date, this gap increased at an alarming rate.
>
> (Banerjee-Guha, 2006: 210–211)

Siematycki (2006) argues that the motivation to build a new subway system
in metropolitan Delhi is the product of pressure from several special interest
groups with competing political and economic agendas. These include tied aid
from the Japanese government, the attempt by property developers to open up
new areas of growth, the attempt by political parties to gain votes, and the desire
of local print media to market the city. Achieving global city status for Delhi in
this reading is to be done by creating a new and modern infrastructure through
neoliberal urbanism (via private–public partnerships, among other methods) and
displacing existing residents along the way:

> This is the vision for a modern Delhi, as promoted by the politicians and
> technocrats leading the development of the metro in their media sound bites
> and inauguration speeches . . . the Delhi Metro experience suggests that
> mega projects are seductive for their potential to reorder space and culture,
> the direction of which is increasingly guided by international meanings and
> aspirations.
>
> (Siematycki, 2006: 285, 290)

While Mumbai and Delhi have been subjects of much literature on global
gentrification and world city making in India, even greater attention has been
paid to two other sites that are perhaps more visibly linked to the global economy,
especially the new information economy: Hyderabad and Bangalore. In the case
of the former, the transformation of the city into a hub for information technology
(IT)–related and business process outsourcing multinational companies was the
main strategy for the regional government. In fact, it was such a success that
the city has become known and marketed as Cyberabad – a development driven
not only by global flows but also by displacement and dispossession (Das, 2013).
But perhaps the best-known example of India's importance in the political
economy of the IT age is the city of Bangalore: once the sleepy 'garden city'
populated by pensioners, today the heart of the software and services industries
on the subcontinent. The Indian central government (and individual states) has
long pursued the strategy of concentrating resources and investment in specific
urban sites for IT-related growth, especially the aforementioned Gurgaon and
Noida, Chennai, and Hyderabad (Fromhold-Eisebith, 2006), but it is in Bangalore
that such policies have arguably had the greatest impact. Nearly one-fourth of
the headquarters of the Indian software industry are now located in Bangalore,

next to India-based IT multinationals such as Wipro and Infosys (Parthasarathy, 2004). Parthasarathy suggests that the transnational linkages Bangalore mobilizes make the city seem more an outpost of Silicon Valley than an Indian version of the latter. A visit to Infosys's 80-acre campus presents a particular vision of globality itself – golf courses, a telecommunication center built as a replica Louvre, shopping malls, gyms and food courts in a replica Sydney Opera House, cell phone stations made to look like British telephone booths, fancy auditoriums and leisure areas – that would not be out of place in the proposed townships and gated communities envisioned in the case studies described in later chapters. Beyond the walls of the campus lie farmland and informal settlements, all amidst new transit and housing construction – again, a familiar sight in peri-urban regions of Indian cities today. And that includes Kolkata.

The transformations that are taking place in contemporary India in general and in Kolkata in particular today are being driven, to a large extent, by the logic of neoliberal urbanism in which city services are increasingly privatized, public space is captured or corroded, and the desire to (re)build a global city trumps considerations of social justice or equity. Global gentrification helps us to conceptualize in particular the role of the diaspora in this dynamic, as the potential 'beautifiers' whose aesthetics and symbolic presence herald the coming of a new (and supposedly better) urban space. Smith's (2002) concept of the revanchist city and its aggressive desire to recapture the city from "undesirable elements" also has its echoes in this case. Kolkata's own 'lower classes' throughout the city – rural commuters, hawkers, domestic workers, agricultural labourers and fishers, workers in the informal economy, squatters, and refugees – are all obstacles to be removed on the road to recovering the city's greatness – living signs of decay whose very presence is an affront to middle-class sensibilities and aspirations.

One of the questions these debates and the developments in cities like Kolkata have brought up is whether current transformations of urban space are wrought at the behest of the middle classes. We understand that world cities are constantly being produced and reproduced all around us and that the process is underwritten by concepts such as neoliberal urbanism and gentrification. But if Kolkata is being rebuilt *for* someone, who or what is the subject of the aspirations of urban planners and civic leaders? Are the townships and housing developments meant only for local elites, or are they meant to entice others to populate them? In other words, if an important component of world/global city formation is an international aesthetic and the demonstration of international linkages, is it then crucial to actually attract the diaspora back home? Can diasporic transnational subjects then be conceived of as a category of 'global gentrifiers' whose presence or presumed tastes are enough to herald and justify urban renewal processes? Bridge argues strongly against such a view, saying that

> there is no global gentrifier class based on occupation, knowledge, aesthetics, or use of space. There are certain global cities where a range of middle-class strategies over social reproduction can be sustained. The downtown neighbourhoods of these global cities are, however, increasingly occupied by a

global elite of the superrich, who might be called global supergentrifiers but whose particular mix of economic and cultural capital suggests that they have very different aesthetic affiliations distinct from something we might call gentrification. In all other urban spaces across the globe where gentrification is found it is unlikely that there is the reproduction of a set of occupational, knowledge, aesthetic, or taste characteristics that can be associated with a distinct urban new middle class. . . . Gentrification thus has to be considered separately as an urban process from a process of class constitution, and neither points to its coherence as a global phenomenon.

(Bridge, 2007: 43–44)

Davidson (2007) similarly suggests that it is important not to see a global gentrifier class as the drivers of urban transformation but to focus instead on the capital flows and processes that allow the formation of local middle-class elites whose interests fit the new cityscapes under construction. My own position lies somewhere between those of Davidson and Bridge on one hand and Ley on the other. So far, it is clear that globalization, neoliberal urbanism, and gentrification are processes that create the conditions for the rise of the global city. But without the bodies and beliefs of the transnational diasporic subject to draw upon, fetishize, commodify, and market, it is hard to imagine selling the project of world city building to residents of a city – at least the middle-class citizens with whom and about whom civic leaders might be concerned. In the final section of this chapter, then, I will explore the potential of Kolkata to claim aspirational global city status and therefore its need to capitalize on its expatriates to help rebuild its stature and remake its landscape.

The importance of place

It appears that stories of the return of the Global Indian and the facilities he or she inhabits are used as evidence of Kolkata's resurgence from a site of urban decay through much of the twentieth century to one of revitalization and growth, as discussed in the next chapter. But while Global Indians are not the reason for the adoption of neoliberal urbanization strategies by governments of all stripes in Kolkata, their presence – both physical and ideological – helps to represent and thereby materialize the city's connections to global circuits of capital, labour, and ideologies (Roy 2011). It is therefore the Global Indian – and locals of similar status – who is meant to populate the industrial parks and high-tech suburbs on the fringes of Kolkata built to attract large corporations and multinationals.

Given this scenario, it is worth asking just how important Kolkata itself is in the imaginings of its diaspora. Try as many Indian governments might, attempts to fundraise for various nation-building projects in putative homelands have been far less successful than the efforts of 'hometown associations' or the more common informal transfers of funds between family members, as discussed in the previous chapter. The ties that bind are more often to specific places – regions, districts, cities, or neighbourhoods – than to a grand notion of an imagined community in the form of the nation–state. The connection to place, therefore, should not be automatically linked with nation. Cities are particularly interesting sites for investigating the transnational connection and their relations with place-making. It is from urban centers that many immigrant groups leave, and it is primarily to urban centers that many such diasporas journey. In the US, for example, the vast majority of immigrants settle in just six states – New York, California, Texas, Florida, Illinois, and New Jersey – and in a handful of large cities within them (Portes and Rumbaut, 2006).

None of this means that the nation does not matter. Indeed, for many diasporas that do not come from a nation–state with which they identify, the dream instead is of a country of their own, as on the part of elements of the Sikh, Kurdish, and Sri Lankan Tamil diasporas. Still, the claim to 'place' and 'home' is based primarily on what De calls the "territorial referent" rather than on the necessity of the nation–state:

> [While] the statehood demand is not a must for nationalism, a territorial referent is. Nationalism proceeds to define people in terms of shared institutions, economic, social and/or political (such as language, religion, customs, etc.) and defends or seeks to increase their autonomy. All the while this demand for autonomy is made in terms of belonging to a particular territory.
>
> (De, 1992: 15)

This emphasis on place and a territorial referent should not be taken as an argument for the primacy of static or immutable spaces that produce 'pure' diasporic identities. Indeed, as my later discussion on the cultural construction of transnational attachments illustrates, the territorial referent – while indeed important in the formation of diasporic identity – is a malleable, adaptive, and transportable concept, though it may not always be characterized as such by those who utilize it.

In this context, it is therefore significant to ask whether Kolkata functions as such a territorial referent and helps to locate or anchor the migrant living overseas. After all, the diaspora from Kolkata and West Bengal has neither the long history nor the sheer quantity of the Punjabi, Gujarati, or Keralite population abroad, not to mention all the many others who are putatively gathered within the folds of the 'global Indian.' And yet we can find traces of a Calcuttan diaspora – both intentional and unwitting – in both the past and the present. Carter and Torabully, in their poetic study of migration, memory, belonging, and the construction of a diasporic identity among indentured labourers from India in the Caribbean, recount the stories of individuals going to Calcutta from rural villages for day labour and ending up thousands of miles away:

> The promised service was in Calcutta, not Mauritius. . . . Karoo was enticed to Calcutta with the promise of work on road repairs, and when the promised job did not materialize, was, like many others, inveigled into the emigration depot.
>
> (Carter and Torabully, 2002: 19)

Many others have left more recently, following paths of employment, education, and empire. For some, such as the smaller Anglo-Indian, Chinese, and Jewish communities of Calcutta, the city has become less and less inviting (Blunt, 2005; Oxfeld, 1996). For others, especially the Bengali Hindu professional classes and intellectuals who have left Calcutta over the past 40 years, either for other parts of India and Asia or for Europe, North America, Australia, and other parts of the Global North, the lure has most often been jobs and a better standard of living. Yet even for some of the latter, the city is remembered with ambivalence, with both its decay and its grandeur foremost in the minds of many. Certain streets, sounds, tastes, and smells of the city continue to be recalled through nostalgia and sepia tones; Suraiya suggests that

> the emigrant experience is perfectly suited to a transplant of Calcutta. And since this can't be done with the real city, a mythical one has been invented to fit the need, an emotional precinct of love and squalor. Beyond the reach of urban blight and civic neglect, this portable city of the mind flourishes all the more as the real one declines.
>
> (Suraiya, 2007: 121)

While it is not a landscape that we see reproduced through Bollywood in the way that Delhi, Mumbai, or even New York and the Swiss countryside are, Kolkata does speak to the Bengali migrants that left. We see it through art-house cinema, an occasional biopic of Mother Teresa, or perhaps a documentary on poverty and prostitution (Hutnyk, 1996). Calcutta does appear considerably more widely in literature – in the writings of Jhumpa Lahiri or Amitav Ghosh, for example. And its most exotic and Orientalized features are the stuff of Anthony Bourdain and Gordon Ramsey's culinary adventures. Intellectuals and academics are not reticent to talk about it either, as the intellectual professions in the West are full of individuals who themselves constitute a Bengali or Calcuttan diaspora. How do they and others see the changing face of the city itself? How is this transformation conceived? To Suraiya, there are indeed many who might care:

> Calcutta may not know it – and if it does, like a somnolent cat it might not care – but there are a number of offshoots of the community flourishing across the globe . . . a diverse cross-section of people of various backgrounds and occupations who, scattered across the world from Melbourne to Memphis and from Hounslow to Hong Kong, maintain a tenuous but lasting long-distance connection with Calcutta, the city they once lived in. Perhaps no other place exercises quite the same kind of lure, composed of about equal parts of nostalgia and anger. With its frailties and foibles, its all too human shortcomings and lapses, Calcutta is like a rundown old relative – eccentric, cantankerous, infuriating, impossible to live with perhaps, but equally impossible to cut oneself off from.
>
> (Suraiya, 2007: 122)

To some extent, my material suggests that it is in fact the very hybridity, indeterminacy, and fluidity that Gilroy (2000) and others have championed that bears some responsibility for the schizophrenic nature of diasporic existence, an existence particularly characteristic of parts of the Kolkata and Bengali diaspora. Place and attachment to it – or distance from it, return to it, and avoidance of it – become simultaneous and contradictory impulses. Bharati Mukherjee, a novelist based in the US, says that during her first years after leaving India,

> I thought of myself as an expatriate Bengali permanently stranded in North America because of destiny or desire. My first novel, *The Tiger's Daughter*, embodies the loneliness I felt but could not acknowledge, even to myself, as I negotiated the no man's land between the country of my past and the continent of my present. Shaped by memory, textured with nostalgia for a class and culture I had abandoned, this novel quite naturally became an expression of the expatriate consciousness.
>
> (Mukherjee, 1997)

Salman Rushdie also bears testimony to the sense of alienation and longing for roots that has characterized much of the postcolonial migration experience. For him, the search is for something that is ultimately difficult, if not impossible to find: "We will not be capable of reclaiming precisely the thing that was lost. . . . We will, in short, create fictions, not actual cities or villages, but invisible ones, imaginary homelands, Indias of the mind" (Rushdie, 1991: 10). How do the Indias – and in this case the Kolkatas – of the mind compare to the changing landscape of Kolkata? That is the question that the following chapters examine in much greater detail.

References

Amin, A. and S. Graham (1997). "The ordinary city." *Transactions of the Institute of British Geographers* **22**(4): 411–429.

Andrucki, M. and G. S. Elder (2007). "Locating the state in queer space: GLBT non-profit organizations in Vermont, USA." *Social & Cultural Geography* **8**(1): 89–104.

Atkinson, R. and G. Bridge, Eds. (2005). *Gentrification in a global context: the new urban colonialism*. London, Routledge.

Baecker, D. (2013). "Mapping a city onto itself: a note on the reconstruction of Beirut Central District." Retrieved May 12, 2014, from http://papers.ssrn.com/sol3/papers.cfm?abstract_id=2229687.

Banjerjee-Guha, S. (2006). Post-modernism, post-Fordism and flexibilized metropolis: dialectical images of Mumbai. *Colonial and Post-Colonial Geographies of India*. S. Raju, M. S. Kumar and S. Corbridge. New Delhi, Sage: 205–222.

Bastida, U. and T. C. Huan (2014). "Performance evaluation of tourism websites' information quality of four global destination brands: Beijing, Hong Kong, Shanghai, and Taipei." *Journal of Business Research* **67**(2): 167–170.

Beaverstock, J. V., R. G. Smith, P. J. Taylor, D.R.F. Walker and H. Lorimer (2000). "Globalization and world cities: some measurement methodologies." *Applied Geography* **20**(1): 43–63.

Bell, D. and M. Jayne (2009). "Small cities? Towards a research agenda." *International Journal of Urban and Regional Research* **33**(3): 683–699.

Blunt, A. (2005). *Domicile and diaspora: Anglo-Indian women and the spatial politics of home*. Oxford, Blackwell.

Brenner, N. and R. Keil (2006). *The global cities reader*. London, Routledge.

Bridge, G. (2007). "A global gentrifier class?" *Environment and Planning A* **39**(1): 32–46.

Brown, G. (2008). "Urban (homo) sexualities: ordinary cities and ordinary sexualities." *Geography Compass* **2**(4): 1215–1231.

Buckley, M. (2012). "From Kerala to Dubai and back again: construction migrants and the global economic crisis." *Geoforum* **43**(2): 250–259.

Carter, M. and K. Torabully (2002). *Coolitude: an anthology of the Indian labour diaspora*. London, Anthem.

Çinar, A. and Bender, T., Eds. (2007). *Urban imaginaries: locating the modern city*. Minneapolis, University of Minnesota Press.

Das, D. (2013). Ordinary lives in extraordinary Cyberabad. *Transforming Asian cities: Intellectual Impasse, Asianizing Space and Emerging Translocalities*. N. Perera and W.-S. Tang. New York, Routledge: 112–122.

Davidson, M. (2007). "Gentrification as global habitat: a process of class formation or corporate creation?" *Transactions of the Institute of British Geographers* **32**(4): 490–506.

Davis, M. (2006). *Planet of slums*. London, Verso.

De, S. (1992). *Nationalism and separatism in Bengal: a study of India's partition*. New Delhi, Har-Anand Publications.

Derudder, B. (2008). "Mapping global urban networks: a decade of empirical world cities research." *Geography Compass* **2**(2): 559–574.

Derudder, B. and F. Witlox (2005). "An appraisal of the use of airline data in assessments of the world city network." *Urban Studies* **42**(13): 2371–2388.

Eckerd, A. (2011). "Cleaning up without clearing out? A spatial assessment of environmental gentrification." *Urban Affairs Review* **47**(1): 31–59.

Florida, R. (2012). *The rise of the creative class revisited*. New York, Basic Books.

Friedmann, J. (1986). "The world city hypothesis." *Development and Change* **17**(1): 69–83.

Friedmann, J. and G. Wolff (1982). "World city formation: an agenda for research and action." *International Journal of Urban and Regional Research* **6**(3): 309–344.

Fromhold-Eisebith, M. (2006). Infotech industries and regional disparities in India. *Colonial and Post-Colonial Geographies of India*. S. Raju, M. S. Kumar and S. Corbridge. New Delhi, Sage: 162–181.

Geniş, Ş. (2007). "Producing elite localities: the rise of gated communities in Istanbul." *Urban Studies* **44**(4): 771–798.

Gibson, T.A. (2004). *Securing the spectacular city: the politics of revitalization and homelessness in downtown Seattle*. Lanham, MD, Lexington Books.

Gillen, J. (2010). "Tourism and entrepreneurialism in southeast Asian cities." *Geography Compass* **4**(4): 370–382.

Gilroy, P. (2000). *Against race: imagining political culture beyond the color line*. Cambridge, MA, Belknap Press of Harvard University Press.

Glass, R. (1964). *London: aspects of change*. London, Centre for Urban Studies.

Glasze, G. and A. Alkhayyal (2002). "Gated housing estates in the Arab world: case studies in Lebanon and Riyadh, Saudi Arabia." *Environment and Planning B* **29**(3): 321–336.

Goh, D.P.S. (2014). "Walking the global city: the politics of rhythm and memory in Singapore." *Space and Culture* **17**(1): 16–28.

Gold, J.R. and M.M. Gold (2008). "Olympic cities: regeneration, city rebranding and changing urban agendas." *Geography Compass* **2**(1): 300–318.

Harris, A. (2008). "From London to Mumbai and back again: gentrification and public policy in comparative perspective." *Urban Studies* **45**(12): 2407–2428.

Hartman, C. (2002). *Between eminence and notoriety: four decades of radical urban planning*. New Brunswick, NJ, Center for Urban Policy Research.

Harvey, D. (2003). *The new imperialism*. Oxford, Oxford University Press.

Harvey, D. (2008). "The right to the city." *New Left Review* **53**(September-October): 23–40.

Hutnyk, J. (1996). *The rumour of Calcutta: tourism, charity, and the poverty of representation*. London, Zed Books.

Jayne, M., C. Gibson, G. Waitt and D. Bell (2010). "The cultural economy of small cities." *Geography Compass* **4**(9): 1408–1417.

Kavaratzis, M. (2007). "City marketing: the past, the present and some unresolved issues." *Geography Compass* **1**(3): 695–712.

King, A. D. (2004). *Spaces of global culture: architecture, urbanism, identity*. London, Routledge.

Le Goix, R. and C. Webster (2008). "Gated communities." *Geography Compass* **2**(4): 1189–1214.

Lees, L. (2012). "The geography of gentrification: thinking through comparative urbanism." *Progress in Human Geography* **36**(2): 155–171.

Lefebvre, H. (1996). The right to the city. *Writings on Cities*. E. Kofman and E. Lebas. London, Blackwell: 63–184.

Ley, D. (1996). *The new middle class and the remaking of the central city*. Oxford, Oxford University Press.

Ley, D. (2003). "Artists, aestheticisation and the field of gentrification." *Urban Studies* **40**(12): 2527–2544.

Ley, D. (2004). "Transnational spaces and everyday lives." *Transactions of the Institute of British Geographers* **29**(2): 151–164.

Li, W. (2009). *Ethnoburb: the new ethnic community in urban America*. Honolulu, University of Hawai'i Press.

Lopez-Morales, E. (2011). "Gentrification by ground rent dispossession: the shadows cast by large-scale urban renewal in Santiago de Chile." *International Journal of Urban and Regional Research* **35**(2): 330–357.

Ma, L. and F. Wu (2013). *Restructuring the Chinese city: changing society, economy and space*. London, Routledge.

McCann, E. (2004). "Urban political economy beyond the 'global city.'" *Urban Studies* **41**(12): 2315–2333.

McFarlane, C. (2008). "Urban shadows: materiality, the 'Southern city' and urban theory." *Geography Compass* **2**(2): 340–358.

McFarlane, C. (2010). "The comparative city: knowledge, learning, urbanism." *International Journal of Urban and Regional Research* **34**(4): 725–742.

Marcuse, P. (2009). "From critical urban theory to the right to the city." *City: Analysis of Urban Trends, Culture, Theory, Policy, Action* **13**(2–3): 185–197.

Mukherjee, B. (1997). "American dreamer." Retrieved May 14, 2014, from http://www.motherjones.com/commentary/columns/1997/01/mukherjee.html.

Mycoo, M. (2006). "The retreat of the upper and middle classes to gated communities in the poststructural adjustment era: the case of Trinidad." *Environment and Planning A* **38**(1): 131–148.

Oxfeld, E. (1996). Still guest people: the reproduction of Hakka identity in Calcutta, India. *Guest people: Hakka Identity in China and Abroad*. N. Constable. Seattle, University of Washington Press.

Parthasarathy, B. (2004). "India's Silicon Valley or Silicon Valley's India? Socially embedding the computer software industry in Bangalore." *International Journal of Urban and Regional Research* **28**(3): 664–685.

Peck, J. and A. Tickell (2002). "Neoliberalizing space." *Antipode* **34**(3): 380–404.

Perera, S. (2011). Gated communities as packaged fantasies: a meeting of the local and the global and the standardisation of taste in urban Sri Lanka. *Urban Navigations: Politics, Space and the City in South Asia*. J. S. Anjaria and C. McFarlane. New Delhi, Routledge: 239–264.

Portes, A. and Rumbaut, R. (2006). *Immigrant America: a portrait*. 3rd edition. Berkeley, University of California Press.

Purcell, M. (2002). "Excavating Lefebvre: the right to the city and its urban politics of the inhabitant." *GeoJournal* **58**(2–3): 99–108.

Right to the City Alliance. (2014). "Home page." Retrieved August 27, 2014, from http://www.righttothecity.org.

Roy, A. (2009). "The 21st-century metropolis: new geographies of theory." *Regional Studies* **43**(6): 819–830.

Roy, A. (2011). "Slumdog cities: rethinking subaltern urbanism." *International Journal of Urban and Regional Research* **35**(2): 223–238.

Roy, A. and A. Ong, Eds. (2011). *Worlding cities: Asian experiments and the art of being global*. Oxford, Wiley-Blackwell.

Rozenblat, C. and D. Pumain (2007). Firm linkages, innovation and the evolution of urban systems. *Cities in Globalization: Practices, Policies, and Theories*. P. J. Taylor, B. Derudder, P. Saey and F. Witlox. New York, Routledge: 124–149.

Rushdie, S. (1991). *Imaginary homelands: essays and criticism 1981-1991*. New York, Penguin Books.

Sánchez, L. (2009). "Puerto Rico and Puerto Ricans: place, space and society." *Southeastern Geographer* **49**(4): 323–325.

Sassen, S. (2001). *The global city: New York, London, Tokyo*. Princeton, Princeton University Press.

Sassen, S. (2012). *Cities in a world economy*. Thousand Oaks, CA, Sage/Pine Forge.

Seto, K. C., B. Güneralp and L. R. Hutyra (2012). "Global forecasts of urban expansion to 2030 and direct impacts on biodiversity and carbon pools." *Proceedings of the National Academy of Sciences* **109**(40): 16083–16088.

Shin, H. B. (2009). "Property-based redevelopment and gentrification: The case of Seoul, South Korea." *Geoforum* **40**(5): 906–917.

Siemiatycki, M. (2006). "Message in a metro: building urban rail infrastructure and image in Delhi, India." *International Journal of Urban and Regional Research* **20**(2): 277–292.

Simone, A. (2004). *For the city yet to come: changing life in four African cities*. Durham, NC, Duke University Press.

Simone, A. (2010). *City life from Jakarta to Dakar: movements at the crossroads*. London, Routledge.

Slater, T. (2006). "The eviction of critical perspectives from gentrification research." *International Journal of Urban and Regional Research* **30**(4): 737–757.

Smith, D. A. and M. Timberlake (2002). Hierarchies of dominance among world cities: a network approach. *Global Networks, Linked Cities*. S. Sassen. London, Routledge: 117–141.

Smith, N. (1996). *The new urban frontier: gentrification and the revanchist city*. New York, Routledge.

Smith, N. (2002). "New globalism, new urbanism: gentrification as global urban strategy." *Antipode* **34**(3): 427–450.

Smith, R. G. (2013). "The ordinary city trap." *Environment and Planning A* **45**(10): 2290–2304.

South City Projects (2014). "Home page." Retrieved May 11, 2014, from http://southcityprojects.com.

Suraiya, J. (2007). *Calcutta: a city remembered*. New Delhi, Bennet, Coleman and Co.

Taylor, P. J. (2001). "Specification of the world city network." *Geographical Analysis* **33**(2): 181–194.

Vandergeest, P., P. S. Bose and P. Idahosa (2007). *Development's displacements: ecologies, economies, and cultures at risk*. Vancouver, UBC Press.

Vora, N. (2011). "From golden frontier to global city: shifting forms of belonging, 'freedom,' and governance among Indian businessmen in Dubai." *American Anthropologist* **113**(2): 306–318.

Wang, J., M. Su, B. Chen, S. Chen and C. Liang (2011). "A comparative study of Beijing and three global cities: a perspective on urban livability." *Frontiers of Earth Science* **5**(3): 323–329.

Wolch, J. R., J. Byrne and J. P. Newell (2014). "Urban green space, public health, and environmental justice: the challenge of making cities 'just green enough.'" *Landscape and Urban Planning* **125**: 234–244.

Zook, M. (2008). *The geography of the Internet industry: venture capital, dot-coms, and local knowledge*. Oxford, Blackwell.

Zukin, S. (1995). *The culture of cities*. Oxford, Blackwell.

Zukin, S. (1996). Space and symbols in an age of decline. *Re-presenting the City: Ethnicity, Capital and Culture in the 21st Century Metropolis*. A. D. King. New York, New York University Press: 43–59.

5   The context of Kolkata

> One cannot understand Calcutta without looking at it from two angles . . . there is
> no major event or influence of India that has not found an echo in Calcutta's bub-
> bling cauldron. It is Calcutta where for centuries sahibs and bhadralok, babus and
> pavement dwellers, socio-religious reformers and terrorists, authors and activists
> have mingled. A brilliant symbol of power and wealth, Calcutta was the second
> city, after London, of the greatest empire in the world. But as the decay set in,
> Calcutta became a symbol of misery, the problem city par excellence.
>
> (Racine, 1990: 51)

This narrative of Calcutta as a city in decline is a powerful one that has preoc-
cupied residents, urban scholars, and politicians alike. The city's decline is
especially troubling because of its history as a global city before the term was
invented – the industrial, financial, and political locus of a world power in Asia.
Intensifying the bemusement of observers, Calcutta in its current incarnation, its
squalor and decrepitude notwithstanding, remains credibly global. Here, then, is
the conundrum: how can a city be at once global and yet parochial? For understanding this puzzle, the city's history is an invaluable guide. But before delving
into history, it would be useful to take note of what has become the common
view of Calcutta's endemic malady. It is one that has taken an especially stub-
born hold in the post-Independence period – the dominant understanding is one
of Calcutta as a city that does not work, one that is overcrowded, polluted,
inefficient, directionless, bloated, and fading. Chattopadhyay (2006: 2–3) suggests
that, beyond India, Kolkata serves in urban studies as "a metaphor for urban
disaster, as the worst possibility of urbanism, as modernity gone astray." But
such negative representations are not created outside alone. Locally, owing to
its diminished economic growth, the city's reputation has long been in tatters.
For many of the leftists who ruled West Bengal for over 30 years in a Marxist-led
government, the city remained an ambivalent site. It is the political and cultural
center of Eastern India and for decades held the title of a cultural capital, only
recently outshone by the likes of Mumbai and Delhi. But as Roy (2003: 9)
argues, it did also constitute "horrible urban capitalism" for those on the Left,
who saw progress and development emerge through three decades of reforms in

the countryside. Until recently, middle-class urbanites saw Kolkata left behind, bypassed politically by Delhi, outdone economically by Mumbai, and cast out of the global limelight that falls on Bangalore.

It appears that former Indian Prime Minister Rajiv Gandhi, who famously dismissed it as a "dying city" in 1985 was not alone (Bhattacharya, 2007), nor the first of Calcutta's detractors. Starting with *Hutom Pyanchar Naksha* (1862, *The Old Owl's Tale*), Kaliprasanna Sinha's satire of decadence and the chaotic coexistence of rich and poor in the new urban center, tales of doom have been present throughout Calcutta's relatively brief history. Under colonial rule, outright hostility towards what was an extremely challenging urban environment was voiced – not surprisingly – by many, including Rudyard Kipling, who famously described Calcutta's dark side:

> As the fungus sprouts chaotic from its bed,
>   So it spread –
>   Chance-directed, chance-erected, laid and built
>   On the silt –
>   Palace, byre, hovel – poverty and pride –
> Side by side.
>
> (Kipling, 1911: 283)

In the twentieth century, both before and especially after Independence, Calcutta has been witness to multiple traumatic events. This includes the Bengal famine of 1943 and the violence and waves of refugees that accompanied both the Partition of India and the Pakistani civil war that gave birth to Bangladesh. The largest influxes of refugees from these latter two events settled in the Calcutta metropolitan area (Weber, 2006: 65). The sudden appearance of so many newcomers, coupled with the trauma of the events that drove them to the city, seems in many ways to have overwhelmed Calcutta both literally and figuratively. We see evidence of such a sensibility in the work of major Bengali artists of the 1950s, including the filmmakers Ritwik Ghatak and Satyajit Ray, whose films develop a local idiom of urban decay in Calcutta after Partition and Independence (Raychoudhuri, 2009; Ganguly, 2010). Common themes in their cinema include the loss of status as a capital, a sense of yearning and absence among refugee characters, the deprivation of a hinterland upon which the city had once depended, and the lack of investment in infrastructure seen through images of life and physical space in cities that are literally falling apart (Sarkar, 2009).

Since the beginning of the current millennium, however, as Calcutta has become Kolkata, its reputation has risen and, in the eyes of many, the city has been rehabilitated. While at the state level, scandals and political violence led to the eventual defeat of the Left Front government in West Bengal, even before its demise, the Marxist coalition in West Bengal had focused much of its energy on Kolkata in the post-1991 liberalization era. As early as 1997, a series of initiatives and reforms ushered in an era of neoliberal politics and governance in West Bengal, a trend that has been mirrored by municipal agencies and by the Trinamool Congress government now heading the state. For many in the middle classes, the dominant story now is that Kolkata is a city on the rise, as evidenced, they consider, by more effective governance, the return of multinational corporations, the creation of new IT-focused townships, and an explosive growth in upper-end real estate. New malls, highways, and flyovers dot the city; Internet cafés and global restaurant chains abound; while various initiatives to 'clean up' and 'beautify' public space are underway – a set of processes this book explores in greater detail in the next three chapters.

If shiny new buildings are the signifiers of a city's march towards global status, then Kolkata seems on its way, even if large sections of the population seem to be en route to a different destination. In the light of this multitude of perceptions, we need to look at Kolkata's history in some detail. This chapter provides an overview, with the first section of the chapter presenting a summary of Kolkata's history, focusing especially on the early colonial period of its ascendance; the second section charting decline throughout much of the twentieth century; and the last section dealing with what is known in India as the era of liberalization, emphasizing in particular the post-1997 period. From this time onwards, political parties of various stripes in both municipal and state government have embraced a series of neoliberal reforms in order to rehabilitate and reshape the city in image, form, and style. These initiatives include major infrastructure development projects – often in the form of public–private partnerships – the privatization of some city services; forced evictions of squatters and slum and pavement dwellers in the name of health and the environment; and the construction of luxury apartment buildings and their attendant facilities, both inside the city and along its peri-urban fringes. Taken together, these trends are meant not only to reclaim Kolkata's place in India but also more broadly on the world stage. As we will see in the three case study chapters that follow, Kolkata will become a global city again only if it is able to build modern infrastructure, reclaim its wild spaces, and turn them into an urban landscape fit for the lifestyles of the desirable cosmopolitan subject – such as the Global Indian. Such a motivation was a recurrent theme among many of the civic leaders and urban planners who I interviewed.

Background: from colonial city to imperial center to postindustrial wasteland

Rumour has it that Calcutta is a city of between ten and fifteen million people. Located on the banks of a tributary of the Ganges, it has known human settlement for something over three hundred years. As a trading post for the British East India Company, and geopolitical centre of British imperialism, the untold wealth of the subcontinent passed through its port. Portrayed as an overcrowded place of poverty and despair, of desperation and decline, the rumour of Calcutta travels all over the world. Yet popular Western notions of this incredible city are scant, wrong, contemptuous, ideological, vicious, shitty. There is little good said about the place, and what is said is so often extreme: Calcutta, crowded and stinking, brutal and dark, black hole and slum: saved only by the vague association with the Missionaries of Charity. Calcutta suffers from a bad press.

(Hutnyk, 1996: vii)

The fledgling settlement that became Calcutta was known as 'Golgotha' to the British soldiers, sailors, tradesmen, and clerks who accompanied Job Charnock, its dark nickname a nod to the high mortality rate it inflicted upon Europeans in those early days (mainly due to malaria). Through its nineteenth-century affluence and the energy of a vigorous proto-nationalist and anti-colonial movement, it became known as a city of palaces and political movements. But a darker reputation was insistent: from Kipling's depiction of a crowded city blanketed by a "dense wet heat" and the cries of "yelling jackals" (Kipling, 1891) to Rajiv Gandhi's labeling of Calcutta as a "dying city," bereft of industry, activity, and hope, Calcutta-watchers remarked on its urban dysfunctionality. Eventually, negative stereotypes began to circulate worldwide, setting aside its earlier fame. Dominique Lapierre's novel *City of Joy* (1985) and its movie rendition have served, in many ways, to reinforce the Orientalist perception that it was a city in need of a literal white knight to save it. One might argue that the fame of other saviours like Mother Theresa could only have been achieved in a place like Calcutta, where only the miraculous might apparently stem the tide of poverty and despair.

The city and its proponents do not, of course, seek to actively market it through such negative representations. By the mid-2000s, for example, the West Bengal Industrial Development Corporation (WBIDC) was trumpeting Kolkata as "the gateway to the Asian tigers . . . offering the shortest distance to the rich treasure trove of the Asia Pacific region" (WBIDC, 2006) – a flattering and hopeful view. All of these sobriquets assigned to Kolkata/Calcutta reflect its multifaceted history, from colonial glory to economic failure and social decline. Today, the hopeful and self-proclaimed resurgence claimed for the city remains similarly marked by contraries, especially the proximity of affluence and deprivation and the heterogeneity of the urban space itself.

The city's global image has suffered from what Hutnyk (1996) refers to as a poverty of representation, depicted most often through the lenses of charity (developmental and philanthropic projects); poverty (a 'black hole' of despair, emptied of industry); pollution (human and environmental); and tourism (a decaying colonial remnant). Yet even for those locals who have themselves internalized such a view, Calcutta remains an important touchstone and symbol. For some, it was an antithesis to the idea of the positive reforms taking place in rural Bengal, an urban site that combined the ruins of imperial grandeur with an inefficient, corrupt, and incompetent postcolonial city. Paradoxically, the city thus provided fecund soil for a neoliberal rebirth as part of a wider urban resurgence across the nation. As such, it became a crucial node in the construction, maintenance, and reformulation of Bengali identity – urban and rural, diasporic and local. In order to understand the ebb and flow of Kolkata's fortunes, we must turn, in part, to a brief history and profile of the city itself.

Kolkata is the capital of the state of West Bengal, located on India's east coast and flanked by the states of Assam, Sikkim, Bihar, and Orissa. The borders of the state are also international, adjoining Bangladesh, Bhutan, and Nepal. The southeast quadrant of the state is what this discussion is most concerned with; however, it is worth noting that it is the northern and particularly the northeastern regions of West Bengal that continue especially to suffer political turmoil, situated as they are in an area of considerable political instability due to tribal and Maoist insurgencies in neighbouring states and ongoing conflict and violence in countries like Nepal. Indeed, this continuing violence in the northeast contributes as a push factor for migration into Kolkata itself (McDuie, 2013; Nath, 2005), the latest in a history of large numbers of people arriving into the city for both economic and humanitarian reasons. This constant influx of people has for decades remained a potent factor of the instability and decline that is a staple of the bad press Kolkata continues to receive.

Kolkata is an old port city, bounded on the west and northwest by the Hooghly River and on the south and southeast by the coast and low-lying wetlands and salt lakes, towards which the city gently slopes and into which it drains. The core of the city is flat, with few elevations more than 2 m above sea level. The name Kolkata refers to both the city proper and the administrative district of West Bengal in which it lies, usually referred to as Greater Kolkata. The core city consists of roughly 185 km², with an older, more congested section in the north, while to the south lie more residential, slightly better-planned neighbourhoods or *paras* (Bhatta 2009). The old Calcutta Business District is located near the center of the old city core, along with the state legislative buildings, town hall, several other government offices, and corporate or regional headquarters for banking and other industries. As with much of the rest of the city, old Calcutta's downtown is a mix of multi-story office blocks, colonial buildings, and the hovels of slum- and pavement-dwellers.

The urban agglomeration of Kolkata includes several municipal corporations, municipalities, city boards, police stations (or *thanas*, a form of urban units in the region), and villages. It represents the third-largest urban agglomeration in India after Mumbai and Delhi, and the 2011 Census put the population of the city at 14,617,882, with the population under the Kolkata Municipal Corporation standing at 4,486,679 (Census of India, 2011). While India may still be a country of many villages (with nearly 70 percent of the nation still rural), mega-cities like Kolkata are increasingly the sites in which we see the concentration of many of the problems that confront the contemporary Indian nation as a whole. These rapidly urbanizing cities with increasing population growth and concentration are the population hubs that are marked by issues of mass unemployment, widespread illiteracy, the explosive growth of slums, snarling traffic congestion, loss of public and green spaces, alarming levels of water and air pollution, and a general deterioration of infrastructure and services.

Three centuries ago, the thought of the sprawling city that present-day Kolkata came to be would have been hard to entertain. At that time, the area around Kolkata was part of a largely rural district in the delta of lower Bengal, a flat rice swamp interspersed with patches of jungle and a few scattered villages on the riverbanks. The area was a region integrated in networks of considerable trade and cottage industries, mainly concerned with textiles and thread; however, the center of Bengal at the time was the city of Murshidabad, some 60 miles to the north (Gupta, 1993: 32). It was from here that Job Charnock, an agent of the East India Company, obtained trade rights in 1690 for the area around the villages of Kalikata, Sutanuti, and Govindapur. The venture was not particularly successful; Charnock died 3 years later, and in 1698, the British East India Company purchased rentier rights to the villages from the Mughal government. As the new landowners (*zamindars*), the Company enlarged the existing garrison and trading post. By 1699, the British had decided to develop Calcutta as a Presidency city, a primary node in the command and control of their commercial enterprise. This decision proved to be a major stimulus for increasing urbanization, and the prospects for employment and commercial opportunities drew increasing numbers of rural people into the burgeoning settlement. By 1707, the British began building Fort William on the Hooghly River to further protect their holdings, adding a wharf and a great number of storehouses in the years that followed. A town began to grow up haphazardly around the fort, which was completed in 1715. While the white bachelor clerks and soldiers stayed in their quarters within the fort, married officials often chose to reside with their families in civilian personal dwellings nearby. As a result, private European houses started cropping up around the fort (Gupta, 1993: 37). Also, local Bengali peasants and intermediaries from trading backgrounds in addition to the existing trading classes began to settle in and around this new town, flocking to the nascent city and adding density to the previously sparse population. Thus, the process of urbanization began to blossom on the grounds of the three former villages. By 1717, the area originally rented by the British was overwhelmed by this unorganized growth, and the British felt pressured to obtain the Mughal Emperor's permission to purchase land rights in another thirty-eight villages from local zamindars in 1717. Of these, five were on the other side of the Hooghly River (in the area which became what is now Howrah), while the rest were contiguous to the three original villages.

Soon what had begun as trade turned into politics, as developments both within the region and across the subcontinent began to play a prominent role in the growth and structure of Calcutta. The Maratha raids of western Indian warlords and their armies against both the Mughals and European traders led to a general exodus from the western side of the Hooghly River, with the fugitives choosing to settle predominantly in British territory on the eastern bank. The presence of the newly built fort attracted more settlers, thus accelerating the process of rapid urbanization. In 1727, a civil court and the municipal corporation were formally established with the appointment of the first mayor, William Hallwell. The growing prominence of the new town was boosted when the Nawab of Bengal ousted the English from Calcutta and renamed the city 'Alinagar,' an episode during which the infamous 'Black Hole of Calcutta' incident occurred in which a group of British captives was killed. But following the Nawab's defeat in the equally mythologized Battle of Plassey in 1757, British supremacy in the region was re-established. By 1765, when Lord Clive gained control over Bengal, Bihar, and Orissa from the titular but increasingly enfeebled Mughal Emperor, Calcutta's place as the center of the empire was assured. In fact, by then, migrants to the city included diasporic groups, including Armenians and Jews, who settled there either in pursuit of specific jobs or of the new opportunities for trade and commerce. To accommodate the growing population, whole neighbourhoods were built, and in 1772, Calcutta became the capital of British India when the first governor–general, Warren Hastings, transferred all offices from Murshidabad.

The nineteenth century saw the rapid emergence of Calcutta as the "city of palaces" and the "cultural capital of the sub-continent" (Sanyal, 1993: 42–44). This was in part due to the concentration of political and economic power in the city and also as a result of its location as a center for educational institutions and the arts. The Royal Asiatic Society, the Calcutta Madrassa, the School Book Society, Sanskrit College, Fort William College, the Calcutta Medical College (the first in Asia), the Hindu College (later renamed Presidency College), and eventually Calcutta University were all founded over the course of the nineteenth century. A public sphere flourished in the form of publications, both in English like the *Calcutta Gazette*, *The Bengal Gazette*, and *The Statesman*, as well as in the vernacular with Bengali publications such as *Bangadarshan*, *Digdarshan*, *Samachar Chandrika*, *Sambad Koumudi*, and *Sambad Timirnashak*. Coffee shops, museums, bookshops, art galleries, and a lively theatre scene nurtured lively debates and public discourses, all of which bore testimony to the refined culture of the city.

A multiplicity of architectural monuments also emerged during this period, ranging from impressive colonial buildings like the Ochterloney Monument (now Shaheed Minar) and the Government House (now Raj Bhavan) to the palaces of rich absentee landlords and the more modest but ubiquitous multi-storied homes of local traders serving colonial elites and the emerging indigenous middle class. The colonial residences were essentially Western or rather Orientalist in design, while the homes of the affluent locals were also embellished with massive pediments; long colonnades; ornate capitals; and stucco terra-cotta–cast iron decorations, railings, and figures (Chattopadhyay, 2006), although their layout – for example, closed courtyards and covered verandas – spoke a vernacular language. A proliferation of associational life, often related to ethnic and religious identity, led to the construction of churches, temples, mosques, synagogues, gurdwaras, and Buddhist and Zoroastrian sites of worship. As Calcutta evolved and grew, the built environment of the city increasingly reflected the multicultural and pluralistic nature of the population and its everyday life.

The development of infrastructure has also played an important role in shaping Calcutta's character (Chaudhuri, 1990: 148–149). In 1854, the first railways in India connected Calcutta to the rural district of Hooghly, the center of the jute industry, while 1873 saw the first horse-drawn tram car in inner-city Calcutta. Motor cars appeared on its city streets in the late nineteenth century, while an electric tram car line serving the center was inaugurated in 1902 to run from Esplanade to Kidderpore Street. Such developments were an important part of colonial necessities. Throughout the nineteenth century, trade had been increasingly promoted across the region by the British. With the growth of commerce, the need for a better-developed communications and transportations infrastructure was clear. Accordingly, the necessary means were built to transport goods, people, and troops throughout the region. Prior to 1860, the Kolkata port had occupied only a small area of the riverbank in the Hooghly, Howrah, and 24 Parganas districts on the eastern shore of the river. These docks served ships exporting raw materials from Bengal, Bihar, Assam, and part of the northwest provinces. Initially, exports from Kolkata to Europe consisted of raw materials such as indigo and cotton and, later, cash crops such as opium, jute, and tea. In 1866–1867, jute from West Bengal accounted for 21.6 percent of India's export earnings, but by 1870–1871, this had declined to 12.4 percent (Bhattacharya, 1991: 18). The declining importance of jute was partly due to growing demand for products such as tea from the mountains of West Bengal and Assam and partly due to low prices resulting from overproduction. Good dock facilities were also crucial for importing goods, troops, and settlers from Europe. With the advent of the industrial revolution in England, demand for coal and iron ore greatly increased, and imports from India were used to supplement local supplies. The export of industrial processes from England to India also meant that during the nineteenth century, factories and mills began to produce greater volumes of processed and finished products for export to Britain, Europe, and America (King, 2004: 204–205).

It is crucial to bear these developments and especially Calcutta's flourishing state in the nineteenth century in mind as we turn to the next hundred years and to our case study of the development of the East Kolkata Wetlands. From a historical perspective, it appears that these contemporary developments cannot simply be interpreted as the imposition of 'alien' ideas of modernity, progress, and development in order to remake the city. The very foundation and evolution of the city is intimately and inextricably connected with ideas about modernity, and as Calcutta's history is, in many ways, the history of colonialism (certainly of colonialism in the Indian context), its postcolonial state owes much to these earlier histories. It was once a primate city (Sassen, 2012) – one that was disproportionately dominant politically, economically, and culturally and was so not only regionally and nationally but also internationally.

Not surprisingly, such a profile has attracted migrant labour to Calcutta for a long time, from all across the subcontinent to work in industries, agriculture, and domestic service in and around the city. Calcutta was even an important node in the extension of the British Empire, serving as a key trans-shipment point for indentured Indian labourers, bound for plantations newly freed of slaves. The city's pre-eminence seemed clear. What led, then, to its apparently precipitous decline?

Calcutta in the century of conflict

At the dawn of the twentieth century, Calcutta's future seemed predictable and optimistic. Throughout the early part of the century, more and more technological aspects associated with 'modernity' materialized: more railroads, an early airport, improved port facilities – all of these signified vibrant economic activity. The city was also teeming with cultural life. But in the course of the last decades of the nineteenth century, the province of Bengal had been slowly whittled down for administrative efficiencies. In 1905, in a radical move, the Viceroy of India, Lord Curzon, partitioned the province of Bengal, carving off the eastern section and large portions which today belong to the states of Assam and Bihar and establishing Dhaka as a rival hub and center of the new region. Interpreted by many as punishment for the anti-colonial sentiment spreading in the province, this resulted in widespread agitation, which united Bengali-speaking Muslim and Hindu communities alike. But it is also important to note that early advocates of Muslim self-determination embraced the move because it promised freedom from Hindu landholding elites as well (Chatterjee, 1994). In 1912, another blow was delivered to the city, when – amidst nationalist mobilization – the British moved the capital of India to Delhi. The protests in Calcutta against these acts reached fever pitch by the middle of the decade. Eventually, the British gave in to vehemently raised demands by increasingly influential political leaders and reunited the two halves of Bengal in 1917.

However, this reunification was to be short-lived. In 1947, Bengal was broken into two and divided for good in the Partition that accompanied Britain's departure from the subcontinent. The eastern, mostly Muslim-populated region of the province became East Pakistan, in what was a traumatic and violent process of separation, a lengthy and ongoing one that affected Calcutta severely and for decades to come. This was a near-mortal blow to a city that had already been through war, increasing communal tensions and violence, and the terrible famine of 1943 that killed between 1 and 4 million people (Maharatna, 1994; Sen, 1981). These events left Calcutta reeling as it tried to absorb increasing numbers of refugees both political and economic, with rising turmoil within the city.

After India's Independence, Calcutta was now the mere regional capital of a diminished province and suffered a decline on both economic and political terms. Soon the municipality was overwhelmed by an enormous influx of refugees, somewhere between 3 and 6 million in the period directly after Partition alone. Housing, sewage, and transport became a problem not only in the refugee colonies but also in areas that enjoyed good service in earlier times. In addition, the jute industry, already in decline, was now crippled by the fact that though most of the factories were based in West Bengal, mainly in and around Calcutta, the jute-growing regions that supplied the factories were now across the border in East Pakistan. In the decade leading up to Partition, sectarian violence had increasingly plagued the city, including communal violence and riots in 1926 and 1946 (Das, 1991). While the major wave of refugees and violence occurred in 1946, refugees continued to cross the border for 50 years, the last major wave in 1971 when, through civil war, East Pakistan became the independent state of Bangladesh.

Calcutta did not, of course, disappear from the Indian political and economic scene. West Bengal in the 1950s was still a leading industrialized state with an established economic infrastructure and an extensive manufacturing sector (including automobiles, chemicals, and consumer goods), with a relatively stable middle class. But as Delhi had replaced Calcutta as the political capital 40 years earlier, this period saw the rise of Bombay. Apart from Partition, Calcutta's decline was linked to other factors, such as the Freight Equalization Policy (1956), which controlled the prices of items such as steel and coal and negated the comparative advantage of mineral-rich states like West Bengal within the national economy. There were also increasing problems with Calcutta's port, whose infrastructure was gravely weakened by the lack of additional investment (Tan, 2007).

Moreover, India's basic economic politics of Import Substitution Industrialization (ISI) and the Infant Industries Model (IIM) for commodity production had a profoundly adverse effect on Calcutta (Rapley, 2002). It lacked heavy industries, which were located in smaller urban areas and newly created industrial towns like Durgapur and Rourkela (Roy, 2007). While other core cities had new roles in the administration, large public sector offices, and headquarters of the private sector, Calcutta was only presiding over the largely unindustrialized hinterland. Thus, the 1960s saw considerable economic stagnation in the state and substantial capital flight from the city as the management of many companies was taken over by the state government. Political turmoil resulted from these processes, with centrist, leftist, and radical forces violently competing over control in West Bengal and on occasion joining against common rivals. For example, centrist and mainstream leftist forces, principally the Communist Party of India (Marxist) (CPI-M), combined during the 1970s to crush the Naxalites, a radical Maoist revolutionary movement that took hold of many parts of the Bengal countryside and was able to control large swathes of countryside for some years. The political violence that spread during this period enhanced Calcutta's reputation as a hotbed of left-wing politics and anti-industrialization governance. In addition, the influx of a second large wave of refugees caught up in the Bangladesh independence war added to its problems and political instability in 1971.

During the preceding period, the centrist Congress Party had ruled West Bengal, as they did much of the rest of the country, by mobilizing massive majorities. But this changed in 1967, when Congress was displaced by a coalition of leftist and communist parties known collectively as the Left Front, comprising members such as the CPI-M, Communist Party of India (CPI), Revolutionary Socialist Party (RSP), All India Forward Bloc, West Bengal Socialist Party, and Marxist Forward Bloc. Although the Congress Party returned to power in 1971, the Left Front won the next elections in 1977. This initiated major changes in Calcutta's fortunes, for the Left Front concentrated resources on rural development, agrarian reform, and village-based governance – measures later adopted as amendments to the Indian Constitution in 1992 (Kohli, 2001). But for Calcutta, the electoral success of the Left Front on the back of these measures implied negligence, as the flight of capital continued until 1991. The city's gradual de-industrialization was accompanied by rapid degeneration of its aging public infrastructure and the growth of corruption and lack of efficiency in urban governance.

By the 1980s, both municipal and state authorities introduced measures to reverse the urban decline by instituting large-scale public works programs and centralized regional planning initiatives in order to improve economic and social conditions in the city. Regional development authorities had been actively planning the new township of Bidhan Nagar (Salt Lake), which presented a large-scale exercise in urban planning. While many smaller improvements in the Greater Kolkata region still suffered delays from (among other things) political gridlock, larger public infrastructure projects were actually launched (Kolkata Metropolitan Development Authority [KMDA], 2001), including internationally funded prestigious global projects such as a metro transportation system. The construction of the Kolkata Metro, Asia's first underground rail network, took many years. Its (relatively) smooth operations stand in stark contrast to the chaotic Kolkata streets above. Service began in 1984, linking southern residential neighbourhoods with the business and financial districts in the center and the old North Calcutta neighbourhoods. Since then, the line has been extended and links what were once outer suburbs to the south of the city with the area around the airport in its far north, although the actual link to the airport is still under construction (Mohan, 2008).

A second major project was the Eastern Metropolitan Bypass along which most of the new developments discussed later in this book have been built more recently. Initially, it only linked the southeastern edges of the city with the township of Salt Lake. Also notable among the major projects have been a series of bridges across the Hooghly River, including the Vidyasagar Setu completed in 1992 and the Nivedita Setu completed in 2007 (Roy and Tassin, 2013). These two modern cable-stayed bridges have become as iconic in their own right as their aging peers in crossing the Hooghly – namely, the cantilevered Howrah Bridge (Rabindra Setu) and the multispanned Bally Bridge (Vivekenanda Setu).

What were initially isolated large projects have accumulated into a series of prestigious sites of redevelopment in Kolkata: the international airport has been upgraded with new runways and terminals, while several high-rise office blocks comprising some of Kolkata's tallest commercial buildings have been built in the business district near the central sections of the city. Keenly aware of its dearth of green space, city planners have also actively created new parks, including the Millennium Park, a "gift" from the KMDA to the city in 1999 (KMDA, 2001).

Many commentators, while lauding the developments, saw these as too little, too late, as middle-class Calcuttans have since the 1990s become increasingly disenchanted with the Left Front's politics of wooing large rural vote banks. They saw that the decay of their once-glorious city was evidence of the reluctance of the CPI-M and its allies to invest in urban areas. Anti-CPI-M feelings were strong among urbanites, who were conversely targeted by Marxist rhetoric and derided for their bourgeois sensibilities. Left Front activists routinely contrasted the decaying capital city with the imagery of a "Sonar Bangla," the 'Golden Bengali' countryside that represented the heartland of political mobilization and renewal (Roy, 2003: 9). But such simplistic interpretations obscure the complex and difficult processes at work – for example, the complex network of peri-urban, rural, and urban interactions, such as the link between ongoing distress migration from villages and the growth of urban slums, or the regional, ethnic, and class politics being played out at the edges of the city. As Roy notes, the Left Front increasingly depended on poor rural voters, who were illegally squatting on urban public land, in order to swing elections:

> On the one hand, the Left Front has sought to engage in a new set of developmental strategies. On the other hand, it has attempted to maintain old populisms, for example its mobilizational alliances with the rural-urban poor. This tightrope balancing, inevitably manifested spatially, has created a quite amazing impasse, most notably the unrelenting cycles of evictions and resettlement to which the poor are subject. But there is also a broader sense in which developmental projects, including those sponsored by the state, remain stalled in Calcutta . . . the very regulatory ambiguities that have allowed the regime its territorialized flexibility have also created the basis for great political challenges – from opposition parties as well as from commercialized factions within the Left Front itself. Put bluntly, the Left is unable to capitalize on the very tracts of urbanizable land that it so savagely has carved out for itself.
>
> (Roy, 2003: 12–13)

The project that the Left Front helped to build the conditions and momentum for – speculative large-scale urban development, primarily for domestic and global middle classes and elites – has continued apace, as this book describes. The Left Front itself, however, has been unable to overcome the obstacles and dilemmas that its ideological positions and baggage left it in, as the final section of this chapter describes.

Post-liberalization developments: a changing picture

After 1991, India entered what is generally known as the liberalization era, when it was forced to undertake reforms to its financial system in order to qualify for a set of emergency loans from the International Monetary Fund (IMF) and World Bank due to an economic crisis, as detailed in an earlier chapter. Foreign investment was welcomed into 31 high-priority sectors. Fifty-nine percent of foreign direct investment (FDI) in the post-liberalization period in India was concentrated in five states: Gujarat, Karnataka, Maharashtra, Tamil Nadu, and West Bengal (Sen, 2005). Belying its national and regional reputation as a state in decline, West Bengal was second among its peers in attracting FDI (behind Gujarat). Moreover, within West Bengal, 35 percent of the small-scale investment was located in the Kolkata metropolitan area (Bannerjee, 1997).

Considerable streams of funding directed towards Kolkata have been made available to the service sector (including office complexes, theme parks, and transportation), as well as manufacturing in the industrial suburbs (Pal, 2005). The bulk of investments has targeted two ports outside of Kolkata itself: Haldia and Kulpi, approximately 50 and 80 km away, respectively (Tan, 2007). Central government development plans during this period include the KMDA's implementation of the Government of India's Mega City Programme (KMDA, 2000). Under this initiative, Kolkata is one of five agglomerations (Mumbai, Chennai, Bangalore, and Hyderabad are the others) that receive special funding for one-off infrastructure improvements. Moreover, the bulk of state (both federal and the Government of West Bengal) investments have been made in the city and its immediate surroundings, which made up 80 percent of metropolitan investment between 1991 and 2003 (Pal, 2005).

On a different level, this period also saw an explosive growth of private and public–private partnerships in order to redevelop the city through new urban housing projects aimed at an emerging and global middle class. As the previous sections show, recent changes in the urban landscape are closely related to the political economy of the city, which in turn are essential to understanding how the Left Front managed to gain the support of many urban middle-class voters, and were later on deserted by precisely this section of the electorate. In the early 2000s in particular, the Left Front plans received strong support from the upper and upper-middle classes, including the non-Bengali business community, as seen in its successful performance in northeast Kolkata and in the Salt Lake municipality, a professional and IT-oriented township to the east. Having embraced a critical stance towards liberalization, the Left Front was a latecomer to industry-related reform. Shaw and Satish (2007) suggest that, as a result, the Left Front adopted its business-oriented reforms notably later than much of the rest of India. They argue, however, that when finally adopted, the reforms introduced for implementation by former Chief Minister Buddhadeb Bhattacharya were extremely effective. Beginning in 1994, West Bengal's industrial policy was restructured, a high-profile Member of Parliament was brought in to head its Industrial Development Corporation, and the Chief Minister undertook the first of numerous missions to Europe and North America in order to court investors. Various policies, including helping to repeal the previously mentioned national Freight Equalization Policy and thereby potentially re-energizing West Bengal's attractiveness to national and international mining areas, were revived. The Left Front also engaged in other actions that made it attractive to middle-class voters, including promoting industrialization and inviting a wide range of private investment to West Bengal and launching attempts at restructuring ailing public sector undertakings like steel companies. In addition, the existing agro-based industries were increasingly directed towards exports to other states.

During this period, the Left Front also adopted a more cosmopolitan and business-friendly attitude, geared towards attracting entrepreneurs, mainly through educational and trading incentives. Long-term plans for urban restructuring designed to support these efforts, like collaboration with Japanese firms to construct flyovers, directed significant funds towards middle-class consumers and their interests. Notably, such initiatives were as unpopular among the urban poor as the implementation of a water tax to re-order municipal balance sheets. The question why the Left Front felt it necessary to make this turn to urban middle-class voters when its political strategy had kept it in power for several decades is a complicated one. In part, it may be that the idea of long-term industrial stagnation suggested to its strategists that the rural vote was, in the end, a losing proposition for a sustained majority government. Even following its last state election victory, however, some critics warned the Left Front that its attempt to woo middle-class voters left it dependent on an unsustainable and unstable voting bloc (Basu, 2007).

Regardless of the dangers and criticisms, the Left Front pushed ahead with its reforms. As a result of some of these changes and the 'business-friendly' attitude of the state government, Kolkata has seen a rapid growth of financial and producer service sectors since the mid-1990s, including – as elsewhere in India – the proliferation of call center firms servicing US and British multinationals. The Left Front government declared IT a utility, whereby unions are not allowed to mobilize in the parts of the city set apart for this industry. Set up adjacent to the up-market middle-class township of Salt Lake, investment in these sectors has been significant, and massive subsidies have improved infrastructure services such as phone and electricity supplies in Kolkata in order to attract such businesses to settle there. While Salt Lake and the IT giants are certainly highlighted to show how Kolkata has advanced, critics have suggested that the bulk of investment in IT-related industries lies in the much less dependable and more *ad hoc* sector comprising the outsourcing operations that are found across the city. Shaw and Satish (2007), in their comparison of Bangalore and Kolkata – the first often cited as an example of a newly globalizing city connected to the information economy and in a tier far above the latter – note many interesting similarities. They note that Kolkata is currently the fifth most popular destination for the IT industry in India because of its significant educated workforce, among other assets, although this investment is mostly in the relatively less high-tech outsourcing sector. It should also be noted that most of this investment is domestic, not foreign.

In order to create an investor-friendly image of the city, the Government of West Bengal and the Kolkata Municipal Corporation (KMC) initiated a series of urban 'renewal' and 'regeneration' measures aimed at 'cleaning up the city' from the mid-90s onwards. Among them was the euphemistically titled "Operation Sunshine" in 1996 directed at driving hawkers and pavement-dwellers out of central areas, which included their forced removal and relocation to urban fringes. While this program was still being widely criticized by its middle-class audience, the campaign for the 'beautification of Calcutta' was undertaken in 2003–2005, which included multiple evictions of illegal slum- and pavement-dwellers and functioned rather smoothly. Justified through both developmental and environmental concerns, middle-class voters had by then accepted the 'need' to claim some of the public spaces the urban poor were occupying for more exclusive land-use projects. To illustrate the extent of these contestations, Table 5.1 provides a list of the main areas of the city targeted by such drives.

Table 5.1 Evictions in Kolkata

Area	Date	Persons affected
Tolly Nullah	22 September 2001	20,000
Tolly Nullah	10 December 2002	40,000
Beliaghata	2 February 2003	7,000
Beliaghata	6 March 2004	100,000
Bagbazar and Cossipore	15 December 2003	75,000
Lake Gardens	2 March 2005	50,000

Source: Asian Coalition for Housing Rights, 2006

The evictions carried out at the time were characterized by a lack of notification for residents, of plans for either rehabilitation or compensation, and by the use of extensive force executed by armed policemen and paramilitary forces (Dasgupta, 2003). Like similar actions carried out in other metros, they were carried out when only women and children were home. But while protests were mounted locally, mobilization was, on the whole, very muted (Bandyopadhyay, 2009; Rao, 2010). Encouraged by the lack of effective opposition, the Left Front then embarked on much grander projects of appropriation outside Kolkata. These, however, did not go unchallenged. Attempts to create special economic zones for foreign and domestic investment and the conversion of agricultural land to industrial production in Nandigram and Singur met with vocal and violent protests (Bardhan and Mookherjee, 2012). It is safe to assume that these moves did eventually contribute to the leftists' fall after three decades in power.

However, the reforms introduced by the CPI-M and its allies resulted in sea changes, which they seemed to be able to turn into political clout in the regional and local politics of West Bengal. As recently as 2007, the Left Front was celebrating 30 years of continuous rule in West Bengal, the longest-serving democratically elected communist government in the world. Federal, state, and municipal elections up until 2011 had confirmed the popularity and power of the coalition; at each level, the political partners increased their share of both the popular vote and representation in legislatures, state assemblies, and city halls. In 2005, the Left Front took power in 50 out of 80 municipalities statewide, including a victory in Kolkata, traditionally a stronghold of the centrist Indian National Congress (INC). Both in municipal elections and in the 2006 state elections, the Left Front solidified its power, increasing its representation in the legislature, capturing 235 out of 293 available seats and continuing the trend of extending its reach beyond traditional rural strongholds and into urban centers and municipalities (Chakrabarti, 2006).

Yet fast forward only a few years, and the ground seems to have collapsed beneath the Left Front. In the 2009 general election, the Left Front saw its federal representation significantly diminished by a resurgent All-India Trinamool Congress Party (TMC, a regional breakaway from the INC) in the general elections. The rise of the TMC and its populist female leader Mamata Banerjee was facilitated by problems with corruption and clientelism by now endemic in the Left Front parties (Banerjee, 2010).

The fate of the Left Front was sealed when the 2010 municipal elections resulted in even greater losses, especially in suburban constituencies such as Salt Lake, and only 39 out of 139 wards in Kolkata were left under its control. Today, the capital is entirely governed by the TMC, which won the 2011 West Bengal elections, thereby ending 34 years of communist rule through a landslide victory, winning 227 out of 294 seats, while the Left Front was reduced to a mere 62 seats, a decline of some 171 from the previous election.

But while Mamata Banerjee, the new Chief Minister, has vowed to help the urban poor, the departure of the Left Front from the halls of power in Kolkata has not ushered in a new era of redistributive policies at the state or municipal level. Instead, the TMC has continued to promote what can best be described as the ideology of neoliberal developmentalism championed by its predecessors. And as the case studies will demonstrate, the same means are employed to 'develop' the city; thus, evictions and exclusions of 'undesirables' – i.e. poor residents and squatters, hawkers, and rickshaw pullers continue. Furthermore, as Sengupta (2006) suggests, while there is a land scarcity for all classes in Kolkata for housing, there has been a notable shift in policies where the provision of subsidies for development is concerned. Essentially, the poor and their needs are ignored, while investment in real estate for middle-class buyers is encouraged, with only minimal attention paid to affordable housing for all. Then, as now, such policies are accompanied by legal changes, which allow anti-poor reforms to be enacted. Among them are the deregulation of housing finance, the creation of public–private partnerships, and the shift by government out of rental public housing by privatizing or selling to tenants. Also in the same category are the new laws that allow for developments to emerge in slum areas, which have opened a market for previously protected tenancy arrangements. All of these measures disproportionately disadvantage the poor:

> With such reform initiatives, private sector investment and participation in housing is forthcoming but the reform is yet to yield any remarkable change for low-income households that comprise around 80% of the population.
>
> (Sengupta, 2006: 270–271)

Slums (*bustees*) have existed in Calcutta since its foundation (Kaviraj, 1997), and it is estimated that today around 5,000 such settlements – formalized to different degrees – can be found in the city. Urban sprawl, the informal settlement of poor migrants, remains a significant concern (Bhatt, 2009). Yet the state government, Kolkata's municipal corporation, and regional planning authorities continue to focus their efforts on townships and new ventures that have no capacity to address the needs for shelter of the urban poor. Indeed, as we will see, urban sprawl in the shape of middle-class housing complexes poses significant challenges, whether through forced evictions, ecological impacts, or economic imbalance. But driven by confidence and optimism about the future of the Bengali middle class, electoral politics promote the idea of a new Kolkata that proceeds from the neoliberal economic, political, and cultural redrafting of the urban imaginary. It appears that transformation of the built environment rather than existing socioeconomic inequalities constitutes a major element in the semiotics of that definition. Thus, it appears that construction sites and new developments are indeed the main sites in which the vision of a neoliberal urban future has become real in a city that prides itself on a revolutionary past and – until recently – a leftist present. In the following chapters, I will examine how some of these visions become manifest across the urban landscape throughout the city.

References

Bandyopadhyay, R. (2009). "Hawkers' movement in Kolkata, 1975–2007." *Economic and Political Weekly* **44**(17): 116–119.

Banerjee, D. (1997). The political economy of imbalances across Indian states: some observations on 50 years of independence. *Calcutta Occasional Paper No. 166*. Calcutta, Centre for Studies in Social Sciences (CSSSC).

Banerjee, M. (2010). A left front election. *Diversity and Change in Modern India: Economic, Social and Political Approaches*. A. Heath and R. Jeffery. Oxford, Oxford University Press: 243–266.

Bardhan, P. and D. Mookherjee (2012). Political clientelism and capture: theory and evidence from West Bengal, India. *WIDER Working Paper, 2012*. Helsinki, United Nations University (UNU).

Basu, P. P. (2007). "'Brand Buddha' in India's West Bengal: the left reinvents itself." *Asian Survey* **47**(2): 288–306.

Bhatta, B. (2009). "Analysis of urban growth pattern using remote sensing and GIS: a case study of Kolkata, India." *International Journal of Remote Sensing* **30**(18): 4733–4746.

Bhattacharya, D. (2007). "Return of the native." *The Telegraph*. Retrieved March 30, 2014, from http://www.telegraphindia.com/1070401/asp/7days/story_7592256.asp.

Bhattacharya, M. (1991). Municipal Calcutta and evolutionary perspective. *Calcutta's Urban Future: Agonies from the Past and Prospects for the Future*. B. Dasgupta, M. Bhattacharya, D. K. Basu, M. Chatterjee and T. K. Bannerjee. Calcutta, Sree Saraswaty Press: 8–21.

Census of India (2011). "Census of India." Retrieved March 30, 2014, from http://censusindia.gov.in.

Chakrabarti, A. (2006). "Left Front: 235." Retrieved May 12, 2006, from http://www.telegraphindia.com/1060512/asp/frontpagestory_6214770.asp.

Chatterjee, J. (1994). *Bengal divided: Hindu communalism and Partition, 1932–1947*. Cambridge, Cambridge University Press.

Chattopadhyay, S. (2006). *Representing Calcutta: modernity, nationalism and the colonial uncanny*. London, Routledge.

Chaudhuri, S., Ed. (1990). *Calcutta: the living city Volume II: the present and the future*. Delhi, Oxford University Press.

Das, S. (1991). *Communal riots in Bengal, 1905–1947*. Delhi, Oxford University Press.

Dasgupta, K. (2003). "Evictions in Calcutta: creating the spaces of 'modernity.'" *City: A Quarterly on Urban Society* **4**(31): 3–14.

Ganguly, K. (2010). *Cinema, emergence, and the films of Satyajit Ray*. Berkeley, University of California Press.

Gupta, N. (1993). Urbanism in India in the colonial period. *An Urban Historical Perspective for the Calcutta Tercentenary*. H. Chakrabarti. Calcutta, General Printers and Publishers: 32–39.

Hutnyk, J. (1996). *The rumour of Calcutta: tourism, charity and the poverty of representation.* London, Zed Books.

Kaviraj, S. (1997). "Filth and the public sphere: concepts and practices about space in Calcutta." *Public Culture* **10**(1): 83–113.

King, A. D. (2004). *Spaces of global culture: architecture, urbanism, identity.* London, Routledge.

Kipling, R. (1891). *The city of dreadful night and other places.* Allahabad, A. H. Wheeler & Co.

Kipling, R. (1911). *Rudyard Kipling Volume XVII: early verse.* New York, Charles Scribner's Sons.

Kohli, A. (2001). *The success of India's democracy.* Cambridge, Cambridge University Press.

Lapierre, D. (1985). *The city of joy.* Garden City, NY, Doubleday.

McDuie-Ra, D. (2013). "Leaving the Northeast borderland: place-making and the inward pull of citizenship in India." *Eurasia Border Review* **4**(1): 1–17.

Maharatna, A. (1994). "The demography of the Bengal famine of 1943–44: a detailed study." *Indian Economic and Social History Review* **31**(2): 169–215.

Mohan, D. (2008). "Mythologies, metro rail systems and future urban transport." *Economic and Political Weekly* **43**(4): 41–53.

Nath, L. (2005). "Migrants in flight: conflict-induced internal displacement of Nepalis in Northeast India." *Peace and Democracy in South Asia* **1**(1): 56–72.

Pal, A. (2005). Metropolitan decision-making – a case study of Kolkata. *Life in the Urban Landscape – International Conference for Integrating Urban Knowledge and Practice.* Gothenberg, Sweden.

Racine, J., Ed. (1990). *Calcutta 1981: the city, its crisis and the debate on urban planning and development.* New Delhi, Concept Publishing.

Rao, U. (2010). "Making the global city: urban citizenship at the margins of Delhi." *Ethnos* **75**(4): 402–424.

Rapley, J. (2002). *Understanding development: theory and practice in the Third World.* Boulder, CO, Lynne Riener Publishers.

Raychaudhuri, A. (2009). "Resisting the resistible: re-writing myths of partition in the works of Ritwik Ghatak." *Social Semiotics* **19**(4): 469–481.

Roy, A. (2003). *City requiem Calcutta: gender and the politics of poverty.* Minneapolis, University of Minnesota Press.

Roy, B. C. and D. M. Tassin (2013). "Second Vivekananda Bridge, Kolkata, India." *IABSE Symposium Report* **101**(12): 1–9.

Roy, S. (2007). *Beyond belief: India and the politics of postcolonial nationalism.* Durham, NC, Duke University Press.

Sanyal, R. (1993). Public societies and civic institutions in Renaissance Calcutta. *An Urban Historical Perspective for the Calcutta Tercentenary.* H. Chakrabarti. Calcutta, General Printers and Publishers: 71–76.

Sarkar, B. (2009). *Mourning the nation: Indian cinema in the wake of Partition.* Durham, NC, Duke University Press.

Sassen, S. (2012). *Cities in a world economy.* Thousand Oaks, CA, Sage/Pine Forge.

Sen, A. (1981). *Poverty and famines: an essay on entitlements and deprivation.* Oxford, Oxford University Press.

Sen, K. (2005). Financial policies and investment in post-reform India: macro and micro perspectives. *Workshop on Indian Economy: Policy and Performance 1980–2000.* Centre for India and South Asia Research, University of British Columbia, Vancouver, BC, Canada.

Sengupta, U. (2006). "Government intervention and public–private partnerships in housing delivery in Kolkata." *Habitat International* **30**(3): 448–461.

Shaw, A. and M. K. Satish (2007). "Metropolitan restructuring in post-liberalized India: separating the global and the local." *Cities* **24**(2): 148–163.

Tan, T.-Y. (2007). "Port cities and hinterlands: a comparative study of Singapore and Calcutta." *Political Geography* **26**(7): 851–865.

Weber, R. (2006). Women's role in the development of refugee colonies in South Calcutta. *Refugees in West Bengal*. P. K. Bose. Calcutta, Mahanirban Calcutta Research Group.

West Bengal Industrial Development Corporation (WBIDC) (2006). "Gateway to the east." Retrieved May 17, 2006, from http://www.wbidc.com/old/overview/gateway.htm.

6   The East Kolkata Wetlands

One of the primary sites in which we see the transformation of fading Calcutta into resurgent Kolkata is along the eastern fringes of the city. The area has long been seen as one of the prime sites for urban expansion, claiming and developing the last remnants of the once-vast wetlands that used to surround the city. Yet, as we will see, these areas have also been a contested territory, imagined in very different ways by various stakeholders. The East Kolkata Wetlands (EKW), as they are known, have played an important role in recent decades of urban development, accelerated from 1997 during the period that is the primary focus of this book. They are home to several reclamation projects, among them the construction of large townships like Salt Lake and Rajarhat, aimed earlier at the upper-middle class and more recently at information technology (IT) companies and their employees. The desire to develop even more of the EKW has led to a backlash and struggle by local environmental groups, who have succeeded in securing a framework for their protection (Dembowski, 2001); in spite of this, illegal construction of new housing projects continues in the region. What started as suburban development has now turned into a wave of redevelopments, building similar projects increasingly within the city itself, as we will see in the final chapter of this book. To begin, I will provide some background on what the Wetlands area is and its ecological, economic, and social significance within Kolkata. Next, I will look at the idea of the EKW as a site for developmentalism through the history of reclamation and the building of townships in the Wetlands. Then, I will discuss the struggle to redefine the EKW as a conservation area. The final section of the chapter will consider the problem of illegal filling and construction in the EKW.

Ecological, economic, and social significance

Five km from the eastern edge of Kolkata proper lies a body of brackish water consisting of tidal pools, creeks, and a series of large, interconnected shallow ponds (*bheris*) – low-lying areas that have long played a pivotal role in the ecology and economy of the area. By the end of the nineteenth century, these were flourishing fisheries fed by the tides of the Bay of Bengal (Sarkar, 1991: 173). Natural processes and human intervention, however, caused the tidal flow to dry up, and thousands of fishers were faced with the loss of their livelihoods by the early twentieth century (Sarkar, 1991: 174). In the 1930s, an ingenious system was developed whereby domestic wastewater from Calcutta would be used as an alternative source of water and protein for the fisheries (Hazra and Goel, 2009). While this might seem a somewhat strange solution to the issue of both pisciculture and waste management, many scholars argue that what has emerged in the EKW is an innovative and sustainable system (Chattopadhyay, Dutta, and Ray, 2009).

Covering over 12,000 ha, the eastern fringes of the city are an ecologically important yet potentially fragile zone threatened by urban sprawl (Bhatta, 2009). As a result, urban development has been allowed to take place in a gradual and planned manner and was executed by the regional planning authority, the Kolkata Metropolitan Development Authority (KMDA), and the Kolkata Municipal Corporation (KMC). Careful management of the Wetlands was necessary, so the authorities argued, in order to manage the waste produced by the city. The EKW are home to the Dhapa landfill, where 95 percent of the city's garbage is deposited (Chattopadhyay, Dutta, and Ray, 2009), and it is the primary site of solid waste treatment (Hazra and Goel, 2009). While the location of the landfill site is the result of land pressures, the latter system of waste management stems from collaborations between scientists, ecologists, urban planners, municipal authorities, and local farmers and fishers. This has led to decades of innovative waste recycling and water management programs that have made the EKW "highly regarded [worldwide] as a model for wastewater aquaculture" (Bunting, Kundu, and Mukherjee, 2002: 6). Today, the Wetlands provide approximately 150 tons of fresh vegetables and over 10,500 tons of fish daily for urban markets within Kolkata and benefit the working poor directly.

Though often imagined as a wet wasteland, the area has a total population of between 62,000 and 100,000 people who live in several semi-rural villages dotted across the landscape. They constitute an extensive workforce. According to the 2011 Census, 8,500 men and women were employed directly in cooperative or private fisheries, with another 6,000 working in wastewater-fed rice fields and 4,000 people engaged in vegetable farming on garbage (Hazra and Goel, 2009). Furthermore, an additional 20,000–25,000 men and women work as waste pickers at the Dhapa landfill. In addition, many are engaged in supplementary income-generating activities like selling vegetables grown in the area. One of the more comprehensive surveys of the population of the Wetlands area in recent years shows that it is evenly split along gender lines, but 85 percent of the population belongs to the so-called Scheduled Castes or Scheduled Tribes, communities that are officially recognized as historically oppressed and economically marginalized. The majority of the population (82 percent) is Hindu; the remaining inhabitants are Muslim (Bunting and Mukherjee, 2002: 29–30). The same study lists the major occupation as fishing, followed by daily wage labour and agriculture close behind. The study indicates that although many residents originate from outside Kolkata and/or West Bengal, migrants constitute a minority. The demographic evidence suggests that the majority of the population is economically marginal, with some 70 percent living below the poverty line and a large majority from low-caste backgrounds. Bunting and Mukherjee's research indicates alcoholism to be rampant, with over 80 percent of male residents affected (2002: 32).

My own site visits to several villages gave me mixed impressions of the area. On one hand, the ecological, social, and economic importance of the area is clear. On the environmental front, the EKW are an integral part of the Ganges estuarine ecosystem and are part of the much larger Sunderban mangrove forest. As such, they provide vital flood and hurricane protection for the region of Bengal. They provide an important habitat for wildlife, especially birds and several endangered species (Dutt, 2000), and the waste management system performs a crucial function for the overburdened metropolis. The Wetlands also sustain diverse livelihoods in fisheries, horticulture, and the informal economy. Furthermore, the EKW's ecological and cultural value as one of the last remaining extensive green spaces in the Kolkata metropolitan area should not be understated; ironically, the green spaces are promoted as a selling point by some of the very developers whose projects encroach upon them.

Yet despite the clear significance of the Wetlands as an ecological area, they do not constitute some kind of paradise. As the demographic details discussed previously show, the population living and working in the Wetlands is over-whelmingly poor and marginalized. Most of the villages I visited lack even basic infrastructure and services. While some primary schools serve the area, no secondary school exists. Most of the roads are dirt tracks inaccessible to vehicles. Few of the houses in the villages I visited are of the *pucca*, brick-built type; most are *kachcha*, made of mud or bamboo with tile, straw, or corrugated tin roofs. These flimsy shelters are commonly found throughout the Wetlands area. Most of these homesteads lack electricity, sanitation, and tube wells. Open ponds provide most villagers with the bulk of their water needs, with concomitant health hazards. Although several of the newly built private hospitals are within view of some settlements, no healthcare is provided for many of the villages.

Residents also raise other complaints about their circumstances. While most earn their livelihoods through fishing, farming, and daily wage labour, siltation of the sewage canals and fishponds over time has already reduced the available water for pursuing the opportunities for fishing activities necessary for their daily economic survival and sustenance. Even the wage opportunity from delivering solid waste for use as fertilizer on the vegetable farms has become inconsistent due to the privatization of the city's waste collection services, as several villagers told me. One of them attributed the breakdown of the system to corruption and incompetence alike:

> How did the company that brings the fertilizer get chosen? The man who owns it, his brother pays all of the city officials. And he hires his own family and his friends. And we receive nothing.

Many peasant farmers and fishers have therefore been forced to take up casual jobs and day labour, which are putting them into direct conflict and competition with others already working in this sector. In any case, such jobs are hard to find. Unemployment among unskilled men is high in Kolkata, and the levels are very high in the Wetlands area in particular (Bunting and Mukherjee, 2002). Compounding this problem is the fact that many of the youth of the region are not interested in continuing in the same occupations as their parents. As one said to me:

> There is no future in this village and in farming. If I want to make money I have to take a job building the new city.

Another's view of the wastewater-fed fisheries was far less positive than many of the scientists and urban planners who admire their efficiencies and innovative nature:

> Every year more garbage comes to be dumped in the ponds. Is it my future to pick through the garbage to get the fish? Or to pick the garbage itself? There are better jobs in the city.

It was not only those with seemingly little opportunity but also others with more possibilities who exemplified this trend for youngsters to seek a life outside the EKW. For example, I interviewed a man from the village who worked and lived in the city proper, yet returned to the village on weekends. His stable employment in a middle-class household in the city allowed him to invest his savings (and borrow against them) in order to build a better home in the village. His relative prosperity had also meant that he was able to send his son to attend a secondary school outside the Wetlands. His objective over the long term had been to create more land for himself and his son to farm with. But he now felt that this strategy had backfired, as he said with some chagrin:

> I am building a house in our village. It will be the finest and biggest house in the entire village. I work here in the city as a cook all the year round. I send money back to my wife, my son and my three daughters in the village. I want my son to have more land to farm than I do. Now he wants to come to the city, but he does not want to work with me here or in farming back home. He has been in school in the village and has matriculated. He has gone to school outside of the village. He wants to work with computers. But how can I afford to pay for him to do additional school? I must give dowries for my daughters and I must still pay the village moneylender for the money I borrowed to build my house.

Many others were concerned about the growth of crime, illegal activities, and anti-social behavior, including trafficking in women and joining criminal gangs – often associated in the minds of locals with corrupt politicians – in and around the Wetlands. The poaching of fish and the stealing of vegetables have also become significant problems. These social problems are often attributed to a sense of the inevitability of failure and hopelessness on the part of the locals, who do not hold titles to land, and feel unprotected. During my interviews, this issue was often raised, as some villagers felt that if their presence could be regularized, it would change social relations and choices within the community. In addition to the lack of legal protection, it was also suggested, the police did nothing to enforce existing laws for protecting the Wetlands, and this contributed to the feeling that law and order were not respected. While this is difficult to prove, several villagers stated that the situation had become markedly worse in the past 10 years, when the illegal practice of filling up ponds to claim them as land for construction took hold (Roy, 2011).

History of reclamation

The peri-urban regions of Kolkata have long been seen as the primary area for the city's continued expansion. Due to its riverbank location, Kolkata has histori-cally expanded towards the north and south rather than the west or east. The west banks of the Hooghly River were traditionally an industrial site, filled with factories and port facilities; the river has more recently been targeted by the KMDA for the building of two new townships and Kolkata West International City, originally in partnership with the Indonesian-based Ciputra Group. However, planners concede that where the middle class they are aiming at is concerned, planners find that former industrial sites are still avoided by Bengali buyers. It is common knowledge that developers and planners began to direct the property boom towards the eastern parts of Kolkata – and for this expansion, the Wetlands needed to be reclaimed.

The direction this expansion takes follows a long-standing pattern in the modern era. By the time of Independence and especially during the post-Partition crisis over how to absorb millions of refugees into Calcutta, the development of the swamps and Wetlands became an urgent concern for civic leaders. Many of the first waves of refugees from East Bengal were mostly middle class and had the social capital and ability to pressure the authorities to provide more permanent housing. Indeed, the issue of refugee housing quickly became an electoral issue and led in part to the need to construct townships, originally planned as settlements for lower-middle-class occupants; in practice, however, they have become increasingly upper-middle-class enclaves over time (Weber, 2006; Chakrabarti, 1990).

After early attempts to reclaim the Wetlands for single-project housing construction proved to be abject failures (Sarkar, 1990), the second Chief Minister of West Bengal, Bidhan Chandra Roy, proposed a more comprehensive approach in the 1950s. This included the development of several satellite townships in reclaimed Wetlands and, accordingly, the state government purchased land in 1955. A Yugoslav company was contracted to reclaim the Wetlands by draining ponds, filling them with sand, and then compacting the soil. The entire process took 7 years and divided the resulting township of Bidhan Nagar (Salt Lake) into five sectors, three of which were earmarked as residential, with the other two reserved for industrial and service sectors (Calcutta Metropolitan Development Authority, 1975, 1976). The size of the township has doubled since the 1960s, with development following the earlier model of reclamation. While this further urbanization is meant to be overseen by various regulatory bodies, in practice, as many of the local critics I spoke with suggested, its growth has often been haphazard and based in part on illegal activities. As a result, Salt Lake has come under fire from pro-poor activists and many within the lower-middle classes (Dey, Samaddar, and Sen, 2013).

Many affluent middle-class families and some employees in housing societies eventually moved to Salt Lake. Numerous offices and government buildings – including the KMDA itself – are today located in Salt Lake. And, most importantly, the nascent IT industry in Kolkata has been built up there. When the question of how to address the ongoing problems of Kolkata and its expansion was raised, the solution built – perhaps naturally – on the successful experience these groups had of Salt Lake (Kolkata Metropolitan Development Authority, 2000). Planners and the media alike point to this model when talking about the pressures on housing, traffic congestion, informal and insecure housing, and even poverty. An urban planner I spoke with at the KMDA went so far as to say that

> Calcutta would have exploded into chaos had Salt Lake not been built. What you see today in Calcutta's revival and development is because Salt Lake allowed us to begin again.

The success of the project led to additional initiatives based on the same model, including East Kolkata Township and Baishnabghata-Patuli Township during the 1980s (Calcutta Metropolitan Development Authority, 1981). Environmental sustainability and a mixed land-use strategy were key components of these carefully planned urban development strategies, which built on the 30-year vision articulated in the Bengal Development Plan 1966–1996. According to a former KMDA planner, these included wide roads and parks every 3 km, as they promoted a holistic and integrated view of the urban system that incorporated local water bodies and emphasized quality of life. He describes the period from 1987 to 1997 as a period of much discussion on how to address Kolkata's complex problems; some asked how environmental concerns could be made a focus of new planning efforts, while others expressed considerable hostility towards such efforts from the outset. A major point of contention was whether planners should focus on growth to the north and west (the majority view among KMDA planners at the time) or whether expansion to the south and east should be pursued. In my interviews, it appeared that initially the discussion was open-ended and that decision-making processes within the KMDA were relatively democratic. There was also widespread support among the city's middle-class electorate for a well-paced and well-designed urban development strategy. Even in the 1990s, it seemed that expansion towards the north and west of the city would be favored. That this was not going to happen became evident after the publication of the first Environmental Management Plan for Kolkata and the adoption of the Mega City Scheme announced by the Government of India, initially in Annual Plans published between 1990 and 1992 and eventually in the Eighth Five Year Plan 1992–1997. Both plans targeted the EKW for expansion, with Salt Lake claiming 500 ha and the other aforementioned townships to be constructed on more of the Wetlands (Kolkata Metropolitan Development Authority, 2001).

All of the townships constructed under KMDA leadership envisioned the housing to be primarily for middle-class residents, especially those connected with the new IT sector, which was to be located in industrial parks within their boundaries. Only very small social housing projects intended to relocate poor communities displaced by development projects within the city were included (Kolkata Metropolitan Development Authority, 2014). Baishnabghata-Patuli Township and East Kolkata Township in particular sought to balance social, economic, and ecological priorities through a mixed-use planning strategy in order to provide adequate green space and retain some of the *bheris* (ponds), though more for aesthetic than commercial reasons (Calcutta Metropolitan Development Authority, 1981).

Nevertheless, as even early critics remark, such a planned development of peri-urban regions bristled with major problems. For one thing, these plans always characterized the Wetlands as essentially uninhabited, a wild frontier to be tamed and utilized for the needs of the city and its denizens. Yet, as early observers pointed out and as the previous section shows, the EKW area is anything but unpopulated (Sarkar, 1991). It is an economically and ecologically vibrant region with a considerable semi-rural/semi-urban population. The city of Kolkata depends upon it for much of its food supply – both protein and vegetables – and cheap labour, and the Wetlands constitute an important natural barrier against floods. Moreover, the idea that this area had not already been utilized to some degree by those imperiled by Kolkata's myriad problems is to ignore its historical usage. It has been a site for migration from other parts of Bengal and for many refugees during the fallout of the Bangladesh war of independence in 1971. Many of them established their own colonies and communities, by *jabar dakhal* or forcible occupation, on the outskirts of the Wetlands to the east of the city proper (Bose, 2000).

The EKW were therefore always productive and inhabited, and yet by the 1990s it was to this area that regional authorities turned their attention for the next phase of planned urban growth for Kolkata. The series of plans developed to exploit the EKW suggested ambitious visions comparable to other such makeovers for metropolitan areas in the new post-liberalization India. They reflected the gradual embrace of a global perspective by municipal and state authorities in the region. They focused on development along the Eastern Metropolitan Bypass – the highway that skirts the eastern edges of the city along the Wetlands – with townships, amusement parks, hotels, hospitals, and country clubs dotted around the existing landscape. Particularly controversial was the plan to create a World Trade Centre in an enclosure of 784 ha (Banerji, 2013). Importantly, as in the cases of Salt Lake City, East Kolkata Township, and Baishnabghata-Patuli Township, the lead agency was to be the KMDA in concert with the KMC. It was at this juncture, however, that the plans were challenged and curtailed by a surge of opposition from a host of different groups, as the next section will discuss in detail.

Contested space: protecting the EKW

The plans to expand the city into the EKW during the 1990s encountered significant and increasingly vocal opposition. According to one of the leaders of the protests, this began with a small group of civil servants, social and environmental activists, and scientists concerned with ecological degradation. An environmental advocacy group formed in 1982 called People United for Better Living in Calcutta (PUBLIC) took up the cause and began to sponsor lectures on topics, including some on illegal land transfers in the EKW. The group also lodged official complaints with the KMDA, KMC, and other stakeholders in the proposed developments. They argued that the Wetlands should be protected not only for the sake of their biodiversity and environmental value but also for the livelihoods they provide for local residents and the important social, economic, and waste management benefits derived from the EKW.

Soon, other interest groups joined these lobbyists, including a number of non-governmental organizations (NGOs) concerned with environmental issues. These groups comprised local farmers and fishers whose livelihoods would be lost along with the fields and working fishponds in the region. Another organized group comprised those working in the garbage disposal areas. In addition to alienating these citizens, the proposed plans created fissures between local/regional planners and state and federal government agencies, with officials from the West Bengal Pollution Control Board and the Federal Ministries of Agriculture and Forests and Environment increasingly concerned about the potential effects that urban development would have on the Wetlands ecosystem. Lastly, social workers and social justice advocates working in the city proper feared that any reduction in locally grown produce would affect local food resources and therefore the urban poor adversely (Bunting, Kundu, and Mukherjee, 2002). Thus, beyond these environmental issues, critics pointed out that displacement and loss of livelihood would be an inevitable byproduct of the plans to build new townships in the Wetlands (Ray and Niyogi, 2014). Some of these social and economic effects were discussed extensively in public hearings, such as the one organized by the People's Commission on Eviction and Displacement in 2002 (*Times of India*, 2002).

However, initially, these protests and advocacy work were unsuccessful. As an activist from PUBLIC who had been very closely involved in the struggle suggested, at the time, the issues raised did not resonate with the wider population and certainly not with local politicians. As a result, PUBLIC took a different approach and filed a legal appeal to halt construction, with lawyers and advocates working pro bono to help protect the Wetlands (Dembowski, 2001). The case went to the Calcutta High Court and left many local planners (including some employed by the KMDA) conflicted as to what position to take. Several of my informants – some of whom worked for the state or central government – found that they were called by their superiors and asked to explain why they opposed the plans for further urbanization. However, the political landscape and the support for those concerned about the effects the plans would have on the environment were rapidly changing; in the end, the central government reversed its position and finally supported the case for conservation. In its final decision, the High Court stated unambiguously that expansion could only continue west and north of the existing city limits and thereby put a halt on all further development by the KMC and the KMDA at its eastern fringes (Wetlands International South Asia, 2010). This decision, which was supported by the central and West Bengal governments, represented a 360-degree turn in planning the apparent fate of the Wetlands, which moved from being a site of development to one of conservation (Dembowski, 2001).

But following the decision, the direction that the opposition was taking became unclear. Some local stakeholders advocated the status quo of slowly reclaiming the EKW as a space of mixed land use, while others focused their efforts on getting a moratorium in place that would prevent all future construction. Many were worried that despite the High Court ruling, development would proceed unless more meaningful protection could be institutionalized. As a result, a growing number of agencies – especially among the state and federal bureaucracies – sought to bring the EKW under the mandate of the international intergovernmental treaty on the protection of Wetlands known as the Ramsar Convention. This Convention, which operates on national and international levels, expects participating member countries

> to maintain the ecological character of their Wetlands of International Importance and to plan for the "wise use," or sustainable use, of all the wetlands in their territories.
>
> (Ramsar Convention, 2014)

Although its supporters in Kolkata were clear that such an agreement would not by itself preclude further developments in the EKW, they hoped that it would establish a set of benchmarks and accountability measures to promote the evaluation of such plans and support the way they are monitored. Protection under the Ramsar Convention would also prioritize environmental concerns in any future discussions of the EKW, something that had not previously been the case.

Why did the Indian central government, which had at best shown indifference to the threat to the EKW, take such drastic measures to have it protected? Activists with PUBLIC, planners in Kolkata, and former civil servants at both the state and federal levels seem to agree that the turnabout may have been an important part of the Government of India's increased involvement with international environmental affairs, including India's representation on the standing committee of the Ramsar Convention between 1993 and 1996. In keeping with that involvement, the Government of West Bengal and the Government of India finally declared the EKW to be a Ramsar site in 2002. This important step was followed by the passing of the East Kolkata Wetlands (Conservation and Management)

Act of 2006 in the West Bengal legislature and the creation of the Kolkata Wetlands Management Authority in 2006. These measures also confirmed the working nature of the Wetlands in that they also defined the Wetlands as a Waste Recycling Region (WRR), highlighting their role in Kolkata's urban functioning. All these measures were taken to emphasize ecological, economic, and social reasons to protect the area from unauthorized development.

This explains why the fact that the Wetlands are protected by their status as a WRR is crucial for any discussion of the development and the legal issues involved in protecting the Wetlands. As the area is primarily zoned for agriculture, pisciculture, and horticulture, all applications for residential or commercial uses are subject to extremely rigid review; however, the authority of the regulatory body that provides such oversight remains unclear to many petitioners and is disputed by the KMC, the KMDA, and a number of other agencies. Nearly a quarter of the WRR is included within the borders of the city of Kolkata, while the actual boundaries of the Wetlands themselves remain a contentious issue. As mentioned previously, state, federal, municipal, and regional authorities all have claims on planning and governing the area, often leading to a situation of contradictory directives and administrative backlogs. The regulations relating to development (or the lack thereof) in relation to fisheries-based purposes, a priority set out by the WRR status, are most rigid. According to the Inland Fisheries (Amendment) Act (1993), water bodies measuring 5 *kathas* (350 m^2) or more that are capable of being used as fisheries cannot be legally converted to other uses (Kundu *et al.*, 1997). Other government acts and regulations, including some of India's oldest environmental laws, apply to Wetlands as well, such as:

- The Indian Fisheries Act (1857)
- The Indian Forest Act (1927)
- The Wildlife (Protection) Act (1972)
- The Water (Prevention and Control of Pollution) Act (1974)
- The Territorial Water, Continental Shelf, Exclusive Economic Zone and Other Marine Zones Act (1976)
- The Water Prevention and Control of Pollution Act (1977)
- The Forest (Conservation) Act (1980)
- The Environmental (Protection) Act (1986)
- The Coastal Zone Regulation Notification (1991)
- The Wildlife (Protection) Amendment Act (1991)
- The National Conservation Strategy and Policy Statement on Environment and Development (1992).

The Ramsar Convention provides the EKW with both visibility and protection, though the actual authority to enforce such agreements is limited. In reality, despite this multitude of possible protection mechanisms, urban development in the EKW continues unabated. Even prior to the most recent increase in housing and township development in the region, the Calcutta Environmental Strategy and Action Plan Report warned in 1997 that "fierce interest group competition to secure access to the resources has stimulated unauthorized use of land on an extensive scale" (1997: 47). Such trends have only intensified in the years that followed. Social movements and popular struggles have long decried urbanization in the region, but local development authorities and municipal officials have consistently claimed that development – especially after the signing of the Ramsar Convention – is not taking place within the Wetlands (Wetlands International South Asia, 2010).

This is partly supported by confusing the boundaries defining the area to which such protection applies and that to which it does not, for the boundaries are sometimes unclear. During my time in the field, for example, a dispute arose regarding what exactly constituted the protected area. Most environmentalists and scientists claim that the figure is approximately 12,500 ha, while many developers and even some state agencies have identified a much smaller area consisting of only 8,000 ha. The controversy culminated in 2007, when some officials supporting development publicly claimed that though the Wetlands were an officially registered Ramsar site, no map of the exact boundaries existed, a claim that the Convention staff were quick to correct (Banerjee, 2012). The more recent clarifications notwithstanding, confusion over boundary issues was compounded by the already-existing problems of administrative and jurisdictional conflicts and competition. Furthermore, a significant lack of law enforcement regarding the existing protection is apparent, with little funding provided at the state, municipal, or federal levels for staff; evidence of considerable corruption in monitoring compliance on the part of developers is on record. As a result, many existing regulations are simply ignored. In order to see the dynamics involved, the following section examines the processes through which the Wetlands have and are being reclaimed.

Illegal filling in the EKW

Despite apparent triumphs of conservation legislation in the region, encroachment into the EKW continues. This occurs in spite of the long history of mixed-use wetland development, the area's pivotal role in Kolkata's waste management, the court cases won by opponents of further expansion, and the international treaties signed. One large part of the problem is illegal activities, often small-scale and local, such as the practice of filling ponds and construction work on top of the fillings. Another example of shady practice is the preponderance of illegal land transfers and questionable rezoning practices. So the question beckons: why can such blatantly illegal activities continue despite considerable public and media support for preserving the Wetlands? A major issue here, as elsewhere in India, is the acceptance of multiple meanings of property ownership and land titles in the area. As elsewhere on the subcontinent, some land is privately owned, while other areas belong to the state of West Bengal, are looked after by the Indian government, or are under municipal administration. Furthermore, large areas are cooperatively owned and managed (especially several of the working *bheris*), and others still are entangled in legal disputes regarding ownership. Most of the land within the EKW is vested, for the most part, with the state, while roughly 80 percent of the fishers and farmers are members of cooperatives but have no legal title to the land on which they work. Across the region, subleasing and absentee ownership are common. When interviewed, many interlocutors in the EKW suggested that titles in land are subject to manipulation by those with political clout and physical muscle, with criminal gangs and corrupt local politicians intimidating residents.

Much of the original development and land reclamation in the Wetlands area was carried out by the state for the purposes of easing population congestions in parts of north and south Kolkata through the strategic creation of townships. As I mentioned earlier, such state-led planning has not ceased; indeed, this is attested by the major new development of Rajarhat, a township near Salt Lake (though nearly three times its size), and of the EKW to the northeast; two other new townships are planned in the west at Dankuni and West Howrah. In the EKW, planned and state-led developments ground to a halt following successful opposition by the broad coalition of groups described previously. However, construction did not stop, as private developers, either on their own or in partnership with the state government and/or local municipalities, are actively appropriating large swathes of land, and many small projects have already been completed. This is possible, as control over land is much more dispersed than in the 1970s when the last large state-led project was finished. While at that time much of the land in the EKW was obtained from a few families who held the titles, by the 1970s political party organizers had mobilized locals against these landowners and offered protection in exchange for votes. Thus, those living and working in the EKW did not, for the most part, receive any official title to their lands but became de facto owners because they enjoyed the patronage of local politicians. When it became apparent that KMDA-led development would not materialize, developers and promoters either partnered with state agencies or approached landlords directly and convinced them to sell their property at below-market costs. Many landowners were happy to do so, as they were not benefitting from holding the land in the first place. As one told me:

> The price I was offered for my land was far less than it should be valued for. But I was receiving nothing, no rents, no money at all. I ended up selling for a rate of 5,000 rupees per acre. I have heard that the developers that I sold to have resold the same land for over 100,000 rupees per acre. I do not have the same connections that they do.

Yet even a legal title does not automatically guarantee the start of construction. While most of the region is still protected by the various aforementioned environmental regulations and treaties, some of the formerly working fisheries have become progressively less productive. Often, the depth of the ponds decreases over time due to siltation, and without regularly being cleaned, they often become unsuitable for pisciculture (which requires a depth of some 4–5 m). As a consequence, some wetland areas – including some not owned by the fishers who work them – have been sold to developers. But other parts of the Wetlands are in fact being filled illegally, as the police and the government are often complicit in the act and the legal bodies refuse to prosecute. While those in power benefit from these illegal activities, they have resulted in a significant loss of livelihoods and residences. During my time in the field, I could observe the process of such illegal filling and the displacement of residents on many occasions. In most cases, such processes began with a developer – usually a private one, whether working alone or with a public sector partner – approaching a landlord or leaseholder. The protected status of much of the land does pose a problem, but it is solved by removing one of the primary sources of livelihoods and a major resource under protection: the fish. This can be achieved by introducing water hyacinth, a highly invasive plant that often covers an entire pond and chokes off sunlight and the sources of food and protein for the fish. It is when the pond is no longer suitable for pisciculture that developers send their trucks up to the pond and the process of filling it up and preparing the ground for construction begins.

The loss of ponds has already led to a massive displacement of fishers and a loss of ancillary livelihoods. The resulting pressures have also led to considerable strife in the local communities. As in similar processes elsewhere, some of those actively involved in the filling of the ponds – for example, the planting of water hyacinths – are local fishers hired by developers to carry out their dirty work. The fishers who do so are, of course, well aware of the consequences and that their actions are destroying their livelihood; however, they expect immediate compensation and are promised long-term and relatively lucrative employment within the burgeoning construction industry by the same developers who hired them to poison the ponds. As one fisherman said to me:

> Why do I want to keep fishing? Why do I want to keep catching fish that smell like filth? What can I do instead? Work at Dhapa? Pick rags? Grow vegetables on garbage? The builder here has promised us all jobs in the construction business, more money, steady jobs. These fools who want to keep fishing in filth can do that but I am no fool.

Apart from the direct impact on livelihoods and cohesion of the local community, there are also considerable ecological impacts that illegal pond filling triggers. As charted by opponents of the Wetland development plans, the loss of green space; destruction of habitats for migratory birds, small marine mammals, and local wildlife; and increased pollution of water bodies are all serious consequences resulting from encroachment (Wetlands International South Asia, 2010). For Kolkata, a city with a desperate need for more green spaces, this is a deeply alarming trend.

Furthermore, the disruption and potential destruction of the century-old waste management system is a further concern. As critics have argued for decades, it is not clear how a city of so many millions can cope without this sophisticated and ingenious arrangement in place (Hazra and Goel, 2009). There certainly does not appear to be the will nor the funds to pay for a substantial waste management infrastructure that will surely be required should the current system collapse. Lastly, some experts have warned that the entire drainage of Calcutta is affected by the development of the Wetlands, with river levels of the Hooghly already having risen over the past decade by 1 cm, a rise forecast to reach 4 cm soon. If this process cannot be halted, Kolkata will be submerged in a few decades (Mukherjee, 2011).

Private–public partnerships and development deals have also served to speed up the scale and pace of construction all along the corridor. With official approval and frequent financing from the state, existing townships and areas are being expanded, especially New Town and East Kolkata Township and the Baishnabghata-Patuli area. Along the Eastern Metropolitan (EM) Bypass, there are large new shopping malls already built or under construction, as well as international hotel chains, entertainment parks, playgrounds, and massive new apartment complexes of the type seen in Delhi's infamous Gurgaon. Within the city, several connectors and flyovers have been constructed to ease traffic congestion in the urban core but significantly and explicitly also to facilitate easy access to the Bypass. These have led to further displacements, with hawkers and squatters along those new roads evicted (Mukherjee, 2004) who now often have to travel long distances to reach their workplaces. As a result, the lives and livelihoods of many are stretched, as one of the drivers I hired in Kolkata asserted:

> On some weekends I go to help with the harvest. Once we lived in a village in the Wetlands. Now my family must farm in a village farther away in the country. I drive a car all week and on Friday I take a train for an hour and a half out to my family, work on the harvest on Saturday and Sunday, and take the train back in to the city Monday morning. When I drive past the Wetlands like this, I remember our home.

The implications of the unplanned development of the EKW and the state-led sites newly included in plans to expand the city are therefore more far-reaching than simply providing new homes for the middle class, including those who are putatively connected to global networks of capital, labour, and identity. Whole communities are actively displaced and find themselves without homes, livelihoods, and cultural networks.

How to save the Wetlands

While the overall picture is grim, organized mobilization against the destruction of the Wetlands is still going strong: the *Jalabhumi Bachao Andolan*, the Save Rajarhat Wetlands Committee, or various fishers' organizations actively oppose the illegal pond filling. Across the EKW, small fishers' huts carry the banners of these groups, and members of these organizations clash regularly with the developers' affiliates, even when they are assaulted by criminal gangs, which is often the case.

Most who find themselves displaced are left without any support. This has been particularly true in the recent development of Rajarhat, where fishers, hawkers, and farmers who were promised compensation or sale prices have yet to be paid; some people have now taken legal action (Dembowski, 2001). As a KMDA planner argued, it is common knowledge that development in the EKW is taking place "at the barrel of a gun." Another KMDA staffer agreed and suggested that faced with the scale of illegal construction in the EKW between 2002 and 2012, the state has chosen a policy of retrospective regularization. Returning to India in 2012, I spent some time at the East Kolkata Wetlands Management Authority (EKWMA) interviewing staff about their experiences with protecting the EKW. Almost all suggested a lack of political support at both the government and local levels. As a compliance officer pointed out:

> The location of land is such a tempting target for real estate developers. And many of those who are most active are large developers, prominent in the city and with many ties to local politicians. Everyone knows them and everyone knows that they will build if they want to.

This was seconded by another EKWMA staffer, who argued that

> there is a lot of encroachment going on. A lot of encroachment. But we have no real authority. We can request but we cannot require compliance, even with the Ramsar Convention. Our director has written to the ministry to say that we need resources and to help actually enforce the rules.

Even police officers agreed that a lack of political support and resources led to apathy towards encroachment. As one said to me:

> Wetland filling is for us a low priority. It is indeed not a priority. We must deal with violent crimes and property crimes, what does filling mean in the context of these? And remember, we have much crime in the wetlands itself, with alcohol and theft and beatings and so on.

As a result, staff at the EKWMA reported that in spite of existing legal provisions protecting the EKW, there are no means to enforce them. When they receive a report of illegal filling, a compliance team is sent to check out the situation, take pictures, and on occasion file a First Information Report (FIR), an official report filed by the police in India based on a given offense. Between 2006, when it came into existence, and 2012, when I conducted my interviews with them, EKWMA had lodged 203 FIRs regarding illegal filling. Of these cases, a grand total of one case had proceeded to prosecution.

In this instance, which occurred in November 2011, a developer had openly drained and filled a pond in the Wetlands, and local activists had contacted the EKWMA and lodged a FIR. The NGO that had led the fight to protect the Wetlands (PUBLIC) took up the call and began protests at the site, which soon received significant media attention. The developer received a stop work notice, but the filling continued, according to activists, during night-time construction.

The protestors then wrote an open letter to the Chief Minister of West Bengal (who declined to intervene), and PUBLIC began to prepare a broader campaign, including pursuing public interest litigation against illegal filling. Unexpectedly, the decision not to prosecute was suddenly reversed, and the unfinished structure that had been hurriedly placed on the fill site was demolished in the presence of activists. Environmentalists argue that those who ended up being prosecuted were functionaries merely standing in for the real culprit, a developer with strong links to the ruling party at the municipal and state levels. Although the filling and construction came to a halt, at the time of writing, the site has not been restored to its original state.

These examples, both of failed attempts to prosecute but also of the negligible effect of successful prosecution, speak to a larger problem of the opposition to development in the EKW – namely, their use for different interest groups. While they are home to migrants and residents, fishers, farmers, and waste management workers on whom so much of Kolkata depends, to many in the city the Wetlands are "the place that breeds all the mosquitoes for the city" – a comment that many EKWMA staff stated that they had heard from residents of Kolkata. The notion that the Wetlands were a blank canvas before the developers arrived, which is so widespread among middle-class Kolkatans, poses very serious problems for an assessment of their beneficial aspects. As the director of the EKWMA said,

> How much are the citizens of the city aware of the services or knowledge-able about what the Wetlands provide to Kolkata? All of these new projects that are coming up are large projects based on groundwater abstraction. How much water will they use, how much land will they take, how much waste will they create? These are people they want to put into these new flats who have upper middle class consumptionist [sic] lifestyles, environmentally affective lifestyles. At whose cost will their comfort be? You cannot have everything for cheap. This city is going to face an ecological disaster if the EKW disappears.

In the next chapter, I will therefore turn to examining how the Wetlands are being reconstructed as an essential part of plans to avert an ecological disaster associated with the quest for Kolkata's revamped global prominence.

References

Banerjee, S. (2012). "The march of the mega-city: governance in West Bengal and the wetlands to the east of Kolkata." *South Asia Chronicle* **2**(2012): 93–118.

Banerji, S. (2013). "NGOs and wetlands." *The Statesman*. Retrieved April 24, 2014, from http://www.thestatesman.net/news/26332-ngos-and-wetlands.html.

Bhatta, B. (2009). "Analysis of urban growth pattern using remote sensing and GIS: a case study of Kolkata, India." *International Journal of Remote Sensing* **30**(18): 4733–4746.

Bose, P. K., Ed. (2000). *Refugees in West Bengal: institutional practices and contested identities*. Calcutta, Mahanirban Calcutta Research Group.

Bunting, S. W., N. Kundu and M. Mukherjee (2002). Renewable natural resource-use in livelihoods at the Calcutta peri-urban interface: literature review. *Land-Water Interface Production Systems in Peri-Urban Kolkata DFID-NRSP Project Working Paper*. Stirling, UK, Institute of Aquaculture, University of Stirling.

Calcutta Metropolitan Development Authority (CMDA) (1975). Anchal development strategy, Report 13. Calcutta, CMDA Directorate of Planning and Development.

Calcutta Metropolitan Development Authority (CMDA) (1976). Area development strategy for Salt Lake Township, Report 6. Calcutta, CMDA Directorate of Planning and Development.

Calcutta Metropolitan Development Authority (CMDA) (1981). New area development at extension of Baishnabghata-Patuli Township, Report 156. Calcutta, CMDA Directorate of Planning and Development.

Chakrabarti, P. (1990). *The marginal men*. Kalyani, Lumiere Press.

Chattopadhyay, S., A. Dutta and S. Ray (2009). "Municipal solid waste management in Kolkata, India – a review." *Waste Management* **29**(4): 1449–1458.

Dembowski, H. (2001). *Taking the state to court: public interest litigation and the public sphere in metropolitan India*. Delhi, Oxford University Press.

Dey, I., R. Samaddar and S. Sen (2013). *Beyond Kolkata: Rajarhat and the dystopia of urban imagination*. New Delhi, Routledge.

Dutt, S. (2000). "Megacities of joy: a case study of Calcutta's environmental problems in an age of globalization." *Australian Journal of International Affairs* **54**(3): 373–388.

Hazra, T. and S. Goel (2009). "Solid waste management in Kolkata, India: practices and challenges." *Waste Management* **29**(1): 470–478.

Kolkata Metropolitan Development Authority (KMDA) (2000). Calcutta development: programmes and projects. Kolkata, KMDA Publications.

Kolkata Metropolitan Development Authority (KMDA) (2001). Vision 2025: perspective plan of CMA (interim draft). Kolkata, KMDA Directorate of Planning and Development.

Kolkata Metropolitan Development Authority (KMDA) (2014). "Basic services to the urban poor sector." Retrieved April 24, 2014, from http://www.kmdaonline.org/html/bsupsector-info.php.

Kundu, N., M. Bhattacharya and A. Mukherjee (1997). *Managing wetlands: a policy perspective*. Calcutta, Institute of Wetland Management and Ecological Design.

Mukherjee, D. P. (2011). "Stress of urban pollution on largest natural wetland ecosystem in East Kolkata – causes, consequences and improvement." *Archives of Applied Science Research* **3**(6): 443–461.

Mukherjee, S. (2004). "Fast forward on flyovers." *The Telegraph*. Retrieved August 27, 2004, from http://www.telegraphindia.com/1040827/asp/calcutta/story_3678779.asp.

Ramsar Convention (2014). Retrieved May 15, 2014, from http://www.ramsar.org/cda/en/ramsar-about/main/ramsar/1–36_4000_0__.

Ray, S. and S. Niyogi (2014). "Heart of East Kolkata Wetlands under siege?" *The Times of India*. Retrieved May 15, 2014, from http://timesofindia.indiatimes.com/city/kolkata/Heart-of-East-Kokata-wetlands-under-siege/articleshow/28418032.cms.

Roy, A. (2011). Re-forming the megacity: Calcutta and the rural-urban interface. *Megacities: Urban Form, Governance and Sustainability*. A. Sorensen and J. Okata. Tokyo, Springer: 93–110.

Sarkar, A. N. (1990). The East Calcutta Wetlands. *Calcutta: The Living City Volume II: The Present and the Future*. S. Chaudhuri. Delhi, Oxford University Press: 173–175.

Sarkar, S. (1991). Indian democracy: the historical inheritance. *The Success of India's Democracy*. A. Kohli. Cambridge, Cambridge University Press: 21–46.

The Times of India (2002). "People's commission hears evictees' pleas." Retrieved August 28, 2014, from http://timesofindia.indiatimes.com/city/kolkata/Peoples-commission-hears-evictees-pleas/articleshow/23007066.cms.

Weber, R. (2006). Re(creating) the home: women's role in the development of refugee colonies in South Calcutta. *The Trauma and the Triumph: Gender and Partition in Eastern India*. J. Bagchi and S. Dasgupta. Kolkata, Stree: 59–79.

Wetlands International South Asia (2010). East Kolkata Wetlands. *Newsletter*. Kolkata, East Kolkata Wetlands Management Authority. **1**.

7 The Kolkata Environmental Improvement Project

The second case I want to present exemplifies the way in which Kolkata is being remade in a form that is simultaneously global and intensely local. My example is that of the Kolkata Environmental Improvement Project (KEIP), a multi-million-dollar partnership between the city, the state government, and several international development agencies aimed at a drastic overhaul of infrastructure with a focus on the wider environment of the city and its surrounding areas. The planned projects include new sewage and drainage systems, clearing of silted canals, improvements to local parks and ponds, construction of new housing for the urban poor, and conversion of a significant part of the East Kolkata Wetlands (EKW) into spaces of conservation and ecotourism. It is on the latter three initiatives that this chapter is primarily focused, as I argue that such projects are integral to the new visions for the city that have taken shape over the past two decades. Global or world cities are often synonymous with modernist landscapes depicted in terms of well-planned and efficient urban spaces. As we have seen in Chapter 5, Kolkata has a reputation for being the absolute opposite of a modern city; instead, it is represented as congested, polluted, crumbling, and marred by corruption. It is therefore its reputation and representation that the new vision for Kolkata aims at changing through a range of environmental improvement initiatives. The KEIP is, however, more ambitious than a focus on infrastructural improvement alone might suggest. The explicit goal of the program may be to reverse environmental degradation in Kolkata. But if planners and politicians in Kolkata are to achieve the aspiration of remaking Kolkata into a global city, the work of the KEIP must provide the foundation for such dreams. The KEIP is thus about more than sewage and drainage, cleaning canals, or creating sites to reinterpret nature. It is a program whose components and articulation bring together multiple themes and discourses, including those on global environmentalism, middle-class sensibilities, transnational spaces, international development, and local politics.

I will start the chapter by looking briefly at the idea of environmental renewal as a middle-class project aligned to the global forms of gentrification discussed in Chapter 4. In particular, I explore the notion of bourgeois environmentalism and the ways in which it may construct both the city and its legitimate inhabitants. Next, I examine the genesis of the KEIP initiative, its structure, and its present status. In the following section, I look more closely at three particular parts of the KEIP that have particular relevance to the book. First, I examine plans to rehabilitate existing water bodies and ponds within the city, paying special attention to the diverse and often opposed interests of different groups of users. Second, I look at replacement housing built by the KEIP for those displaced by (some of) its work, contrasting these with the types of housing developments envisaged for Global Indians. Third, I analyze the plans proposed for conservation, education, and profitability related to the Wetlands and put forward by the KEIP, which often intersect, overlap and, at times, conflict with the new developments described in Chapter 8.

Bourgeois environmentalism in the remaking of cities

'Cleaning up' a city is not by any means a new idea, nor is it particular to our day and age. Whether it is the recurrent slum clearances in colonial and post-colonial contexts found across the globe (King, 1976; Hazareesingh, 2001); renewal measures meant to combat 'urban blight' in the industrialized world (Teaford, 2000); infrastructure projects that have long been run roughshod over and through working-class, poor, and minority neighbourhoods in many countries (Groves, 2012; Bullard, Johnson, and Torres, 2004); or the more recent 'beautification' discussed in Chapter 4, the narratives and processes of urban renewal have a long and often sordid history.

Kolkata has certainly had its share of slum clearances and the displacement of 'pavement-dwellers,' (Sengupta, 2010; Ghosh, 2013), squatters, and the like. But in the past, the idea of 'development' that justified such actions was discursively related to ideas of justice and redistribution, poverty alleviation, or public health concerns, with the needs of the poor and the lower middle class highlighted. The environment – while often part of such discussions – has not had the same prominence as now in pre-1990s plans to remake Kolkata. The KEIP, on the other hand, brings such a focus into processes of urban design in Kolkata, following a global trend towards "green urbanism" (Lehmann, 2011). To be clear, while complaints about the city's environmental conditions are widespread, the action undertaken by the KEIP is not a response to popular initiatives or mass mobilization. The KEIP is not a result of a groundswell of environmental activism in Kolkata, nor – as has been the case in other Indian cities like New Delhi – the result of judicial activism and public interest litigation (PIL) aimed at halting environmental degradation (Williams and Mawdsley, 2006; Rajamani, 2007).

Instead, it is a form of institutional environmental action, initiated and implemented at the level of state and local governments in partnership with international agencies, private consultants, and a range of non-governmental organizations (NGOs). The majority of the measures implemented consist of straightforward civil engineering initiatives, including a new sewage system and the clearing of canals so filled with garbage or encroached upon by informal housing that they scarcely function. Many of the other aspects of the KEIP, however, speak to a desire to redevelop Kolkata for the benefit of the middle class – as evidenced by the project's focus on the renovation of parks and ponds, the construction of social housing to remove unsightly slums, and the creation of new outdoor amenities and ecotourism. In contrast to Delhi, these initiatives are not citizen-driven, but the push for environmental renewal in Kolkata is nevertheless congruent with what some have called "bourgeois environmentalism" – the desire of the affluent to 'improve' spaces at the expense of social justice or concerns about equity (Baviskar, 2003; Baviskar and Ray, 2011; Mawdsley, Mehra, and Beazley, 2009). As I have argued elsewhere (Bose, 2013), several of the emerging environmental conflicts in Kolkata are the result of a fundamental clash between visions of the city as it is and the city as it may yet be.

On one hand, these conflicts are fuelled by attempts to renovate and recreate what Roy (2003) has called Kolkata imagined as a middle-class Bengali city – a modern, worldly, and civilized place inhabited by cosmopolitan, genteel, and educated citizens who belong to the old middle class and therefore form a privileged elite. This city is one that is functional, safe, efficient, clean, and connected to global networks of people, industries, technologies, and ideas. It is hard to imagine that such a city can exist at the same time and in the same space as the present incarnation of Kolkata, which is overcrowded, polluted, and only just emerging from decades of apparent neglect. It is even harder to imagine how the current city and its residents would fit into the future visions. For many others in the city today – for example, the third of the population that live in slums (Schenk, 2010) – the city is imagined and understood in terms of basic needs of shelter, food, and hygiene, the fulfilment of which might well trump dreams of environmental futures. This city is one in which survival is the first order of the day, not global prominence. An imagined future Kolkata for such people might place greater emphasis on the provision of public services, a focus on land tenure or affordable housing, food security, or accessible and sustainable employment. And it is clear from what has been said before that this vision of Kolkata is clearly not accommodated within the KEIP version.

There are, of course, many residents whose lives are situated somewhere in between the extremes of great affluence and mere survival sketched previously, and few of these citizens are satisfied with the quality of life in Kolkata. But the city clearly does not work for the majority of its inhabitants, and the question we have to ask is: how will these competing narratives of a possible future for Kolkata play out? To take the example of the pond as an urban space, can there be a middle ground between its perception as a site for leisure activities, cleaned and surrounded by park benches, gated and secured, and the perception of those who see it primarily as a source of water for everyday use and as a working fishery? Equally, we need to ask how the rights of hawkers and the homeless to urban space overlap with the perspective of technocrats and politicians who see the very same spaces as sites for beautification or places that need to make way for new developments. In the contest between these (and many other) visions of Kolkata, the city emerges as a site of struggles, not only over space but also over its representation, the imaginary that uses the present to determine possible futures.

It is also important to recognize that the vision of a clean, green Kolkata in the KEIP is a similarly contested vision of green urbanism or, indeed, of environmental action in general. A range of scholars has pointed to the dissonance between Western environmentalism and the conditions found in the Global South (Guha and Gadgil, 1995), the emergent and evolving forms of green globalism (Lohmann, 1997), and green colonialism (Shiva, Jani, and Fontana, 2011). Others have pointed to the phenomenon of "land grabbing" in the name of environmental protection (Fairhead, Leach, and Scoones, 2012; Levien, 2013a; Rai, 2012) and of "environmentally induced displacement" (Bose and Lunstrum, 2014; Buscher and Davidov, 2014). Of particular relevance for the Kolkata case are Mawdsley's (2004) discussions of emerging Indian middle classes (and middle-class consciousness) and the environment and Baviskar's (2003, 2006) important analysis of "bourgeois environmentalism" in urban India. As Baviskar and others (Guha and Martinez Alier, 1998; Levien, 2013b) have shown, a complex interaction between global environmental discourses – by state actors, NGOs, transnational activists, and multinational corporations, among others – has led to the targeting and blaming of poor and marginalized groups for a range of urban problems.

Within this framework, the survival strategies of the urban poor are redefined as evidence of anti-environmental and, therefore, anti-social behaviour. Viewed as they are through the lens of the bourgeois environmentalist, trash heaps on the streets, polluted waterways, a lack of trees and green space, and urination in public are no longer seen as indicators of inadequate planning, lack of sanitation, or hazardous industries but as products of the ignorant and indifferent attitudes of the poor, who are oblivious to the needs of nature. At best, we are told, the poor lack facilities like time and space to consider the environment. At worst, as one environmental activist I interviewed claimed, they just don't care:

> The poor have more pressing things to worry about than the environment. As a result their own environment is greatly degraded. One cannot expect them to take the initiative to protect the land; without proper education or opportunity how would they even know what is necessary?

Such a view of the urban poor was not common among all of the environmentalists I interviewed, but it was hardly unique. These opinions have clear consequences, whether in Kolkata or elsewhere. The characterizations of the urban poor as careless polluters of the environment have led, in many instances, to drastic actions in the name of better urban quality of life and the beautification of the city; their consequences, including evictions, slum clearances, and 'renewal' efforts, as well as the loss of jobs through closures or relocations of whole industries; and restricted access to resources in the name of conservation. In the most dramatic cases, these actions also included direct violence and led to deaths, as in Baviskar's (2003) example of the killing of an urban youth by a middle-class mob after he defecated at the border of a middle-class enclave.

In an attempt to analyze these processes, Baviskar suggests that what we see emerging through such cases in India is "a complex interrelationship between two forms of environmentalism, with the green agenda of the rich leading to greater social and economic marginalization of the poor and their concerns over fair distribution of resources and safe working conditions" (Baviskar, 2003: 89). In this context, she states that "middle class assumptions of the working class as inferior shaped the articulation of the 'public interest' in Delhi at the expense of the interests of the poor" (Baviskar, 2003: 89). This is an important point, even if we acknowledge that, as Mawdsley (2004: 94) reminds us, there exists considerable "diversity and dynamism within the middle classes in relation to the environment." She therefore calls for a situated understanding of 'the environment' itself (Mawdsley, 2004: 88–89), while both scholars emphasize the need to understand the wider processes at stake.

Context of the KEIP

This is the complex context within which the KEIP took shape, intended as "a multi-agency endeavour to arrest environmental degradation and improve the quality of life in Kolkata" (KEIP, 2014) – a tall order indeed. But how does this project fit into the broader scheme of conflicting environmental and future visions of Kolkata, as discussed previously? In order to find an answer, I must discuss the project in greater detail.

In terms of specific goals, the KEIP's main objectives are pollution reduction, provision of basic services (primarily sanitation) to slums, upgrading the sewerage and drainage system for the metropolitan area, improvement of solid waste management for the city, rehabilitation of drainage canals, improvement of recreation facilities for parks and water bodies, and the provision of affordable housing for squatters along the canals (KEIP, 2014). Furthermore, among the overall goals is the general improvement of the delivery of municipal services.

The project was triggered when the Government of India applied in 1998 to the Asian Development Bank (ADB) for a loan to fund measures that would address environmental degradation in India's mega-cities. The proposal built on long-standing efforts by regional planners to secure international funding for much-needed infrastructure improvements: the best part of Kolkata's existing sewage and drainage infrastructure, for example, is a legacy of the colonial era, with precious little upgrading since then. Kolkata was identified as the most appropriate location for the initiative, and a multi-partner effort to develop a large project plan was underway by the next year. The stakeholders included the Kolkata Municipal Corporation; the Kolkata Metropolitan Development Authority (KMDA); the Bengal Chamber of Commerce; an NGO called Concern for Calcutta; the federal Government of India departments of Urban Development and Economic Affairs; and West Bengal's departments of Municipal Affairs, Environment, and Finance. In a first step, the steering committee representing these bodies commissioned several pilot studies conducted by domestic and international consultants in engineering, waste management, environmental assessment, and urban development (KEIP, 2014). Out of these initial explorations arose a project underwritten by a complicated series of direct and matching

Table 7.1 KEIP funding structure (US $, millions)

Source	Original funds	Supplementary	Total	Percent
Asian Development Bank	177.77	80.00	257.77	64.22%
Government of West Bengal	54.60	19.50	74.10	18.46%
Kolkata Municipal Corporation	55.40	14.10	69.50	17.32%
TOTAL	287.77	113.60	401.37	100.00%

Source: KEIP, 2014

loan agreements among several bilateral and international partners, as well as supplemental funding agreed to 5 years into the project. Table 7.1 shows the funding structure for the project.

According to the original plans, the project would have been completed by 2007, but at that point it had become clear that costs were rising, as delays and increasingly ambitious programs envisioned by project staff meant that more time and funds would be needed. Inter-agency squabbling, redundancies, and duplication signalled the need to some of the partners that capacity building needed to be an integral part of the overall plan. A good illustration of this problem is the complex hierarchy that existed between different personnel and organizations from the outset of the project. For example, while the director was chosen from the federal Civil Services of India to lead the project, much of the responsibility for planning lay with KMDA staff, while the implementation of plans lay with Kolkata Municipal Corporation (KMC) officials. In addition, a team of foreign and domestic consultants provided project management and financial oversight. On top of this complex set of interdependencies and relation-ships, project evaluation and monitoring were handled by outside experts. As a senior member of the management team commented, this structural complexity led to multiple tensions within the teams:

> There were big debates about what the project should and could do. There were big debates about who were our primary stakeholders and who we were accountable to. There were big debates about what we were expecting to accomplish and what we could actually finish. I don't think we were ready for the number of debates when we started the job and how much they would slow us down.

As a result, not only did the ADB, Government of West Bengal (GoWB), and KMC all provide extra monies which amounted to over a hundred million dollars in supplementary funds, the UK Department for International Development (DFID) contributed US $42 million exclusively for the training of KMC staff. This money was provided in addition to the ADB funds, which were structured as 30 percent grant and 70 percent loan for the extended period of the project between 2007 and 2010, although at the time of writing, many components have still not been completed. As discussed in the following, some parts of the plan are so time-consuming that they will not be completed within the foreseeable future for 5 or 10 years, if ever. Thus, issues of feasibility and responsibility have raised significant obstacles to the success of the project as a whole. That these are serious concerns was apparent when KEIP planners discussed in interviews how a parallel proposal, intended to improve the existing sewerage and drainage infrastructure through World Bank funding, fell through precisely because of concerns with accountability raised by the funder. Furthermore, some of the KEIP consultants expressed their surprise at the expected levels of transparency and responsibility in the ongoing project. As a consultant remarked:

> I have found very low levels of accountability or oversight demanded by our own project funders. The ADB has been relatively disinterested other than when it comes to rehabilitation and resettlement of canal dwellers. The KMC's chief concern seems to be in immediate gains linked to political outcomes.

The goals of the KEIP

The core parts of the KEIP as it stands involve building sewerage infrastructure, including trunk and secondary sewers and stormwater drainage and pumping stations, and upgrading and constructing treatment plants. Other activities include replacing open containers for municipal solid waste with closed ones; increasing the number of containers; purchasing new compactor trucks, bulldozers, and mechanical road sweepers; important actions to dredge and desilt canals, including the building of new pumping stations; and the building of numerous foot and single-lane vehicle bridges to cross these waterways (KEIP, 2014). All of these are capital- and labour-intensive initiatives and not surprisingly have taken up the majority of the project staff's attention and the majority of funds. Beyond improving the sewerage and drainage system as a whole, the KEIP included funds to address emergency works – essentially short-term investments to fix critical infrastructure that had broken down. Such a focus responds to what representatives of multiple agencies involved in the KEIP see as the major issues facing Kolkata today. A KMDA engineer, for example, said that

> our streets are polluted and the collection systems are not efficient. If we are to grow Kolkata properly, we must improve them. We must remember that solid waste collection and disposal is also a serious health as well as environmental concern.

Another staff member at the KMC supported this view of the priorities:

> We can do nothing to solve the issues in Kolkata until we address the question of environment. This begins with proper disposal of waste and the KMC has already undertaken plans to begin this process.

To this, an environmental scientist employed by the GoWB added that the KEIP effort was important to spearhead efforts to raise environmental awareness and action among the citizens of Kolkata:

> Biodiversity needs to be a more central focus for citizens and planners. Parks, playgrounds and lakes need to be improved and maintained. Noise pollution is also a serious concern. We must model good environmental behaviours through our rehabilitation of the city.

Another environmental scientist pointed out the urgency of these measures when he mentioned the greater-than-expected effects of annual floods in 2007 and linked environmental concerns with the presence of the poor in the KEIP's work areas:

> We have had more torrential rain than usual this year, which has helped lead to flooding. The system is badly in need of maintenance and repair. The canals are badly silted and the number of *bustees* [hutment neighbour-hoods] on them increases the problem every year.

Despite their long-term visions of an improved and cleaner Kolkata, most of the staff that I interviewed told me that their primary goal was to lay sewer pipes effectively and efficiently. All seemed frustrated by the slow pace of progress and the political difficulties of conducting their work. A KMDA engineer's complaint is typical:

> The work that we are doing is *ad-hoc* and one-sided. A more integrated system of planning and development is needed. Only developing one sector does not work, nor does working without a broader vision. For example, the new system is designed to accommodate two-meter wide pipes but many Kolkata roads are too narrow for them.

These problems were not only related to staff engaged in the project itself but also stemmed from overlapping jurisdictions, responsibilities, and the relative power of the various partners, as well as poor conflict resolution skills – all of which were clearly major concerns for many of the consultants (both domestic and international). As one said:

> The KMC rather than the KMDA is in charge of the project; but the first is a political body with experience of management rather than development and they tend to see things through short-term political objectives rather than longer-term developmental ones. The KMC is not a development orga-nization and has no experience with development; overall planning is there-fore not undertaken. They want results right away and have no experience in planning. It is also possible that political patronage and corruption also came into play. Too often KMC politicians have used funds for political purposes, to appease constituents or gain favors.

The problem was also felt acutely by staff on the ground. Thus, a project engineer involved with the actual laying of sewer pipes spoke of being inundated with phone calls – not from KMC staff involved with the project but from politicians themselves:

> We receive a call that tells us to place two feet of pipe in one street, five in another, two in another. It does not matter that the pipes are not connected or that it is not part of the overall scheme. The only thing they want is for voters to see that work is being done. Anyway the KMC is more interested in maintaining than building, though it does not really do either particularly well. This makes us worry about the long-term viability and sustainability of the project.

The consultants I spoke with were also frustrated by what they saw as their exclusion from discussions on the emerging EKW management plan drawn up by the GoWB after the Ramsar designation of the site. They had been fighting for a voice at the table but were unsuccessful. Those responsible for sidelining them when it came to planning saw this as a political (and principled) matter rather than a practical or technical one. As one Ministry official stated:

> While technical assistance from outside agencies is always welcome, our legislative approach to environmental management must remain internal. Our development of the East Kolkata Wetlands is a part of a commitment to development in our state. There is overall a problem of development in the state of West Bengal. It is still focused on Kolkata. Developing other parts of the state may decrease the problems faced by the capital city.

This statement was made by a senior civil servant in 2007, when no one could have anticipated the level of controversy and resistance to state-led development of other parts of West Bengal. The fall of the Left Front government, which can in no small part be attributed to failed attempts to introduce such measures in Nandigram and Singur, did not introduce a more even distribution of development projects across the state. Even under the new Trinamool government, Kolkata remains the main focus, with planners and staff still convinced of the benefits that the plan would produce. That this pattern of thought will remain in force is presaged by the comments of a project leader, who stated in 2007:

> Despite my concerns and reservations, the project will have an impact by 2010 and will have come a long way. The KEIP will be a significant success simply by building actual infrastructure, though this of course needs to be maintained as well.

That the project has produced new infrastructure – not only by laying new sewer lines but also by constructing houses for the displaced and toilets for slum-dwellers, among other things – indicates a significant accomplishment. But when I returned in 2012, outstanding work had not been completed, and the situation did not look promising. Asked about the delay and a time frame for completion, a senior civil servant explained:

> The KEIP has done some important work – they have managed to desilt the upper reaches of the canals, they have placed some regulators and pumping stations and built some flats, but not much else. The ADB money can be used for sewage and drainage but this is not enough. The project must go back to the Bank to get more money. In the East Kolkata Wetland areas alone they have spent 50-crore rupees but 200-crore rupees are needed to really make an impact. The KEIP is not that useful and I often quarrel with them over what needs to be done.

Despite the skepticism articulated by planners, managers, and staff – which is also shared by outside observers and the general public – addressing the environmental issues plaguing Kolkata is a priority on which any vision of rehabilitating the city hinges. An important part of such strategies is creating a better system for managing waste. As one KEIP staff member said:

> Sewerage and drainage is the lifeline of Kolkata. If we are to help Kolkata become a new global city, then this is the first step.

While both have been partially addressed, the work remains unfinished and, as a result, one can say that the "first step" is yet to be completed.

Environment and the new Kolkata: parks and water bodies

In the final sections of this chapter, I would like to focus on three particular components of the KEIP which are less concerned with waste disposal and more with values and ideals that are consonant with a set of middle-class values and global identities, as discussed previously. These are the restoration of parks and ponds, new housing for those displaced by the cleaning of canals, and the development of ecotourism and environmental education in the EKW. Taken together, they all reveal a very different vision for the new city than the focus on sewage and the cleansing of canals might suggest. These three parts of the project – none of them nearly as capital-intensive as the sewage and drainage components – are important, as they are intimately related to the way the city and the EKW are re-imagined as sites of leisure pursuits. In this vision, 'nature' becomes a site to be protected, interpreted, and profited from to the exclusion of the interests of those working the land or indeed already living on it.

In terms of the proposed restoration of parks and water bodies, the KEIP aims at improving ponds in primarily residential neighbourhoods through landscaping, widening of pavements, repainting of existing walls and buildings, upgrading of lighting, and installation of benches. These measures are designed to make the ponds both more attractive and accessible to local residents. But the plan does not envisage granting that accessibility to everyone, as the improvements include significant expansion of the boundaries of the ponds through the construction of walls with railings and retaining walls and the installation of security and surveillance systems. According to KEIP staff, this last measure was introduced to stop the dumping of waste into ponds allegedly perpetrated by slum-dwellers. In response, increased protection of the water bodies (especially in light of the significant investments in their upgrading by the KEIP) seems a legitimate reaction. Indeed, an important requirement for the success of infrastructure improvements is a set of environmental education initiatives – classes on ecological restoration, wildlife walks, new interpretive signage – aimed especially at local schoolchildren and other users of the new parks. Seen from this perspective, the water bodies in Kolkata are intended for the enjoyment provided by 'nature.'

The work undertaken has focused on ten parks in the first phase (2002–2007); two parks, three lakes, and one swimming pool in the second phase (2007–2010); and one park in the current third phase, which has extended beyond the original life of the project (KEIP, 2014). This section – the installation and operation of a musical fountain and the enforcement of a no-fishing ban in an affluent neighbourhood of South Kolkata – brings the conflicts between middle-class environmental desires and the livelihoods of working-class residents out quite clearly. Many of the staff working on the project are acutely aware of these conflicting interests, as this interview with a scientist with the West Bengal Pollution Control Board demonstrates:

> Most of the work on Kolkata is on wetlands but urban waterbodies and ponds are far less studied. There are over 3600 urban ponds and waterbodies in Kolkata that are used by over 500,000 people to bathe in as well as to catch fish in. It is why they exist and are not filled in because many also supplement income from fish. Local people tended to plant trees, but mostly nicely flowering ones. They realize later on that birds don't tend to use those so they instead have started planting different ones that will attract birds. The green spaces created near/around water-bodies often provide sanctuaries for urban animals (especially birds) and also for people to enjoy.

Urban water bodies perform a host of important functions but have different meanings for different people depending on their backgrounds and class positions. What seems to some a space for quiet contemplation, religious ceremony, or education is to others a source of water for drinking, bathing, cleaning clothes, or fishing, as well as often a source of income. But, crucially, the ponds are also of wider significance for the KEIP more generally because they are part of a wider system of drainage. Thus, in 2007, an engineer explained the ponds' role:

> Ponds can play a major role in the drainage network. We are hoping to incorporate ponds as an integral and practical part of the second phase of the existing project. Currently ponds are often filled by first being used as impromptu garbage dumps, after which they are filled in and construction is begun. We need to halt this.

It therefore appears that the pollution of these water bodies is a pressing concern. But problems arise when a specific set of uses – that of ponds as sites of leisure rather than of sustenance and work – is prioritized over all others in a project that supposedly acts in the interest of all Kolkatans. For one of the environmental engineers at the KMDA, the solution seems straightforward:

> Eighty five percent of the ponds would be cleaned up simply if we removed solid waste before it goes into the water. We cannot achieve North American standards here but still we can achieve minimum safe standards that still allow enough use for local people. We need to wisely use this resource.

To this, a local environmental activist added:

> We have begun an initiative to protect ponds by having them declared important cultural sites. Ponds are the places where people go to have an *adda*[1] beside. It cannot be all ponds of course. It must be one that needs to have a seventy-five to hundred-year history and usually be connected to a famous historical event or (more commonly) to a famous family. This could be a possibly good moneymaking exercise so wealthy people would pay to have ponds protected.

Such an approach also plays into the logic of neoliberal urbanism discussed in Chapter 4. In this case, the need to protect ponds is made profitable and 'efficient' through a focus on user fees and the redefinition of public space on the basis of class and identity. The importance in such a scheme of defining 'residents' in terms of services and their usage was highlighted by another KMC officer, who outlined a plan to penalize those who caused 'environmental degradation':

> We have in mind a scheme to charge polluters for cleaning up their messes. The main polluters are not the slum dwellers. It is actually from the immersion of idols following *pujas* and other ceremonies. This scheme would be an important revenue-generating exercise.

While this official emphasized that the urban poor were not solely responsible for pollution, his was not the majority voice. Indeed, some of the social activists I interviewed spoke of their intervention when some neighbourhood associations tried to restrict slum-dwellers' access to local ponds. In some cases, this meant trying to get police to arrest slum-dwellers who were using ponds for bathing and the like. In other instances, neighbourhood associations joined international environmental organizations and local activists in an effort to urge the KMC to evict slum-dwellers when they were located within the (relatively large) radius of a given pond. This call for eviction and displacement was thus uniquely citizen-led rather than organized by officials, which has so far been unusual in Kolkata. This provides strong support for Chatterjee's point about a change in the emerging politics of class relations, which he makes in a much-discussed essay, raising the question of whether the Indian city has finally become bourgeois (Chatterjee, 2004). Certainly, some housing and pro-poor activists that I met had scathing critiques of many environmental organizations as instruments of a self-serving bourgeoisie. As one said:

> I am concerned primarily with social justice. I have come into conflict with an environmental organization here in Kolkata that wants to protect a pond from waste by evicting slum dwellers who lived not near it but came to use it. What right do the environmentalists have to evict people from their own homes which aren't even nearby?

Canal clearances and new housing development

An important aspect of the KEIP is the construction of public housing, albeit in a limited form, with only one such project currently underway in Kolkata. When compared to the multitude of projects undertaken by both private developers and public–private partnerships that are driving the high-end real estate developments discussed in the next chapter, this seems quite insignificant. To the KEIP, their work is a central part of their humane attempts to remake the city (though a cynic might see this as little more than neoliberalism with a human face). The KEIP's initiative is primarily aimed at resettlement for those who are displaced by the work carried out under the plan to clean up the canals. These canals carry sewage from the city to the Wetlands and various processing facilities and have become increasingly inefficient due to siltation and squatter settlements located on their banks. Many of those who live there have been there for decades, including refugees from the 1971 Bangladesh war of independence and even from the period around the Partition of 1947.

The canal cleaning work encompasses sites within the city, the EKW, and some outer-city municipalities at seven sites in all. It has led to the planned relocation of some 2,000 families, and according to KEIP staff, new homes were originally conceived as plots of lands with some utilities to be provided to the displaced households. All were expected to construct their own homes, but as the project evolved, these plans were altered in favour of a series of apartment complexes to be built by the KEIP rather than by the displaced on those sites. While the original plan guaranteed that the displaced would not be relocated farther than 2.5 km away from their old residences to allow easy access to their current workplaces, many of the new homes are farther away, as we will see in the following. As the project developed, the plans also became more ambitious, with some 3,626 families to be displaced in total, of which 1,359 had already been resettled in KMDA-built replacement housing by the time I interviewed staff in 2007. Three separate sets of flats totalling nearly 700 had been completed by 2007, with a further 700 under construction.

This experience with rehabilitation and resettlement has been such an apparent success that a second phase of the KEIP included slum improvement and the creation of 'model slums' for the urban poor at no extra cost. The focus of this amendment is on the improvement of the 'environmental conditions' of the slums, with an emphasis on behavioural change through new initiatives on land owner-ship and titling, education, health, hygiene, nutrition, sanitation, and the creation of micro-credit schemes designed to improve livelihoods. The project also includes infrastructural improvements such as widening and realigning neigh-bourhood access lanes, new lighting, open public spaces, and the provision of utilities and supplies to residents.

On the face of it, such planned improvements are welcome. But many of the KEIP staff voiced concerns regarding the long-term viability of these measures, as the displacement of canal-dwellers resulted from the ADB loan, which speci-fied precisely how those affected would have to be compensated – through relocation and rebuilt livelihoods rather than cash alone – a conditionality increas-ingly common in development bank–financed projects (Penz, Drydyk, and Bose, 2011). Thus, it appears that the provision of housing is the exception rather than the norm. In the absence of ADB or similar funding, the future of those displaced by maintenance and further improvement of water bodies in the city is very uncertain.

Furthermore, we need to ask how the resettlement of those affected by the KEIP was handled. While project staff organized the desilting of canals and the construction of new buildings, resettlement and rehabilitation were outsourced to NGOs that the KEIP contracted after advertising in local and national media. A senior planner describes the criteria for selecting the NGOs and the motivation behind the project in these words:

> People who have been living by canals for generations originally really wanted land or plots of land, but now they have apartments. It has been a lottery distribution of the flats themselves, conducted in front of trusted authorities so that there is transparency and accountability. We have chosen NGOs for the R&R through a careful selection process, based on their track record and their professionalism. We have looked at their websites to see proof of this.

The actual process of informing canal-dwellers that they would be displaced and selecting those who would receive compensation in the form of land or housing seems to have followed procedures familiar in the context of major development projects. Thus, the KEIP identified a total of 81 settlements to be displaced by the desilting of canals, and the NGOs in charge of resettlement organized stakeholder consultations with resident squatters living along the canal and set up an information center in each settlement. According to one NGO staff member, there were two types of stakeholders identified in the process:

> We conducted two types of consultation: 1) primary, with representatives, youth clubs, politicians (this helps develop an entitlement matrix that helps to determine utilities, facilities, size of flats, though actual allocation is done

through a lottery) and 2) actual project-affected, who are spoken to about their needs as well. Canal resettlement groups were formed with canal dwellers themselves.

When asked who was deemed to be a legitimate recipient of compensation, the same NGO worker answered that they based their list on a survey conducted in 2000 that was used initially to identify canal-dwellers and issue identity cards. These documents, some of which I was able to see, included a photo, name, date of birth, name of settlement, and a thumbprint. Once this process had taken place, KEIP representatives met the canal-dwellers to determine who would be resettled in which area.

For representatives of the NGOs, the project was not simply about compensating slum-dwellers displaced by a development initiative but one that aimed at transforming the lives of the urban poor more generally. Thus, individual components of the project included attempts to regularize titles to residences and transform informal and insecure relationships into formal land titles or secure housing. Other measures included vocational training and support to open bank accounts and interact with other institutions; in essence, they comprised a system of legalizing the displaced. One of the NGO experts described the effect on those who lived in slums on the edges of the canals in this way:

There was no formal or official social identity for the canal dwellers prior to the project. They cannot get bank accounts and are denied hospitals and educational access, plus have difficulty in getting voter registration cards. Through processes of the project they have now become officially legitimate. Also, the purpose in building the new apartments for canal dwellers is not only housing resettlement but also economic rehabilitation. We have emphasized this through things like a women's self-help group, providing vocational training, and a fair in which women's handicrafts and other products are sold and orders taken.

Other staff echoed the importance of gender-based strategies for the resettlement and rehabilitation scheme:

When an allotment letter is sent out, it is issued in the name of the women. In these communities men often have several wives and this strategy was used to try and prevent abuses of the system and the collecting of more compensation flats than was allowed. Bank accounts were also opened in the name of women. When men objected we advised their wives to simply say that this is a government scheme and these are the rules that must be followed.

These practices reflect notions commonly found among those working for development banks, who frequently express essentializing, patronizing, and gendered views of the poor. Given the strong influence that the ADB has had on the resettlement aspects of the KEIP project, this is therefore not a surprising attitude. Overall, NGO representatives viewed the resettlement as a significant success and asserted that, in their view, the lives of the former canal-side squatters were positively changed as a result of compensation schemes following displacement.

But for many social justice activists in the city, the eviction of canal-dwellers signifies a more complicated story. Many spoke of conflicts between those who had been deemed legitimate and were therefore entitled to compensation after displacement and those who had not been included in such schemes. These activists argued that the process whereby recipients were selected was arbitrary and open to considerable corruption. Ironically, the NGOs themselves also reported a problem that they had not anticipated as a result of the project:

> The project has created real problems for other resettlement projects as the project-affected persons come in demanding the same type of compensation. Their reasoning is that it is the same central government, same state government, same municipality, why can't they get compensation for road-widening, flyover constructions, bridge-building, etc? They too want flats. They say "are canal dwellers gods?"

The squatters themselves were suspicious and distrustful of the entire enterprise right from the outset and have become increasingly vocal in their opposition to evictions and in their criticism of the new housing provided. By 2010, several communities had formed the Brihattaro Kolkata Khaalpaar Bosti Uchhed Protirodh Committee (the Greater Kolkata Committee to Resist Eviction of Canal Bank Slums). According to Nagarik Mancha, an NGO supporting them, they voiced multiple grievances (Nagarik Mancha, 2010). One related to the assurance that their new dwellings would be no more than 2.5 km from their old homes. This has turned out not to be the case, as most of the new apartments are located between 3 and 6 km away from their former residences. The group argued that, in many cases, this rendered existing occupations – primarily in domestic work and daily wage labour – unsustainable. Furthermore, they claimed that some of the sites they had originally been promised had subsequently been turned over to developers.

They also took issue with the information they received from the project planners and the consultation and decision-making processes. Contrary to the KEIP staff's claims, the spokespersons for the displaced communities complained that the process was chaotic and unclear, with the distribution of photo identity cards inconsistent and their purpose often obscure. Because the total size of the families to be displaced was often not recorded during the initial interviews, large families were often allocated single-room apartments as compensation. While each family was originally allotted 215 ft² per three family members in the resettlement sites, the lack of available land and the sheer number of the displaced meant that, in reality, flats of between 163 and 190 ft² with a balcony and a toilet were provided to the canal-dwellers, irrespective of family size. Furthermore, residents complained that within 4 months of taking possession, cracks, water damage, mold, potholes, and salt deposits began to appear. Often, it turned out that running water was unavailable, while the lack of containers for garbage and of most municipal services meant that these developments – created at the behest of an environmental project – soon became sites of considerable pollution. Residents also noted the lack of adequate common green space and playgrounds, as well as lighting for public areas, raising questions of recreation and safety alike.

Canal-dwellers reported feeling pressured to agree to the rehabilitation scheme in order to become legalized as occupants and alleged that the lack of any kind of compensation in earlier cases of eviction was used as leverage to get them to agree. The displaced spoke strongly of their feelings and their sense that they felt they were excluded from the plans to create the new Kolkata. Two excerpts from a study recording the voices of former canal-dwellers reflect this sense of displacement (Nagarik Mancha, 2010: 10–11):

> We are being treated like garbage and that is why we are being thrown towards Dhapa, the dumping ground of Kolkata. In the Megacity of their dreams there is no place for us.
>
> This is just the beginning. They have started with us and soon the slum dwellers, hawkers and pavement dwellers all over will be thrown out from the city to make it beautiful.

Ecotourism in the EKW

The final aspect of the KEIP that I wish to discuss as significant in redesigning Kolkata for a global future is the transformation of the EKW from a working landscape into a site of ecotourism and "edutainment" (Boppré, 2012; Ferreira, 2012). In the preceding chapter, I explored the ecological, economic, and social significance of this area and the long-standing threats to its survival. The leaders and staff of the KEIP are all too aware of such challenges – part of their proposed solution is to change the perception of the Wetlands among the general public from that of a landfill or sewage treatment site to that of a 'transition zone' between different aquatic and terrestrial environments valued by residents. There are other claims on the site; for example, KEIP staff told me in 2012 that the existing fisheries have been pushing to have more raw sewage processed in the EKW in order to increase their yields, a plan that waste engineers I spoke with found unacceptable. As one engineer explained:

> I believe that using sewage for pisciculture is a good thing but existing systems must be approved and I am doubtful as to whether the system would be able to adequately absorb and manage an increase in waste levels. What are the health impacts of so much sewage treatment in the EKW? Waste is a hazard and wastewater needs to be treated properly. Treatment must be done prior to entering the wetlands if possible; however, many fishermen in the area have a myth that treating wastewater prior to it entering the EKW will make it less viable for pisciculture.

Many of the KEIP staff agreed with the objective that "development of the area should not change the current pattern of land use, nor should it result in upsetting the ecological balance" (KEIP, 2014). Yet these same designs call for considerable impact, especially in terms of potential pollution from construction and outflow from the canal desilting efforts. In this context, the KEIP's solution is to develop a new East Kolkata Wetland Park with a Nature and Wetland Interpretation Centre at its core. The Centre would occupy some 30 acres, while the Park as a whole would be spread across a further 2,000 acres, with its primary purposes being the demonstration of wise use and the promotion of ecotourism. Together, these would constitute what the KEIP describes as a "national class attraction" with the following goals (Wildfowl and Wetlands Trust [WWT], 2006):

- to attract as many visitors as possible while maintaining a quiet and peaceful environment;
- to bring visitors and wildlife closer together whilst minimising disturbance;
- to be a centre of education in Kolkata related to conservation education programmes in both formal curricula as well as in extra-curricular activities, with a view to arousing public interest and awareness of ecology and wetlands; and
- to market the EKW effectively on an international scale.

Revenues for the project are to be generated through ticket sales, lotteries, parking, sponsorships, advertising, food and handicraft concessions, parties and special events, gifts, and products. Proposed ticket prices for domestic visitors range from 50 to 75 to 100 rupees, although for public parks and museums, the equivalent prices are in the 5–10 rupee range, which reflects the plan's desired target audience as described in their planning materials: "we wish to attract a substantial number of the Indian middle class while remaining accessible for all" (WWT, 2006). A staff of 40 full-time personnel is required to run the Centre and the Park with the support of volunteers, while the leadership, for reasons that were not explained to me, was to be external. As the project plans outline, "it is desirable – at least initially – for the General Manager to be of expatriate status" (WWT, 2006).

Among the features of this Centre will be exhibition halls dedicated to flora and fauna; an auditorium for audiovisuals; offices and laboratories for scientists; an observation deck; and various learning technologies, including touch-screen kiosks, experiential learning devices, and games. The Park will include a bird sanctuary, observation hides, facilities for boat and bicycle rentals, walking trails, bicycle pathways, interpretive signage, and weatherboards promoting low-impact ecotourism. The plans also include demonstration sites to show off value-added waste recycling production systems, alternative energies, and eco-friendly low-cost housing models. In addition to these tourist-focused activities, the Centre is expected to train villagers in eco-forestry, horticulture, medicinal plant cultivation, naturopathy, and herbal treatment and to create an accurate inventory of human habitation in the EKW. The overall purpose of the plan is described as follows (WWT, 2006):

> Creating a Nature & Wetland Interpretation Centre will help emphasize the importance of the EKW and provide both educational and recreational facilities for the widest range of audiences. Such a Centre will provide a relatively new experience for Kolkatans which on one hand they may have difficulty understanding as a visitor attraction or, on the other, instantly adopt for its uniqueness and edutainment value.

On the surface, this seems like a reasonable, mixed-use approach to conservation in the EKW which would allow the Wetlands to be reinterpreted for consumption by a broader public. But doubts regarding the strategy and its beneficiaries have already been raised, some of them by members of the KEIP staff. These individuals, when interviewed, spoke of being unable to defend the boundaries of the EKW, let alone a proposed Park, from encroachment by developers, with housing projects, golf courses, theme parks, and malls already in the making. Furthermore, even government-funded infrastructures, like the roads connecting Rajarhat and other townships, had become controversial and were constructed in spite of the Ramsar Convention designation and the East Kolkata Wetland (Conservation and Management) Act of 2006. Other employees raised the issue of compensation for farmers and residents displaced by the construction of the actual Centre or for the restriction of their activities in the new Park. Other employees were concerned whether the proposed Park might compromise the EKW's Ramsar status by disturbing sensitive species. Furthermore, as they pointed out, so far there has been little public or governmental support for these plans due to poor management and marketing. Doubts about the idea of ecotourism were expressed by a senior official with the East Kolkata Wetlands Management Authority (EKWMA):

> The only Nature Interpretation Centre in the country that is any good is in Rajasthan. It is true that we need to help raise awareness about the wetlands. But do people really want to see the processing of waste? Do they want to ride their bicycle near the landfill? Will they want to boat in a fishpond? And where will the Centre be? They need to get the actual land to have it and I am not sure where it would go.

This last issue remains a thorny one, as the original plans called for the Centre to be at the site of an abandoned waste treatment plant constructed in the colonial period. But that plant has also been identified as the potential new location for a sewage treatment plant meant to deal with the waste produced by the new housing projects that have emerged in the EKW over the last few years. If this conflict – between addressing the needs of all the new residents of international-style housing developments and protecting the Wetlands – remains unresolved, there is a strong chance that we will see the interests of those protecting the EKW being sacrificed yet again.

Unlike the rehabilitation of ponds and the construction of apartments for slum-dwellers displaced by the cleaning of canals, ecotourism and conservation initiatives in the EKW have not materialized 4 years after the putative end of the KEIP's mandate. Yet the plans testify to a general desire to remake the city in a global mold. Admittedly, the KEIP is designed in multiple ways to just initiate the change expected in any municipality by cleaning and managing waste; transforming, protecting, and limiting access to green space; and relocating and re-educating less desirable communities. But considered against the backdrop of the global discourses and diasporic imageries, the KEIP is part of a larger framework intended to remake Kolkata into a world-class city. Since the global city is not only a modernist fiction but depends on middle-class notions of environmentalism, sustainability, and cosmopolitanism, these aspirations pre-empt claims to social and environmental justice. It is in this sense that the KEIP feeds into the larger project of redesigning the city for the new urban middle class.

Note

1 An informal gathering typical of middle-class Bengali cultural exchange that flourishes on freewheeling debate and discussion that include politics, literature, art, sports, and social gossip.

References

Baviskar, A. (2003). "Between violence and desire: space, power and identity in the making of metropolitan Delhi." *International Social Science Journal* 5(175): 89–98.
Baviskar, A. (2006). "Demolishing Delhi: world-class city in the making." *Mute* 2(3): 88–95.
Baviskar, A. and R. Ray (2011). *Elite and everyman: the cultural politics of the Indian middle classes.* New Delhi, Routledge.
Boppré, M. and R. I. Vane-Wright (2012). "The butterfly house industry: conservation risks and education opportunities." *Conservation and Society* 10(3): 285–303.
Bose, P. S. (2013). Bourgeois environmentalism, leftist development and neoliberal urbanism in the City of Joy. *Locating Right to the City in the Global South.* T. Samara, S. He and G. Chen. New York, Routledge: 127–151.
Bose, P. S. and E. Lunstrum (2014). "Introduction: environmentally induced displacement and forced migration." *Refuge* 29(2): 5–10.
Bullard, R. D., G. S. Johnson and A. O. Torres (2004). *Highway robbery: transportation racism & new routes to equity.* Cambridge, MA, South End Press.
Büscher, B. and V. Davidov (2014). *The ecotourism-extraction nexus: political economies and rural realities of (un)comfortable bedfellows.* London, Routledge.
Chatterjee, P. (2004). *The politics of the governed: reflections on popular politics in most of the world.* New York, Columbia University Press.
Fairhead, J., M. Leach and I. Scoones (2012). "Green grabbing: a new appropriation of nature?" *Journal of Peasant Studies* 39(2): 237–261.
Ferreira, S. (2012). "Moulding urban children towards environmental stewardship: the Table Mountain National Park experience." *Environmental Education Research* 18(2): 251–270.

Gadgil, M. and R. Guha (1995). *Ecology and equity: the use and abuse of nature in contemporary India.* London, Routledge.

Ghosh, S. (2013). "Regional disparities of slums, 2013 – an overview with special emphasis to Kolkata." *International Journal of Humanities and Social Science Invention* **2**(3): 48–54.

Groves, Z. (2012). "People and places: land, migration and political culture in Zimbabwe." *The Journal of Modern African Studies* **50**(2): 339–356.

Guha, R. and J. Martínez Alier (1998). *Varieties of environmentalism: essays North and South.* Delhi, Oxford University Press.

Hazareesingh, S. (2001). "Colonial modernism and the flawed paradigms of urban renewal: uneven development in Bombay, 1900–25." *Urban History* **28**(2): 235–255.

KEIP (2014). "Kolkata Environmental Improvement Project." Retrieved April 27, 2014, from http://www.keip.in/bl3/.

King, A. D. (1976). *Colonial urban development: culture, social power and environment.* London, Routledge.

Lehmann, S. (2011). "Transforming the city for sustainability: the principles of green urbanism." *Journal of Green Building* **6**(1): 104–113.

Levien, M. (2013a). "Regimes of dispossession: from steel towns to Special Economic Zones." *Development and Change* **44**(2): 381–407.

Levien, M. (2013b). "The politics of dispossession: theorizing India's 'land wars.'" *Politics & Society* **41**(3): 351–394.

Lohmann, L. (1997). Resisting green globalism. *Global Ecology: A New Arena of Political Conflict.* W. Sachs. London, Zed Books: 157–169.

Mawdsley, E. (2004). "India's middle classes and the environment." *Development and Change* **35**(1): 79–103.

Mawdsley, E., D. Mehra and K. Beazley (2009). "Nature lovers, picnickers and bourgeois environmentalism." *Economic and Political Weekly* **44**(11): 49–59.

Nagarik Mancha (2010). Canal bank dwellers: displacement in the name of development. Kolkata, Nagarik Mancha.

Penz, G. P., J. Drydyk and P. S. Bose (2011). *Displacement by development: ethics, rights and responsibilities.* Cambridge, Cambridge University Press.

Rai, N. (2012). "Green grabbing in the name of the tiger." *Economic and Political Weekly* **47**(42): 108–109.

Rajamani, L. (2007). "Public interest environmental litigation in India: exploring issues of access, participation, equity, effectiveness and sustainability." *Journal of Environmental Law* **19**(3): 293–321.

Roy, A. (2003). *City requiem, Calcutta: gender and the politics of poverty.* Minneapolis, University of Minnesota Press.

Schenk, W. C. (2010). "Slum diversity in Kolkata." *Columbia Undergraduate Journal of South Asian Studies* **1**(2): 92–108.

Sengupta, U. (2010). "The hindered self-help: housing policies, politics and poverty in Kolkata, India." *Habitat International* **34**(3): 323–331.

Shiva, V., S. Jani and S. M. Fontana (2011). *The great Indian land grab.* Delhi, Navdanya.

Teaford, J. C. (2000). "Urban renewal and its aftermath." *Housing Policy Debate* **11**(2): 443–465.

Wildfowl and Wetlands Trust (WWT) (2006). East Kolkata Wetland Park: detailed project plan. Slimbridge, UK, Wildfowl and Wetlands Trust.

Williams, G. and E. Mawdsley (2006). "Postcolonial environmental justice: government and governance in India." *Geoforum* **37**(5): 660–670.

8 New housing developments
Global living in Kolkata

The most obvious sign of Kolkata's recent transformations is the sheer number of new buildings that have appeared across the city over the past two decades. While planned townships and modest, modern private houses are not a new phenomenon, this latest construction boom is novel in both scale and quality. Today we find a significant number of higher-end realty developments – high-rise apartment towers; bungalows and condominiums; and new neighbourhoods with their own schools, malls, hospitals, leisure facilities, and a host of other amenities – sprouting up all over town. There are many reasons behind the proliferation of so many new projects initiated by a host of different developers. Among these reasons are the gradual move away from building affordable or social housing projects towards public–private partnerships targeting the burgeoning middle classes, the deregulation of the national economy, and the emergence of speculative real estate investment on the local level. Lastly, there is the growing importance of transnational elites in urban imaginaries worldwide.

In this chapter, I explore the impact of the new developments on Kolkata's urban landscape, beginning with a brief review of the range of developments going up all over the city. Next, I look at some of the attempts to market these buildings to potential local and especially international clients, noting how these spaces are advertised and which of their features are highlighted to draw in international elites. Finally, I look in closer detail at three particular cases – Kolkata West International City (KWIC) located in the western suburb of Howrah, Vedic Village in the heart of the East Kolkata Wetlands (EKW), and South City in the southern residential neighbourhoods of Kolkata. These are three distinct architectural examples: the first is a massive satellite township of primarily bungalows, the second a gated condo-and-spa 'eco-village,' and the third a set of luxury high-rise towers. They are set in three distinct locations – the first in a former industrial suburb to the west of Kolkata, the second amidst the reclaimed Wetlands, and the third in the middle of a middle-class southern neighbourhood – yet taken together, these three represent many of the changes we currently see taking place in similar developments all across the city. These three projects sparked my particular interest during my first fieldwork visit in 2004 because of their explicit and self-conscious use of global language and imagery in their advertising and design and in the words of their promoters. I had no idea at the time, of course, that they would each in their own way become among the most well-known and most controversial of the new development projects.

Size and scale of the new construction

As in other Indian cities, notably Delhi, the number of housing developments initiated in Kolkata from the mid-1990s onwards is truly staggering. When I began my field research in 2004, I counted forty projects that fit my criteria for new housing aimed at a transnational or elite audience. Loosely defined in terms of developments with at least 100 units, the vast majority were high-rise towers with a minimum of twelve floors with a set of accompanying amenities. At that point, almost all were in the design stage, with a few beginning to break ground. By 2007, many of the projects I had analyzed in their planning stages were already underway, with dozens more in the planning phase. When I returned in 2012, even more such developments were on the books, while some of the earlier projects had been completed and were now inhabited. My first fieldwork trips documented the rise of these kinds of sites, primarily in the EKW (Bose, 2007). The IT-themed township of Rajarhat in the heart of the EKW is home to most of these new buildings, as has been documented in several excellent studies on the developments (Dey, Samaddar, and Sen, 2013; Dey, 2011; Samaddar, 2012). Today, however, new housing construction has spread across the entire metropolitan region of Kolkata, from the central city to the peripheries and surrounding municipalities as well.

These towers and townships dominate the skyline of metropolitan Kolkata today. A look at the tallest buildings in the city shows that 74 out of 85 of these have been built since 2004, with 66 of them completed since 2010 alone (SkyscraperCity, 2014). Almost all fit the criteria for the projects I examined, which rose from a total of 40 in 2004 to 77 in 2007 and to 120 by 2012. Based on the success of these developments, many more projects are being planned or are in construction. What do these initiatives have in common? They are almost all 'international' in their design, meaning primarily that their architectural design is modernist, replicating features and spatial arrangements that are common to condominiums and apartment towers all across the world. Indeed, such buildings are often meant to have a turnkey or low-maintenance appeal – though unlike many Western examples, the buildings in Kolkata do not usually come with furnishings or appliances. Office complexes in these developments, moreover, cater to the high-technology sector – local offices of national and international companies being scattered throughout. The malls and amenities that come with the buildings are also full of recognizably global retailers and brands and cater to a supposedly transnational clientele. Together, all of these new buildings are meant to house close to a million people, with the target audience identified as middle- and upper-income-bracket earners, according to many of the planners, politicians, and developers I spoke with. One must, however, always be somewhat skeptical of the claims of the proponents of these projects. As Searle has pointed out in her important work on the discourse of developers and promoters of new housing projects, there are many contradictions both within and among such groups, and the desires and projections of the latter may not match those of foreign investors or building residents themselves, a fact that appears to be confirmed by many of my own interviews (Searle, 2014).

Non-resident Indians (NRIs) and housing developments

Even a casual observer can see that housing developments are significant for the city of Kolkata, not only in number and scope but also in the idiom of their representation. With names like "Infinity," "Astral," "Technopolis," "Atmosphere," and "Uniworld," they often evoke a futuristic or exotic cityscape. Such practices are not unique to Kolkata but follow common conventions in the naming of condominium complexes and gated communities (both today and historically) and are certainly not restricted to mega-projects alone (King, 2004). What is unusual, however, is a situation in which the effort to revive a whole metropolis seems to be hinging on its success at marketing a global image through housing. This means being able to materialize its connections to the networked global economy through the presence of transnational capital and transnational subjects – relating both to where they live and where/how they work. As Chakravorty says of the transformation of Kolkata's peri-urban fringes, where the majority of the Global Indian–themed housing construction was initially located, "clearly the planners want this development to contain new (rather than relocated) industry of the type that is high-tech or global in nature" (Chakravorty, 2005: 70).

Who, then, will live in these shining monuments to a globalized and networked future? Who are the ideal inhabitants of the newly reclaimed Wetlands regions to the east of the city, former industrial sites to its west, and 'blighted' neighbourhoods throughout? Furthermore, we need to ask where the considerable resources stem from and which characteristics are shared between individuals and companies involved in developments of this size. Clearly, at this stage, it is not simply a regional planning authority (like the Kolkata Metropolitan Development Authority [KMDA]) or a municipality (like the Kolkata Municipal Corporation [KMC]) that is proposing and implementing a project. Rather, it is the public–private partnerships like those described in Chapter 4 that are so ubiquitous in urban development worldwide today (Grimsey and Lewis, 2004; Theodore, Peck, and Brenner, 2011; Peck, Theodore, and Brenner, 2013) through which the majority of projects are initiated. While public partners certainly continue to play a significant role – in deregulating certain sectors, rezoning parcels of land or providing them to developers at a relatively low cost, and providing municipal services, among other benefits – they are not executing the construction work. Their private partners include local, national, and even some international real estate companies, many with considerable prior experience in the housing industry. Some of the key players in Kolkata's housing boom include both national firms such as DLF, Ambuja, Belani, and Sureka, known for their developments in places like Gurgaon, Mumbai, Ahmedabad, Hyderabad, and

Bangalore, as well as Kolkata-based developers like the Merlin Group, Avani Group, and Team Taurus (Hill and Athique, 2013; Roy, 2011; Nair, 2005).

My initial fieldwork marked the absence of Global Indians themselves in the articulating of these visions for remaking Kolkata. Rather, it was primarily urban planners and politicians who seemed determined to bring back the migrants and capital by creating spaces that they would deem desirable. By contrast, upon my return in 2007, I found more involvement by Global Indians, especially in two notable projects. The first was "Rosedale Garden" in Rajarhat. Conceptualized and spearheaded by two MIT graduates who work in the IT industry in the US, put together a project team, and secured initial financing for the development, the project embodied many of the same luxury features that are seen in the aforementioned undertakings, though the fact that the project was conceived by NRIs played a significant role in the way it was perceived. Saha (2006a) describes the project as follows:

> It would be a slice of Americana on the fringes of the city. They would call it Rosedale Garden, an exclusive NRI habitat in Action Area III of New Town, Rajarhat. It would offer NRIs the standard of living they are used to in the West. The complex would combine the best of both worlds, a blend of the conveniences of the West and the earthy charm of Bengal. It's not just about returning to one's roots, but also an urge, a commitment to make Bengal a better place.

This is certainly not the first and only example of such an imperative; indeed, a number of charitable organizations, philanthropic initiatives, and even cooperative housing projects initiated by NRIs have existed for decades in Kolkata (Toronto-Calcutta Foundation [TCF], 2014). However, this project is very much in the minority of the current globally oriented housing boom in that it includes direct diasporic involvement. As with similar cases in other parts of India, while Global Indians are the target market of promoters and developers or the inspiration for project design, their actual participation as investors or project partners in Kolkata is limited. In Verrel's (2012) study of NRI involvement in the housing market in Bangalore, for example, an average of 10–15 percent of the owners of NRI-styled or NRI-themed housing was actual NRIs. A majority of these were NRIs from the Gulf rather than North America or other, more desirable locations. Very significantly, for many of them, the purchase represented speculative investment rather than a second home, a strategy that Donner (2014) argues is observable in the case of locals as well.

My own research has shown similar patterns (Bose, 2012, 2014). It is therefore not entirely obvious whether developers are successful in attracting their self-certified target clientele or whether they use 'NRI,' as Searle (2013) has suggested with reference to developers in Delhi, as shorthand for 'professional' and upper-middle-class clients. The importance of equivalence with NRIs in the aspirational fantasies of India's emerging urban middle classes has become increasingly apparent, as Brosius (2010) and others have argued. Whether developers are successful in attracting their target clientele is unclear; promoters and developers insist that a large proportion of apartment buyers are, in fact, overseas Indians, but they cannot (or will not) provide data to support their claims. During my research, it appeared that claims like "NRIs live here" were employed for marketing purposes, reinforced by the copy of real estate advertising within the city which depicts such lives and by the discourse of the travelling real estate trade shows held in places like Dubai, Hong Kong, Singapore, London, Houston, New York, Toronto, and Vancouver to attract investors. There are many such fairs organized by different sponsors with different motivations – the 2013 India Property Show in Dubai was, for example, a joint venture between the State Bank of India and *The Hindu* newspaper and explicitly intended for "those who want to buy for future use and for investment purposes and those who want to maintain ties with their homeland" (Sharma, 2013). One of the realtors present claimed that, of their clientele, "75% are expatriates working in the IT sector looking for property that they could use when they eventually settle down in India" (Sharma, 2013). Such an emphasis on significant Global Indian participation in the urban housing boom in India was common among professionals and other groups of respondents, including urban planners and politicians, promoters and developers, and even the workers involved in the actual construction of buildings, as well as social justice activists concerned with affordable housing. Whether NRIs are actually present or not, the imagery of global designs for global buyers powerfully conveys the notion that the housing boom taking place in the city benefits only 'outsiders,' specifically NRIs or Global Indians. Thus, a construction foreman who had worked on several projects told me in 2007:

> Do you see those flats over there? All of them are owned by NRIs like you. But I will tell you what, come back here at night, come back here at nine or ten o'clock tonight and I'll show you something. A hundred flats and only ten lights will be on. Only ten of them will have people in them. All the rest of you are overseas.

Whether the flats have sold or not seems to have depended on the particular projects, as the cases discussed later in this chapter demonstrate. This problem with underoccupancy was indeed an issue raised by local owners of apartments in several different buildings whom I interviewed in 2012. Some of them suggested that the units had indeed sold, it was just that the owners were either NRIs or based in another Indian city. Others believed that the units had been purchased in order to be rented or sublet and that difficulties in securing tenants had kept them empty throughout most of the year. For full-time residents in such housing projects, the issue was a sore point, with some suggesting that security was inadequate and that break-ins, vandalism, and petty theft were not uncommon.

Quite apart from the problem of actually finding global buyers, the 'international style' that has been trumpeted by the builders comes at a considerable cost, one that may be attractive to foreign residents but less affordable for locals. It is the need to secure both markets that has led to a two-fold approach to selling the new housing projects, one aimed at an international audience and the other at the domestic market, both within Kolkata and more generally within India. The diasporic audience has been reached through three main vehicles: traditional mass media, overseas trade shows, and electronic media. Images of the transnational subject are invoked in all of these. King, in his work on the interaction of such bodies and spaces, suggests that

> the international advertising and marketing of substantial suburban residential property apparently based on "Western" styles familiar to the residential locations of the Western-based NRIs has, over the last two decades, with other forms of property development, increasingly become a form of globalized practice . . . in places as far apart as Australia and California, Indonesia, Canada, Turkey, as well as more generally.
>
> (King, 2004: 131)

Housing developers have placed advertisements in a wide range of media, including *desi*-themed television shows abroad, diasporic publications like *India Today* or the international editions of Indian newspapers, and local satellite television stations. Some promoters have also placed advertisements in ethnic newspapers and multicultural broadcasts overseas – for example, in Bengali cultural programming in Toronto and New Jersey (Bose, 2012). Others have travelled, as noted previously, to cities with large Global Indian populations in order to make sales pitches for their buildings, and similar travelling roadshows are touring within India (Bose, 2014). In most cases, these trips coincide with religious and cultural festivals as well as special events that will ensure larger audiences – for example, the celebration of Durga Puja, the annual North American Bengali Conference, and smaller regional events. Furthermore, developers utilize the Internet, electronic messaging, and bulletin boards to reach out to potential clients. This strategy is predicated on the knowledge that many diasporic networks are heavily reliant upon such means of communication to maintain links with families and friends in a dispersed community. Internet sites such as realestatekolkata.com (maintained by the Kolkata Real Estate Board) have been prime vehicles for this form of advertising, offering not only houses and apartments for sale but also rental properties as well. Developers have used such official websites in conjunction with those run by private real estate agencies to market their products, and they directly target diasporic individuals with specific offers sent to their email accounts.

Locally, Kolkata promoters advertise new developments using English- and Bengali-language newspapers, magazines, and television programs. They also make considerable use of billboards to present their messages. Throughout the course of my fieldwork, the lifestyles and life spaces of 'international living' were never more visible than on the hundreds of billboards that dot the city. Their cumulative effect is significant: as important as the towers and construction cranes that announce the arrival of the new city are the massive advertisements that tell one that a particular developer was "born to build," that a particular housing estate is where one can "celebrate the best of east and west," or that another is "where you can give your children a better life" (Bose, 2014). Such messages are common across the many projects I looked at and the others that have come up alongside them and often serve to sell this developer's other, smaller, and more affordable projects. I will look briefly at three examples of such advertising campaigns before exploring my case studies in this chapter in greater detail.

Bengal Silver Spring is a joint venture between the KMC and the Sanjeevani Group, private developers who have also executed other prestigious projects such as Club Town, Space Town, Koyla Vihar, Hari Kunj, and clubs like Space Circle and the Circle, both within Kolkata and in other parts of India. The promotion material for Silver Spring offers "just the kind of place you would see in foreign glossies and regret you'd never get" (Bengal Silver Spring, 2014). It advertises its proximity to leisure facilities like Science City and the Eastern Metropolitan Bypass. Its amenities include landscaped gardens, a shopping arcade, home deliveries of groceries, laundry services, a beauty parlour, two clubs, a temperature-controlled swimming pool, indoor gyms, tennis courts, roller-skating arena, health club, pool room, convention center and conference hall, games arcade, library, coffee shops, and restaurants. It is, in the promoters' words, "where life resides" and "five star inside, five star outside" (Bengal Silver Spring, 2014). With its strong emphasis on 'lifestyle,' the development ties in with larger discourses that allow local middle-class consumers to buy and appropriate self-consciously modern and supposedly 'foreign' aesthetics (Brosius, 2010; Baviskar and Ray, 2011).

The "shopping convenience" advertising campaign, for example, shows a woman in what appears to be a supermarket, an image that evokes the recent introduction of modern, 'world-class' sites in a city dominated by local, traditional markets. Most can be found in the malls attached to the new housing developments and are a convenience aimed at Global Indians and locals who aspire to their lifestyles. Another advertisement, telling the prospective buyer that they may live in the Bengal Silver Spring "with nature," is even more intriguing. The trees that the advertisement uses to signify nature are nowhere to be found in Bengal. They appear to simulate evergreens common on the Pacific coast of the US and suggest an implicit reference to the sites of IT industries there, which are very much dominated by South Asian workers. Another Bengal Silver Spring advertisement promises:

> A luxury condominium lifestyle. Not just one flat above another. But more than 500 luxury apartments. Not just 100,000 square feet of open exotic greens. But a home in harmony with nature. Not just an add-on club for effect. But an integrated lifestyle environment with modern-day comforts and a soothing ambience.
>
> (Bengal Silver Spring, 2014)

In the case of the Rosedale Garden project in Rajarhat discussed previously, half of the apartments in the scheme are reserved for diasporic Indian buyers, although the nationality of the occupants may vary in that expat children might buy them for their parents. In their marketing material, the promoters boast that

> this is by far one of the only projects which has been conceived to get all NRIs under one roof so that the bondage with Indian roots and culture is kept intact regardless of their present location. On this occasion we have even launched our "Senior Citizen Apartments" which is an homage and tribute to our parents of Bengal from their children who have been able to create an identity of themselves out of India.
>
> (Rosedale Garden, 2013)

When asked what the purpose of these apartments was, a promoter told me that they were meant to be a way for NRIs who lived overseas to provide a comfortable home for their parents without their having to leave India.

In addition, Rosedale Garden offers to Global Indians "New Age homes" for "go-getters on the move" with amenities including not only the ubiquitous country club, exercise facilities, yoga and meditation lounges, jogging tracks, pool, steam room, sauna and Jacuzzi, landscaped gardens, medical center, grocery store, and security services but also the unique option to purchase fully furnished apartments. The Rosedale Projects were initially a popular sell to both locals and diasporas, but despite the backing of industry heavyweights, the projects have failed to deliver on their promises (Law, 2011). Much like the international township in Howrah discussed in the next section of this chapter, the whole project is now engulfed in complaints and even lawsuits filed by buyers against the developers.

Yet another developer, Bengal Ambuja, offers three projects at various locations in the mold of what it calls "condovilles" (Ambuja Neotia, 2014). Significantly, these blueprints for condominiums have now been recognized as "Model Housing Projects" by the Housing and Industrial Development Corporation (HUDCO), India's national urban development agency, and are typified by large, open, manicured green spaces and "eco-friendly designs," as well as staggered prices for apartments appealing to different groups of consumers. In Kolkata, the group has developed a number of such 'condovilles,' including Udayan on the Eastern Metropolitan Bypass and Utsa and Ujjwala in the new township of Rajarhat. They are offered in different price ranges, from "Luxury" to "Comfort" to "Efficiency" units. They are marketed as "traffic free community spaces" – an enticing claim, given Kolkata's overbearing issues with congestion – and spaces boasting "international aesthetics and design" for the higher price range. While lower-cost units come unfurnished, at the other end, "Luxury" units include high-end appliances and other amenities. The advertisement materials for these developments feature pastel colours, parked cars, and joggers – as likely to conjure New York as Kolkata. It is not only in advertising, however, that the global city is apparently brought to life. As we will see in the following three case studies, there have been numerous material attempts to make it a reality.

Kolkata West International City

Across the Hooghly River in Howrah, which belongs to the larger Kolkata region but is technically an independent municipality, sits an unfinished satellite township called Kolkata West International City (KWIC). Once touted as the largest foreign direct investment in real estate in Kolkata (and one of the largest in India) – a joint venture of Indonesian capital, local state and private developers, and NRIs – the project has run into numerous problems and delays since its inception. Its initial vision was grand, with a cost of nearly US $20 billion. Spanning close to 400 acres, it would house nearly 36,000 people in more than 6,000 bungalows and four high-rise residential towers. Accompanying these grand plans for residences were three separate IT-focused business parks, a 13-acre country club, a 200-bed hospital, two schools, and four shopping malls (KWIC, 2014a). Its most prominent backer was the former Chief Minister of Bengal, Buddhadeb Bhattacharya, who laid the foundation plaque for the project in 2006. On the occasion, the Government of West Bengal's Urban Development Minister enthused that:

> This township is not only about answering the housing needs of Howrah. The number of jobs it would provide and the environment-friendly units it would promote prove the success of the public-private partnership mode.
>
> (Saha, 2006b)

The original project – to be completed and occupied by 2010 – was a joint venture between the Indonesian companies Salim, Ciputra, and the Djakarta-based NRI Prasoon Mukherjee (who made his own fortune franchising Outback Steakhouses in Asia) and the KMDA. In a newspaper interview, Mukherjee described his motivation for participating in the project:

> I have always wanted to do something like this for Calcutta and it gives me immense pleasure to be able to do this on the west bank of the river, which deserves an address like Kolkata West. Our motto is to create a new integrated township to ensure an international-quality lifestyle with lush, open spaces, stylish homes and a host of amenities in a composite basket.
>
> (Saha, 2006b)

I interviewed one of the KMDA planners involved with the project, who echoed similar sentiments:

> [KWIC] will be at the cutting edge of design, innovation, and modern international-style living. Residents will enjoy many facilities that will bring them close to nature and the township will raise the profile of Howrah as a destination for professionals.

The theme of 'international-style' living is a recurring one in many of the new developments coming to Kolkata today. In the case of KWIC, this means a gated community with plenty of parking for personal automobiles, wide paved roads and sidewalks, tree-lined streets, landscaped parks, sculptures of roadside ballerinas beside benches, a kindergarten and a secondary school taught to 'international standards,' a hospital, tennis courts, supermarkets, multiplexes, an Olympic-sized swimming pool, a sauna, games facilities, and even an air-conditioned bus service to downtown Kolkata. And the cosmopolitan imagery that has given birth to this enthusiasm is visible everywhere. Thus, when approaching via a new highway, one is greeted at the entrance to the township by an enormous arch modelled on the Brandenburg Gate and framed by jet-black sculptures of rearing Arab stallions. The massive gates dominate the view, with a huge mall visible beyond it and row after row of townhouses disappearing into the distance. So-called traditional markets selling fish, vegetables, and spices are designed to give the local touch to residents and remind them that they are still in India. All of these elements create a township that stands in stark contrast to the mixture of industrial sites surrounding it but also to the squatter settlements, residential areas, and water bodies scattered throughout. As Benny Santoso, Chairman of the Salim Group, puts it, the KWIC should not be understood as alien to this part of the city but as offering something new to it:

> We promise to give the residents of Kolkata West a truly international living experience.
>
> (Saha, 2006b)

Such an experience does, of course, by implication mean that services need to be reliable and well-maintained. Given the state of such services in Kolkata at large, the promoters did their best to assure potential customers that they would provide self-contained waste management and water metering services, as well as constant and reliable electricity supplies. In order to achieve such an ambitious goal in a city famous for its power cuts, the state electricity board set up a power station within the township as part of another public–private partnership. House prices range from 16 to 72 lakh rupees in price each (approximately US \$26,000–\$120,000). Such a cost would seem to be at the top end of what domestic purchasers might afford. But promoters see another audience that they might tap – Global Indians:

> There are lots of rich Indians overseas. We intend also to sell to them. They will invest in this project and bring in the dollars. The NRIs want to buy a second home at home.
>
> (Ciputra Group, 2006)

While the appeal to Global Indians is still a priority, promoters are aware of the allure that 'international-style' housing complexes might have for locals. A testimonial on KWIC's website by a new local owner (who has not yet taken possession of his flat) testifies to the appeal of global aesthetics:

> Although I live in the city, coming to Kolkata West International City would surely unleash a new experience of living in a green setting far from the concrete jungle while enjoying all the modern comforts. There's an international sophistication about the look and feel of the township and its architecture is impressive. Wide open spaces and greenery offers an extremely soothing ambience. Living here would enable one to derive value more than the money's worth.

> (KWIC, 2014b)

But the ambitious goals for the township have yet to come to fruition. For most of its brief history, the KWIC project has remained stalled. While sales – especially initially – were brisk, by 2009, fewer than 200 of the projected 6,100 bungalows had been taken. Those owners whose units had been completed were reluctant to take up residence in what was essentially a ghost town. As one middle-class owner I interviewed argued in 2012:

> I have been offered a small amount of interest by management on my purchase amount. But this is much less than the amount of interest I am paying on my original loan to purchase the property. I have heard that the developers are making a profit on the township because they have bought land very cheaply from KMDA but from what we know less than 2% of the construction is complete.

While construction did pick up in 2012 and some of the bungalows and amenities have now been completed, at the time of writing, the township remains mainly a shell. Not surprisingly, owners have now formed a KWIC Buyers Welfare Association to protest against the failure to deliver their housing units (*The Telegraph*, 2013). Some critics have also argued that what we see in such developments is less about real estate and housing than it is about illegal and speculative land grabbing (Donner, 2014).

What has caused this delay? It is certainly not a lack of faith in the international-style development, as the success of Rajarhat and the number of other new buildings being completed shows. Some of the problems with KWIC relate to the poor quality of units that have been completed. The Howrah municipality is moreover aggrieved that services and utilities that it had reserved for the township have not been utilized, which leads to shortages in prospective funding and supplies elsewhere. But there are also more substantial problems, some of which have to do with the location itself. An urban planner with the KMDA with whom I spoke in 2012 pointed out:

> No matter how fancy or international your township is, it will be difficult to convince people that Howrah is a desirable location. You are much better to build in the city or in Rajarhat or Salt Lake where people will want to live and work.

The developers themselves claim that a lack of funds has hampered completion. Two of the original partners – the Salim and Ciputra Groups from Indonesia – found themselves caught up in considerable controversy by 2007 over their broader portfolio of investments in West Bengal. Their joint venture, called New Kolkata International Development, entered into a series of agreements with the West Bengal Industrial Development Corporation, the government of West Bengal, and a number of other regional and municipal partners to spearhead a number of ventures, including investment in industrial infrastructure and special economic zones. The problems around the original plans – a joint venture to locate an automobile manufacturing plant in Singur and a chemical factory and hub in Nandigram – caused considerable political and therefore financial problems for the joint venture. Both of these initiatives came under heavy criticism and scrutiny as local farmers and landowners complained about land grabs and uncompensated displacement. Resistance by villagers and heavy-handed responses by security forces led to increasing violence, while political activists of varying stripes sought to capitalize on the ruling Left Front's connections to the crisis. The notion that a Marxist-led coalition whose reputation was built on rural reforms was now exploiting and marginalizing peasants rapidly undermined the Left Front, and within a few years it was out of office (Bardhan and Mookherjee, 2012).

The association of both Indonesian investors with the violence of Nandigram and Singur seriously affected the reputation of KWIC. In 2010, Ciputra pulled out of the project, and the state government and local agencies began to invest much more heavily in Rajarhat. This township in the Wetlands has also seen controversy over land grabbing and political violence, but at least it is not associated with the scandals of Singur and Nandigram in the way that KWIC is. For now, the township remains in limbo, gathering dust much like the rusting horses that stand atop its no-longer-pristine marble entrance gate.

Vedic Village

Unlike the bungalows and towers of KWIC or the high-rises of South City and so many other new developments in Kolkata, Vedic Village has represented a very different kind of development right from the outset. It was conceived as a 'resort' and a 'spa,' planned along the lines of other similar developments that are becoming more common worldwide (Islam, 2013; Smith and Puczkó, 2013). Before describing Vedic Village and its importance for the imaginary new cityscape further, it may be helpful to describe the transformed landscape in which it is situated, which brings us back to the EKW described in Chapter 6. Today, the former Wetlands rarely live up to their name. Although we can still find villages, farmland, and ponds, shiny new buildings have come up in between, and whole townships like Rajarhat dominate the local scenery. This formerly remote area is now made accessible by highways, framed by omnipresent cranes, glitzy malls, and loosely scattered smaller developments seemingly in the middle of nowhere. Here, McDonald's, Pizza Hut, KFC, and a myriad of other brands and stores are on hand, and billboards scattered throughout New Town advertise ever more real estate to purchase. Everywhere, apartment towers in various states of completion, some identical to those one might find in other urban settings in India, rise many stories high. Much of the construction work is carried out in fenced-off areas, but even a quick peek through the ramshackle fences reveals how large swathes of agricultural land are being transformed into housing for the middle class.

Vedic Village is unique, as it is self-consciously positioned not at the borders of the Wetlands, like the new townships, but in their middle. It is close to but removed from the new townships and set amidst villages and farmland. While the primary focus of the complex (especially after the controversies discussed in the following) is on the spa and hotel, there are over 100 residential units available for purchase. The prices are in the 70–lakh rupee range (approximately US $150,000) for Lakefront Villas, Eco Homes, Aqua Homes, Whirlpool Homes, and Farm Bungalows (Vedic Realty, 2014). As the prospectus points out, the emphasis of the marketing material is not on urban amenities, as in KWIC and South City (discussed in the following). Instead, the emphasis is on the consumption of 'nature' – here implying not the middle-class environmentalism discussed previously but a luxury 'experience.' When I first looked into the plans for Vedic Village in 2004, the advertisements promoted two semiotic fields, which are closely related in Hindu thought and consumerist takes on 'Indian' values: traditional medicine and nature (Brosius, 2010). As a self-described "wellness resort" – an increasingly common phenomenon globally (Crooks *et al.*, 2011) – Vedic Village focuses on offering alternative treatments – for example, 'Western' naturopathy (delivered by an NRI doctor based in Australia) and 'Eastern' therapies, including Ayurveda, from local practitioners. The spa is built in line with what the developer calls Bengali architecture in the "Shantiniketan village style," with "Earth Villas" sporting thatched roofs and mud walls (Vedic Village, 2014). The promoters of Vedic Village have also emphasized the ability to get close to the natural environment, whether as a patron of the spa or as a purchaser of property:

> Man was always meant to live close to nature. Today, caged as we are in concrete jungles, the yearning to return to more natural surroundings moves us as never before.
>
> (Vedic Village, 2014)

Activities offered range from pottery, farming, golfing, boating, and learning about eastern medicines to team-building exercises, and the promotional material suggests that the development "is what reflects the best that Kolkata has to offer to an international audience – a veritable paradise on Earth!" (Vedic Village, 2014).

Yet the story of Vedic Village has been anything but out of this world. Although the area is quite remote and heavily gated, in 2009, when following a contentious penalty during a 'friendly' football match between a local club and a Vedic Village team, nearby villagers proceeded to torch several administrative buildings and halls in the complex (*The Telegraph*, 2009). For realtors involved in the housing developments detailed in this chapter, this incident served as a wakeup call, indicating that security and policing had to be ramped up to protect their investments. The Bengal Chamber of Commerce was particularly concerned by the events and recommended creating a police force encompassing all parts of the metropolitan area, including currently external locales in Rajarhat and Salt Lake (*Times of India*, 2009b). When interviewed in a local newspaper, a realtor warned:

> The fears are real. . . . It needs to be allayed with decisive action by the administration. If people don't feel secure to move into peripheral areas, the city's growth will stop. The incident has made me very apprehensive about future projects in the area. If it recurs, builders will look at other cities. We cannot do business in an environment of fear.
>
> (*Times of India*, 2009b)

But villagers were not simply acting out of sore feelings after they lost a football match, as many reports suggested. Neither was there evidence of habitual crimes against property among the rural population. The villagers asserted that they vented their frustration over the manner in which developers of Vedic Village and their guests had been behaving. After opening in 2004, Vedic Village had quickly gained a reputation as a haven for local criminals and as a destination for sex tourists rather than medical ones. As recently as 2012, a villager told me, upon being asked about this:

> Every weekend they used to drive up in their flashy cars and their expensive clothes. They played music loudly throughout the night. They drank large amounts of alcohol and swore loudly. After the incident, when police raided the complex, they found illegal guns and bombs made by the gang. Ever since the arrests, some of the gang has left, but many are still there.

Whether or not these particular rumours were true, like other tourist sites, Vedic Village did attract young middle-class men to consume alcohol and enjoy music and dancing, all of which is seen as deviant behaviour in conservative middle-class circles and among many villagers. Furthermore, immoral practices followed on, stemming from initial threats and intimidations by thugs who worked at the behest of the land developers. Locals regularly describe land grabs in which realtors collude with politicians of all stripes and at all levels to acquire land – often paying far below market prices. Dey, Samaddar, and Sen (2013) argue that this is not uncommon and was employed in the case of Rajarhat as a whole. In the case of Vedic Village, when questions were raised in 1999 as to why developers of Vedic Village were able to acquire land beyond the 24-acre ceiling imposed by the West Bengal Land Reforms Act, the state government initially seized the additional 50-plus acres that Vedic Realty had purchased. But according to local social justice activists, the private developer sued the government, which responded either half-heartedly or not at all, and by 2002 the state government had leased back that land, along with an additional 75 acres to build an expanded set of condominiums, arguing that it had been persuaded of the merit of the project.

Also central to the villagers' complaints beyond those about rude neighbours and forced land acquisitions was the sense that they were being left out of the transformations taking place in their region. One of the villagers I spoke to in 2012 suggested that spatial segregation was a main reason for this sense of exclusion:

> Only if you can find work in the complex can you pass beyond its gates. Even if you walk by the front gateway you will often be harassed by guards. And our local markets suffer as no one who visits here stops, they just drive to the complex and go in.

While tensions have eased off since the violence in 2009 and most of the criminal activity centered on Vedic Village has disappeared, the developers' plans have not slowed down. In 2010, they partnered with Best Western to become its first Premier hotel in India, focusing primarily on the medical tourism potential of Vedic Village (Saha, 2010). While this is a smart move and increases the 'international' appeal of the complex, more important is Vedic Realty's revival of a plan to build an IT-focused upscale township, including over 2.5 million ft^2 of new homes along with a world-class golf course on some 1,500 acres acquired, again – according to local social justice activists – through dubious means. The violence in 2009 had led the previous state government to shelve the proposed development, as the then-opposition Trinamool Congress (TMC) raised concerns. Once in power, the same TMC gave its blessings to the new development (Basu and Datta, 2013).

This scheme aims at drawing IT companies such as Bangalore-based Infosys and Wipro and their workers into the township, with the state government receiving land from the developers in exchange for building civic infrastructure (including roads) and providing utilities beyond regular municipal services. Critics of the scheme argue that this proposal has also brought back the heavy-handed tactics of developers with regard to land acquisition, which will lead to considerable intimidation of local farmers. Those who object to the expansion of Vedic Village face violent threats from thugs who are well-connected to all political parties concerned. As a new era dawns on Vedic Village, it is worth asking what its impact on local residents has been. This was reflected in a newspaper editorial shortly after the violence in 2009:

> The arson and mob fury at Vedic Village on Sunday shows that the quiet, green countryside which has gone from sleepy village to global village in a matter of years is being wracked by disruptive forces. Mushrooming highrises, malls and eateries have brought in upscale city residents, for whom the village is nothing more than a weekend boutique destination. Villagers not only feel left out of the dazzling show but also know that culturally, they can never be a part of this.
>
> (*Times of India*, 2009b)

South City

Unlike the two other developments detailed in this chapter, the original South City Projects are not located in a peripheral area of Kolkata such as a former industrial site or the Wetlands. Instead, it has been built right in the heart of existing neighbourhoods in the southern part of the city. South City is a township that has come to dominate these residential neighbourhoods and is a joint venture between developers with a track record of constructing such sites at the fringes of Kolkata. As plans for this development became more concrete, billboards that were displayed across the city long before the earth had been broken invited prospective buyers to "live the way the world does" and promised "a lifestyle of international standards" (South City, 2014). The original South City comprises over 30 acres of "eco-friendly design" residential towers (which the promoters describe as "soaring"), a school, a shopping mall, entertainment complexes, and the ubiquitous country club. It prominently features "80% green space" and claims to be "perfect for children to rediscover the wonders of nature." This township, located amidst established, middle-class neighbourhoods, which over the years have become desirable locations, has been an enormous success, selling out all of its units. Building on this success, the same development group recently completed South City Garden and South City Bel-Air, while South City Galaxy and South City Villa are under construction. Unlike the other two cases profiled in this chapter, South City is a considerable success. The consortium of developers that comprise the South City Group has even taken its success abroad, with a project underway to build a South City–style project in post-conflict Colombo, Sri Lanka (*The Hindu*, 2011).

As mentioned previously, one of the main reasons that South City has been such a success is its location, which is in the middle of desirable middle-class neighbourhoods. Another factor is that the developers have had a reputation for successful completion and delivery of previous projects, primarily in the EKW area. South City followed those but went beyond them in size: where earlier projects had comprised a handful of apartment towers, this was an entire 32-acre township located within the boundaries of the city itself. As the developers themselves stated, it is designed to provide "a city within the city" (South City, 2014). Built on the grounds of a former industrial site, it promised to be the largest development in Kolkata, with the tallest towers, the biggest mall in eastern India, the best school, the most exclusive country club, the most beautifully landscaped pond, and so on (South City, 2014). When I visited the city in 2004, the project was little more than a set of plans. By 2007, work on three of its four towers had begun, and by 2012, it had not only been almost completed, but it had also become a landmark, especially because of its mall.

One promoter told me that all the units allotted to him had sold out quickly and often at levels far above the original asking price of approximately US $300,000 for a three-bedroom flat. Indeed, he said that some 1,500 out of 1,740 total units were purchased before a single tower broke ground. In line with the projects in the Wetlands, here, too, the lure of the location, the idea of a global lifestyle, and the fact that perhaps transnational families had invested here had made all the difference. Along the same lines, another promoter boasted that fully 35 percent of apartment owners were NRIs and that some 50 percent of flats were being reserved for overseas Indians and asserted that promoting a building with NRI inhabitants was a great marketing tool to get locals in, echoing the sentiments I discussed previously in this chapter. Once again, when considering what lies behind these statements, we must keep in mind not only the localized self-interest of promoters but also the broader "developer/promoter speak" that Searle argues puts the Global Indian to work in order to sell realty (Searle, 2013).

But although South City has been a far more successful project than either KWIC or Vedic Village, it has encountered its own share of controversy. The main concerns were related to environmental degradation, labor law violations, and forced displacement of slum-dwellers. South City is located on the site of the old and once-prosperous Usha sewing machine factory, which had fallen into disrepair, and borders Vikramgarh Jheel, one of the largest remaining water bodies within Kolkata. Locals have long sought to clean up the increasingly polluted area so that it might function as a mixed-use landscape for recreation, fishing, and other community needs (Vasundhara Foundation Kolkata, 2010). But instead of being able to develop a sustainable neighbourhood space, environmentalists and some local residents found that their small-scale vision confronted a scheme that was built upon large-scale profits and global imageries of affluent lifestyles. As a local environmental activist pointed out:

> When South City engages in this illegal construction and there is no penalty, how can the city penalize others who then also begin to engage in illegal construction? How can we as activists say something to others who flout the laws when the biggest flouters can get away with it? What if there is a small factory on the edge of the pond or a household of slum dwellers who pollute it? Is it fair to penalize them and not South City? The GoWB has made a finding of illegal encroachment – of more than 1 meter of a pond of approximately 10 total meters – the CPM and now the TMC have both said it is encroachment, the TMC have even held mass meetings about it. But nothing is done. This is not surprising – who benefits from South City's construction? Not just the city but the mayor and other political elites.

Many who live in the surrounding areas also wondered how the influx of so many affluent newcomers and cars would affect noise and air pollution levels. Others questioned the wisdom of such dense development within an existing residential neighbourhood, which would no doubt create problems with services supplied by the municipality and create competition for city services. As the towers took shape, protests grew on multiple levels. Trade unions protested the often shoddy and unsafe working conditions that led to several worker deaths during construction (*Sanhati*, 2006). Several residents' groups filed court cases based on grounds of environmental degradation; namely, the increase in noise pollution, congestion, and traffic in the area both during and after construction (Vasundhara Foundation Kolkata, 2010). Housing and poverty activists rallied around Sambhu Singh, one of the few remaining workers associated with the Usha factory, who refused to be displaced for the new developments, though some 7,000 other residents had been unceremoniously evicted already. He died under mysterious circumstances but not before successfully drawing attention to the problems with the South City Projects (Basu, 2011). Environmental groups, mostly from middle-class neighbourhoods around the project, have decried the development's illegal encroachment onto a full acre of the existing water body and have filed lawsuits to halt construction. Several state and federal agencies concurred and ordered that development of the third and fourth towers of South City should be halted (Basu, 2006). But in spite of all these concerns and actions of various stakeholders, the project went ahead with support from government officials, who lauded it as a prestigious project and a landmark development symbolizing Kolkata's renewal. And while activists among some locals christened South City "Towers of Violation" (Vasundhara Foundation Kolkata, 2010), to most it became simply another fact of life in a rapidly changing cityscape.

By 2012, South City was already well-established, and most of the units had been sold – quite the opposite of the experiences of KWIC and Vedic Village. The primary tenants are locals, but a good number of NRIs have also bought flats in the units. The township as a whole is a crowded and vibrant space with a huge glittering mall as its focal point and a destination site in its own right, full of international brands and franchises, designer labels, supermarkets, luxury goods, and omnipresent security on every floor. Testimony to the projects' international allure, the on-site multiplex cinema shows Hollywood and Bollywood films, and an on-site school boasts that it will "bring out the David Beckham, Bill Gates, or President Obama" in the children who attend (South City International School, 2012). For those who can gain entry, South City is the realization of neoliberal, consumerist, and middle-class fantasies – shiny toys, affluence and convenience, and participation in leisure activities apparently occurring everywhere across the globe.

Here, as elsewhere in the new globalized middle-class spaces emerging across urban India, it is the imagined membership in a cosmopolitan community of consumers that lies at the heart of the message that South City's developers harnessed in their advertising. Glossy demonstration units were on hand to entice locals, and massive billboards offered the opportunity to imagine how it would feel to "live in the sky," "own a home with India's biggest swimming pool," and "live the way the world does" (Bose, 2014). On the larger global stage, South City Corporation sends its promoters on the roadshows discussed previously, where they compete with developers from across the country who visit foreign sites with large potential NRI markets or diaspora populations. The message sent to such audiences also invokes 'global living,' but rather than offering the opportunity to enter an aspirational cosmopolitan lifestyle, the focus of such sales pitches has been on providing a dwelling with all the modern conveniences and standards that owners may be familiar with and expect from experience in other parts of the world. If the effort is to sell a second home away from home, prospective clients must be persuaded that they will get value for their money; one of the biggest challenges that one of the promoters told me he faced was in getting NRIs to abandon their preconceived mistrust of buildings and developers in Kolkata and India.

In 2012, I conducted interviews with a number of owners of South City units in order to chart their experiences with the development. While it had sold well and instead of the originally planned three towers, a total of five had been completed by then, it was important to find out whether South City's vision had been realized. In other words, my interviews were probing what 'international-style living' looked like on the ground. Of the South City owners I interviewed, none were full-time residents, but all treated the flat as a second home to be used for annual visits with friends and family. They are based in Australia, Canada, Western Europe, or the US, some of them spending up to 6 months in India. When asked what drew them back to Kolkata, most alluded to family ties, especially care for elderly relatives. Thus, a retired executive from Chicago explained:

> My mother is older now and needs me to be around. My own children are grown and so I am spending half of the year in India. I stayed with her in our family house the first two years but it is old and inconvenient. Now I can be close by to help but still be comfortable.

Explaining why it was so important to live in Kolkata, an architect based in London argued that he felt a strong obligation and desire to return annually:

> I need to return every year. I cut back on other luxuries in order to do it. But I have to admit it is much easier now that I have this flat to stay in.

Many others echoed similar sentiments and related the relief and pleasure they experienced now that it had become so much more "comfortable" and "easy" to stay in the city. A number of my interlocutors spoke approvingly of South City and cited it as evidence that Kolkata was on the right developmental trajectory. Thus, a software engineer based in California said:

> It's about time that Kolkata got its act together. I still don't trust that it truly has, at least as far as the politics goes. But at least all the new construction and Rajarhat and South City show that there is a lot of promise.

Along the same lines, a doctor from Toronto marvelled at the physical changes that developments like South City seem to induce:

> When I first stepped into this flat and came up here to the third floor, I opened the windows and felt a breeze I had never felt before in Calcutta. It was cool and refreshing and clean. I couldn't hear the sounds of the city at all. In fact, I felt as though I wasn't in Calcutta at all.

But South City did not deliver on all fronts; for example, another California-based IT professional complained:

> This is not a cheap apartment. I could have bought one for much less elsewhere. But the developers have a good reputation and the model unit was very impressive. When I came to take possession I was shocked – unfinished, dirty, dusty, completely lacking in the features I was sold on. When I complained to the management it was almost impossible to get them to act promptly.

These complaints were echoed in the comments of a London marketing executive, who also said that the property managers, Jones Lang LaSalle Meghraj, the Indian subsidiary of the global real estate services firm, were not delivering finished flats to the NRIs:

> Every time I have contacted them they fob me off with some excuse. They promise that work will be done and it is not. I feel in dealing with some of them that they think they can trick me because I am not here most of the time. If South City wants to keep NRIs happy, they need to do a better job of delivering on its promises.

While these complaints about the state of the actual flats were common, further problems seem to have arisen in relation to the 'public' green areas, so essential to the notion of 'green living in the city.' The same IT engineer from California cited previously had this to say:

> Where are the water features? Why is the pond half-finished? Where is the opportunity to relax in the outdoors? The township is supposed to be an oasis in the middle of the city. I don't see any of that.

Beyond doubt, the part of the development that has most fully delivered on its promise of "global living" has been the South City Mall attached to the towers. But for many of those who were sold flats in the complex, the success of the mall and the poor condition of their own apartment towers presented a stark contrast. This sore point was addressed by a Toronto-based banker, who felt that

> if they put half the work into the apartment towers that they did into building the mall, I wouldn't have any complaints. It looks like all their efforts went into making that spectacular. Maybe they could have used some of the leftover material to spruce up our building.

One has to admit that the breach between the promise of South City and the disappointments of the aforementioned owners is not limited to an international-style development in a city of the Global South; we might find such complaints by many a condominium owner in many a place, yet the implications in this context are potentially more significant. South City and similar projects in Kolkata are not simply buildings that may fail to live up to their potential. They are indicative of a particular developmental strategy that relies on successful appeals to transnational subjects and local elites alike. If the space between the promise of "global living" and actual life remains so wide, what will be the effect on the remade city? Will the projects eventually lose their appeal and become the hollow shells of migra-villages bemoaned elsewhere (Kapur and McHale, 2005)? For now, residents in South City are not leaving in any numbers. Ironically, the disappointment in the lack of promised amenities seems to be one point on which the Global Indians in South City and locals might make common cause – upon seeing the shabby state of the pond area, the residents' association in the towers reached out to the same environmental organizations that had fought the construction in the first place for help arriving at a solution. This is not perhaps as surprising as it might seem; after all, many foreign owners have many local relations living nearby.

But this cannot distract from the fact that ambitious developments such as South City or Rajarhat still struggle to deliver what lies at the core of their marketing promise – namely, access to global lifestyles and the remaking of Indian cities in that mold. While they constitute modern habitats in cosmopolitan and metropolitan areas and are driven by a sense of exclusivity and of 'having made it,' they struggle to validate Kolkata as a global city, for this validation hinges on little else than these developments. The desire to become such a place has combined with the goal of overcoming its history of urban decay and stagnation to keep the construction industry in Kolkata energized. It has led to a wide array of collaborations – some legal and many illegal – between development agencies, foreign investors, urban planners, civil servants, politicians, local developers, and other actors dreaming of remaking the city. It has also made the concerns of local residents, activists, and even residents fade in the face of the imperative to overcome the challenging reputation of Kolkata by building more and more massive housing projects.

References

Ambuja Neotia (2014). "Realty." Retrieved May 11, 2014, from http://www.ambujaneotia.com/realty/default.aspx.

Bardhan, P. and D. Mookherjee (2012). Political clientelism and capture: theory and evidence from West Bengal, India. *WIDER Working Paper, 2012*. Helsinki, United Nations University (UNU).

Basu, J. (2006). "Key curb on mega estate: law flout alleged, builders deny." *The Telegraph of India*. Retrieved November 25, 2014, http://www.telegraphindia.com/1060301/asp/calcutta/story_5910083.asp.

Basu, M. and R. Datta (2013). "Project to build IT township near Kolkata revived." Retrieved May 11, 2014, from http://www.livemint.com/Politics/lpm7UeZLO357m4mqOJZpYM/Project-to-build-IT-township-near-Kolkata-revived.html?ref=ms.

Basu, S. (2011). "Reeling off the battle against South City Mall." *Deshlai*. Retrieved November 25, 2014, http://deshlai.wordpress.com/2011/02/04/reeling-off-the-battle-against-south-city-mall/.

Baviskar, A. and R. Ray (2011). *Elite and everyman: the cultural politics of the Indian middle classes*. New Delhi, Routledge.

Bengal Silver Spring (2014). "Home page." Retrieved May 11, 2014, from www.thesilverspring.com.

Bose, P. S. (2007). "Dreaming of diasporas: urban developments and transnational identities in contemporary Kolkata." *Topia: Canadian Journal of Cultural Studies* **17**(Spring): 111–130.

Bose, P. S. (2012). Kolkata, transnationalism and the diasporic imaginary. *Indian Transnationalism*. A. Sahoo. New Delhi, Rawat Publications: 75–97.

Bose, P. S. (2014). "Living the way the world does: global Indians and the reshaping of Kolkata." *Annals of the Association of American Geographers* **104**(2): 391–400.

Brosius, C. (2010). *India's middle class: new forms of urban leisure, consumption, and prosperity*. New Delhi, Routledge.

Chakravorty, S. (2005). From colonial city to global city? The far-from-complete spatial transformation of Calcutta. *Globalizing Cities: A New Spatial Order?* P. Marcuse and R. Van Kempen. Oxford, Blackwell: 56–77.

Ciputra Group (2006). "Kolkata West International City." Retrieved July 3, 2006, from http://rc5a.ciputra.com/projects.php?p=kolkata.

Crooks, V., L. Turner, J. Snyder, R. Johnston and P. Kingsbury (2011). "Promoting medical tourism to India: messages, images, and the marketing of international patient travel." *Social Science & Medicine* **72**(5): 726–732.

Dey, I. (2011). New Town labour and transit. *Transit Labour: Circuits, Regions, Borders*. C. Kernow, K. Hepworth, B. Neilson and N. Rossiter. Kolkata, MCRG.

Dey, I., R. Samaddar and S. K. Sen (2013). *Beyond Kolkata: Rajarhat and the dystopia of urban imagination*. New Delhi, Routledge.

Donner, H. (2014). Of untold riches and unruly homes. *Routledge Handbook of Gender in South Asia*. L. Fernandes. London, Routledge: xii.

Grimsey, D. and M. Lewis (2004). *Public private partnerships: the worldwide revolution in infrastructure provision and project finance*. Oxford, Edward Elgar.

Hill, D. and A. Athique (2013). "Multiplexes, corporatised leisure and the geography of opportunity in India." *Inter-Asia Cultural Studies* **14**(4): 600–614.

The Hindu (2011). "Kolkata realtor South City to develop project in Sri Lanka." Retrieved May 11, 2014, from http://www.thehindu.com/business/companies/kolkata-realtor-south-city-to-develop-project-in-sri-lanka/article2433067.ece.

Islam, N. (2013). "New age orientalism: Ayurvedic 'wellness and spa culture.'" *Health Sociology Review* **21**(2): 220–231.

Kapur, D. and J. McHale (2005). *Give us your best and brightest: the global hunt for talent and its impact on the developing world*. Washington, DC, Center for Global Development.

King, A. D. (2004). *Spaces of global cultures: architecture, urbanism, identity*. London, Routledge.

Kolkata West International City (KWIC) (2014a). "Project info." Retrieved May 11, 2014, from http://www.kolkatawest.com/overview/project/index.html.

Kolkata West International City (KWIC) (2014b). "Testimonials." Retrieved May 10, 2014, from http://www.kolkatawest.com/testimonials/index.html.

Law, A. (2011). "Shrachi group fails to deliver on Kolkata luxury apartment project." *The Hindu Business Line*. Retrieved May 11, 2014, from http://www.thehindubusinessline.com/companies/shrachi-group-fails-to-deliver-on-kolkata-luxury-apartment-project/article2729238.ece.

Nair, J. (2005). *The promise of the metropolis: Bangalore's twentieth century.* Oxford, Oxford University Press.

Peck, J., N. Theodore and N. Brenner (2013). "Neoliberal urbanism redux?" *International Journal of Urban and Regional Research* **37**(3): 1091–1099.

Rosedale Garden (2013). "The vision." Retrieved July 13, 2013, from www.rosedalenri.com.

Roy, A. (2011). Re-forming the megacity: Calcutta and the rural–urban interface. *Megacities: Urban Form, Governance and Sustainability.* A. Sorensen and J. Okata. Tokyo, Springer Japan.

Saha, S. (2006a). "A slice of West – an exclusive residential complex on the fringes of Calcutta promises NRIs the standard of living they are used to abroad." *The Telegraph.* Retrieved May 10, 2014, from http://www.telegraphindia.com/1060428/asp/propertt/story_6156981.asp.

Saha, S. (2006b). "West wake-up – a sprawling satellite township that promises a slew of facilities and can house 36,000 people may change the face of Howrah." *The Telegraph.* Retrieved May 11, 2014, from http://www.telegraphindia.com/1060414/asp/propertt/story_6096803.asp.

Saha, S. (2010). "Vedic tie-up with US chain." *The Telegraph.* Retrieved May 5, 2014, from http://www.telegraphindia.com/1100723/jsp/calcutta/story_12705073.jsp.

Samaddar, R. (2012). The social factory: production of the New Town. *Transit Labour: Circuits, Regions, Borders.* C. Kernow, K. Hepworth, B. Neilson and N. Rossiter. Kolkata, MCRG.

Sanhati (2006). "6 workers killed due to negligence: South City construction." Retrieved November 26, 2014, from http://sanhati.com/excerpted/1183/#6.

Searle, L. G. (2013). "Constructing prestige and elaborating the 'professional': elite residential complexes in the National Capital Region, India." *Contributions to Indian Sociology* **47**(2): 271–302.

Searle, L. G. (2014). "Conflict and commensuration: contested market making in India's private real estate development sector." *International Journal of Urban and Regional Research* **38**(1): 60–78.

Sharma, P. D. (2013). "India Property Show 2013 attracts NRI investors." *The Hindu.* Retrieved May 11, 2014, from http://www.thehindu.com/todays-paper/tp-national/india-property-show-2013-attracts-nri-investors/article5130657.ece.

SkyscraperCity (2014). "Kolkata vertical limit – tall buildings guide." Retrieved May 10, 2014, from http://www.skyscrapercity.com/showthread.php?t=1439747.

Smith, M. and L. Puczkó (2013). "Regional trends and predictions for global health tourism." *Wellness Tourism: A Destination Perspective.* C. Voigt and C. Pforr. London, Routledge: 203–213.

South City International School (2012). "Home page." Retrieved November 26, 2014, from http://scis.co.in.

South City Projects (2014). "Home page." Retrieved May 11, 2014, from http://southcityprojects.com.

The Telegraph (2009). "Mob burns resort – fury at murder of teenager in soccer row spills over into Vedic Village." Retrieved May 11, 2014, from http://www.telegraphindia.com/1090824/jsp/frontpage/story_11401133.jsp.

The Telegraph (2013). "Township buyers protest delay." Retrieved May 11, 2014, from http://www.telegraphindia.com/1130925/jsp/calcutta/story_17385595.jsp#.U2_QicalJhM.

Theodore, N., J. Peck and N. Brenner (2011). Neoliberal urbanism: cities and the rule of markets. *The New Blackwell Companion to the City.* G. Bridge and S. Watson. Oxford, Blackwell: 15–25.

Times of India (2009a). "Left out of dazzle and delight, villagers may have struck back." Retrieved May 11, 2014, from http://timesofindia.indiatimes.com/city/kolkata-/Left-out-of-dazzle-delights-villagers-may-have-struck-back/articleshow/4930637.cms?referral=PM.

Times of India (2009b). "Vedic Village mob violence rattles realtors." Retrieved May 11, 2014, from http://timesofindia.indiatimes.com/city/kolkata/Vedic-Village-mob-violence-rattles-realtors/articleshow/4930674.cms.

Toronto-Calcutta Foundation (TCF) (2014). "The Toronto-Calcutta Foundation." Retrieved August 30, 2014, from http://www.toronto-calcutta.org.

Vasundhara Foundation Kolkata (2010). South City controversy: selected documents. Kolkata, Vasundhara Foundation Kolkata.

Vedic Realty (2014). "Type of bungalows." Retrieved May 11, 2014, from http://www.thevedicvillage.com/homes/bungalow.html.

Vedic Village (2014). "About." Retrieved May 11, 2014, from http://www.thevedicvillage.com.

Conclusion

Kolkata, as this book has argued, can be a difficult city. It can be a difficult city to live in and a difficult city to fix, a difficult city to make work. It can be a difficult city to imagine in a new way and a difficult one to imagine operating in any other way than it currently does. But Kolkata can also be a difficult city to let go of, to forget, to hate, or to abandon for many locals and non-residents alike. It is a city that has become synonymous with some with the worst qualities of contemporary urban landscapes – filled with poverty, overcrowding, pollution, and decay (Chattopadhyay, 2006). It is one that is often viewed through a discoloured lens, whether clouded through nostalgia (Suraiya, 2007) or an Orientalist view of an exotic, broken, and barbaric city (Hutnyk, 1996). Yet if this is such a place of disrepute and disrepair, of faded glory and dusty memory, what are we to make of the past two decades in Kolkata's history? Why the explosion of new real estate throughout the city? Why the attempts to materialize connections to global networks of capital, labour, and ideas? Why the investment of time, resources, and ideas into rescuing what appears, from the outside, to be a failed urban experiment? This book seeks to answer these questions by exploring the transformations that are taking place in contemporary Kolkata. To do so, in the preceding chapters, I have examined the processes through which the changes are occurring, analyzed some of the reasons they are taking place, detailed some of their early effects, and speculated on the long-term impacts of this strategy of urban redevelopment.

I argue in this book that what is taking place in Kolkata today represents the intersection, collusion, and collision of a number of different sets of ideas, interests, and flows. We see globalization manifest in many forms – aspects of neoliberal urbanization that are currently sweeping over cities across the planet, the emergence of transnational middle-class identities, the varied discourses of global environmentalism, the old-school developmentalism of international financial institutions, and the unabated practice of speculative land grabbing. But what is taking place in Kolkata is also intensely local and parochial – the politics of individual municipalities and of the state government, the clash between entrenched bureaucracies and radical activists, the reassertion of nativist sentiments and identities, a struggle to define the right to the city among its varied inhabitants, and the corruption and criminality of various actors in different stages of the process of change.

As Roy has pointed out in her important work on cities across the world, one cannot simply see all urban sites as blank canvasses on which global processes can smoothly work to produce a final product (Roy, 2003, 2009, 2011a). Indeed, she has gone so far as to call the fits and starts of Kolkata's transformations a "blockade" on the road to achieving world-class city status (Roy, 2011b). At the same time, Kolkata's struggles to re-invent itself are neither unique nor divorced from what is going on elsewhere. The desire to create a global city is an almost ubiquitous obsession among politicians, planners, and significant numbers of the broader public in urban centers across the world. In Kolkata, as elsewhere, diasporas are heralded as agents of change and ideal bodies in the remade city – even in a place that has little experience or history with return migrants investing in their former home. And managing the contradictions between global desires and imperatives on one hand and local realities and resistance on the other has challenged and, in some cases, overcome some of the key participants in the changes taking place in Kolkata today. Not least of these has been the former Marxist-led state government of West Bengal for whom Kolkata was part of a grand new experiment in neoliberal restructuring, adopting a business-friendly posture in order to woo urban middle-class voters outside its rural power base. As with its higher-profile disasters in rural restructuring, the strategy was a failure, one that led to its eventual ouster (Bardhan and Mookherjee, 2012). Despite the government's downfall, the plans originally initiated by leftist political parties for urban redevelopments in Kolkata's metropolitan region have not been shelved by their successors. To the contrary – if anything, they have been intensified.

At first glance, it seems that the manner in which Kolkata is being remade is one that seems at odds with its history as a center of leftist political activism and reform. But it is through neoliberal urbanism and governance that the Left Front hung on to power until, partly as a result of the changes that it had unleashed, the populist leader Mamata Banerjee and her Trinamool Congress took over. What this new government now claims as transformations they have initiated are in fact largely institutional and legal conditions first brought about under a leftist alliance at the state (and sometimes municipal) level, and it is those that are now continuing under its center–right successors. The creation of a cityscape in accordance with neoliberal policies has been embraced by political leaders, technocrats, outside experts, and much of the middle class. It is an imaginary characterized by privatized services; scarcity of truly public spaces; increasing speculation in land and property; and the growth of public–private partnerships to design, build, and govern the city. Yet this new version of urban life comes at a heavy price for many. From overburdening local utilities and services to restricting the use and access of natural resources, from evictions and displacement to the appropriation or devaluation of land and property, there is evidently little room in the Kolkata of the future for many of its current denizens and their livelihoods and pastimes.

So while the Trinamool Congress may have gained their political power by seemingly championing the rights of the disenfranchised in the face of ill-advised attempts to create special economic zones and foreign investment, once in power, they – not surprisingly – doubled down on a set of strategies aimed to increase globally oriented investments in urban infrastructure as the key to re-imagining Kolkata. As I have argued in this book, a focus on global processes and identities might seem a curious strategy in a place with as limited a history of diasporic emigration as Kolkata and West Bengal (at least when compared to places in India like Gujarat, Punjab, or Kerala). And we must keep in mind the cautions offered by the work of Searle (2013, 2014), Donner (2014), and Brosius (2010) and recognize that the desirability and distinctiveness of Global Indians for promoters, developers, planners, and politicians may be little more than middle-class fantasies being used to justify projects and investments and indeed to simply sell apartments. And yet it *is* Global Indians, not just successful Indian professionals aspiring to middle-class lifestyles, who are being embedded in these new developments and used generically as a key marketing tool. This therefore raises two of the central questions of this book: what is it that makes an 'international-style' housing project so attractive to potential customers? And why would the idea of a city filled with Global Indian bodies and projects meant to house them be so persuasive to civic leaders as a strategy for rejuvenating the city?

To try and grapple with these questions, I have examined in the various chapters of this book both the ideologies behind Kolkata's transforming urban landscape and the processes that seek to bring the global city into being. I have argued that like many other cities, regions, or even nations, Kolkata is being re-imagined through the mobilization of diasporic capital, subjects, and neoliberal ideologies. I have therefore explored the rise of the iconic figure of the Global Indian or non-resident Indian (NRI) at length – and the political and cultural construction of transnational subjectivities – which are interpellated, designed, embraced, and used to justify a specific vision of the urban future. I have also looked at a range of transnational practices and the ways in which diasporas can help to catalyze development in an old homeland – through remittances and investments, through relief efforts and tourism, via philanthropic initiatives and charities. I have also argued that beyond such a material presence (of bodies and capital), we must consider what Maimbo and Kapur (2005) have referred to as the "non-pecuniary" transnational practices through which diasporic groups might help transform their former homes. In this sense, it is almost immaterial how many Global Indians might be purchasing flats in South City, Vedic Village, or Rajarhat. It is the power and the resulting influence of the *idea* rather than the actual physical presence of Global Indians (whether in person or in the form of resources) that are crucial for understanding the ongoing transformations of Kolkata. Thus, we should read the various local demands for amenities that characterize a world-class city in light of the need to attract Global Indians – or those who might wish to live in simulacra of their habitus – back to the city but also understand such demands as an aspirational claim to become like them.

This is not to suggest that what is happening in Kolkata is all fiction and fantasy. Changes are happening on the ground, with very clear winners and losers in contests over space. This, again, is not an uncommon story across the world, and to better situate the Kolkata case, I have examined at length some of the important scholarship and debates regarding global cities, world cities, ordinary cities, and so on. The issue is not one of rankings or determining the boxes that Kolkata must check off to ascend the ladder of the global urban hierarchy; rather, it is to see what kinds of processes and patterns emerge from several decades of world-city building across the globe. Of several important themes that seem to be in common are those of securitization and segregation, gentrification, dispossession, and the struggle over the right to the city (Harvey, 2008; Bridge, 2007; Genis, 2007; Atkinson and Bridge, 2005). While the envisaged transformation of Kolkata might make perfect sense to elites and those who aspire to return the city to its former glory, questions of social justice and citizenship are raised at different junctures throughout this book. The new skyscrapers that dominate the skyline, the glittering malls that fetishize a global consumerist lifestyle, the bypasses and flyovers that allow cars to literally bypass the old city's roads, the entertainment complexes, golf courses, and restaurant chains that bring the promise of global leisure, the 'international' schools all raise the same question: who is part of this new world?

The emphasis on the Kolkata being rebuilt is on a city that works. But for whom? The new city of joy is not imagined as a city of justice – anti-poverty campaigns or programs to improve education and healthcare or build affordable housing receive little notice or funding. The Kolkata Environmental Improvement Project, with its large-scale investment in sanitation infrastructure, relies in large part on external funding and, as this book details, has serious problems in delivering on many of its promises. If the main way through which the urban poor – the vast majority of Kolkata's population – engage with the newly built spaces is by providing cheap labour either in construction or as domestic help, what is their investment in and – more importantly – what is their right to the new city? If the new Kolkata is being built primarily for elites and the aspiring middle classes, how will these developments affect the marginalized, the slum-dwellers, the peri-urban populations, and the nearby villagers? What will be the price they pay for the privilege of living in a global city?

What has become clear throughout my long engagement with urban change in Kolkata is that it has been accompanied by high costs, as in almost all modern metropolises that tailor themselves to the tastes and self-perceptions of a global professional class (Searle, 2013; Atkinson and Bridge, 2005). First, there are the financial resources and the time spent planning this transformation, both of which have to be diverted from other sites. Furthermore, as critics in the city have pointed out again and again, human costs of this kind of development are by no means negligible and may increase in the long term (Dey, Samaddar, and Sen, 2013; Banerjee, 2012; Samaddar, 2009). For local critics of the transformations taking place in Kolkata, the prominence of the Global Indian in justifying the changes may exacerbate the sense that large sections of the population are excluded from the developments surrounding and affecting them. Those who are vocal in their criticism comprise not only activists and the urban poor but also the lower ranks of the local middle class, ethnic minorities, and those belonging to the city's hinterland. For many of them, there is already ample evidence that outside interests and identities are taking precedence over local needs and desires (Ganguly-Scrase and Scrase, 2009). To better understand this sense of grievance and the tangled skein of local and global discourses and priorities intersecting in Kolkata's development, I explore the history and context of the city's growth and some of the long-standing challenges in its expansion over the years. I am particularly interested in how some of the global processes that are of interest to me – transnationalism, urbanization, environmentalism – appear on the ground in Kolkata.

For example, it became clear through the course of my interviews with owners that 'globality' carried only so much weight with the purchasers of many of the flats being sold. Even when they were buying into what they conceive as 'international' – that is, valorized by global, standardized designs – many were bound to, at the same time, refer to local political and social conventions, values, and relationships. As part of such Global Indian middle-class identities, access to 'global' lifestyles works in tandem with excessive references to 'Indian' values (Brosius, 2010; Baviskar and Ray, 2011; Fernandes, 2006). Many of the developers and promoters of projects sought to capitalize on such sentiments by celebrating "Indian-ness" (though, interestingly, less so "Bengali-ness") in the form of 'heritage' and 'tradition' as a way of reproducing a sense of superiority in the middle-class Global Indian. Seen in such a light, the new 'international-style' developments play an important role in what Roy (2003) has called the project to recover the 'genteel' middle-class heritage of Kolkata.

But the category of the Global Indian is a far from stable one; indeed, I have argued in this book that it has been from the outset a highly contested and controversial formation everywhere, with little of the unity that its representation(s) in the official politics and the culture industries might suggest. This is even more the case in Kolkata and West Bengal, neither of which has ever belonged to the remittance-rich economies prominent in India. Thus, while its largely Bengali-speaking Hindu diaspora is small and, in comparison, not as affluent, Kolkata seems, in many ways, an unlikely place for the transnational subject to function as a driver of development. However, as a point of reference in middle-class lives across the nation, the Global Indian continues to be an important icon (Baviskar and Ray, 2011; Donner, 2014) and as an aspirational figure appears important within Kolkata as well. For many of my Kolkata-based respondents, their sense of who was doing the developing – outside of a few unique projects such as Rosedale Garden – was that NRIs were rarely involved. Rather, a common perception was that it was a North Indian business class – *Marwaris* – who were invoked most often as the money, the muscle, and the motivators behind the new projects. But again, it is not important whether such a belief is accurate or not – the housing developments that were springing up all over Kolkata were not in any sense viewed as Marwari or even as diasporic Bengali: they are ultimately global, built in the assumed style of the Global Indian. It is thus perhaps unsurprising that a certain ambivalence towards the new way of life symbolized by Kolkata's newest developments – even among those who live within them – is partly the result of their 'global' imagery.

There are three particular cases through which I have examined the attempts to turn around Kolkata's fortunes. The first is the ongoing struggle to alternately protect and develop the East Kolkata Wetlands, one of the few areas into which the city can expand if it must. The second is an ambitious plan called the Kolkata Environmental Improvement Project, which aims to spend hundreds of millions of dollars (US) on upgrading the city's sewage and drainage infrastructure, as well as a number of other environmental initiatives. The third comprises some of the actual housing projects that have emerged over the past decade, with particular focus on Kolkata West International City in Howrah, Vedic Village in the heart of the Wetlands, and South City Township in south Kolkata. Together, these cases represent a vision of remaking the city to literally clean it up, to make it more attractive for foreign investment, and to make it more habitable for diasporic bodies (or those with 'international' tastes). Such actions will, in theory, help to deliver global city status to Kolkata and re-invent it both as an idea and as a site of a kind of transnational modernization.

As pointed out throughout, this process of re-imagination hinges largely on the creation and population of idealized city spaces correlative to global success stories. The emerging picture is marked by class-specific inclusions and exclusions and is recognizably cosmopolitan. The conditions upon which the new city is built are clear. As pointed out in the chapter on the Wetlands, legal processes enabling development go hand in hand with illegal forms of appropriation, and often the latter precedes the former. The actual restructuring of the city through large-scale environmental infrastructure projects and the construction of affluent enclaves, it is assumed, will attract investors and residents who represent the new global lifestyle, most prominently associated with the information technology (IT) industry. The three cases I look at in detail suggest that development in the form of intervention in Kolkata's urban and peri-urban environment has the potential to redefine the Bengali diaspora's relationship with the homeland materially and ideologically. But at least equally important are the effects it has on the city, its permanent residents, class relations, livelihoods, identities, and equality. Thus, the plans to refashion the city as a transnational site through new plans for housing, roads, open spaces, and sanitation may irrevocably change the lives of current city-dwellers beyond recognition. As a result, the notion of 'Kolkata' itself has become a site of conflict and confusion arising from concerted efforts to fit with a model of dynamic global urbanity.

These complications are, on one hand, those of process, as a variety of actors engage in responding to the policy requirements and practical tasks of Kolkata's development. On the other hand, they relate to core questions regarding the common good. This, in turn, raises the issue of who the people of Kolkata are: are they being increasingly defined by their ability to meet the cost of living in global Kolkata? Does development have to be the result of displacement? This is already a contentious issue, no matter whether people are being displaced by actual diasporic interlopers or by the local beneficiaries of developmental action set in motion by the perceived needs of the diasporic consumer. It is obvious that this kind of top-to-bottom development brings to the fore the rifts inherent in India's economic system, political culture, and social relations. The visible distinction between those who live in gated, air-conditioned towers and those who were evicted from the land on which these residences were built is symbolic of this. We need to ask in light of such dynamics whether the NRI present in the figure of the Global Indian could be seen as a new colonist.

In the frenetic – and so far highly successful – marketing of developments as sites of generic international lifestyles, Kolkata is providing a stark lesson on processes of cultural colonialization. Mimicking the living space and attendant amenities of upscale New York, London, or suburban Toronto gives Rajarhat or South City the cachet of both exclusivity and affluence. Besides, it is easy to persuade Kolkata's elite and Kolkata's diasporic population that their residences must not be less 'international' than those enjoyed by their Bangalore or Gurgaon equivalents. Thus, while marketing succeeds because affluent Indians are competitive, the existing gap between rich and poor in urban India (and not only in India) is in fact growing, especially where cities are supposedly catching up and becoming revitalized. Given that the attraction of a 'world-class' city at the moment draws arguably more locals than diasporic children, the distinction between them can barely be maintained. We need to ask in this context whether those whose economic and social relations span the globe, such as IT workers, construction professionals, and financial executives, can really be defined in terms of their nationality alone. Kolkata seems to be an excellent site to study the transformations that urban restructuring brings about. There is no question that change in the mold of middle-class desires is irreversible, even if it were deemed necessary to right some of the accompanying wrongs. Thus, in Kolkata, as elsewhere in India, the intervention in people's lives via spatial practices has far-reaching implications for civil society, especially the existing axioms of social justice and environmental stewardship in postcolonial India.

Is Kolkata, with its as-yet-incomplete transformation, a cautionary tale then? Is it one in which urban redevelopment has been a failure? Such a claim would be hard to sustain for some audiences, especially in the face of the very real changes that have altered the city's landscape over the past two decades. We must still ask ourselves, however, who it is that stands to gain if the city is remade along 'global' lines. The city's present and future, I have argued in this book, are today at an important juncture, where many decision-makers and large sections of Kolkata's population have invested considerable time, resources, and political influence in its rebirth through 'development' understood in terms of urban infrastructure. If, they argue, twenty-first-century Kolkata is to prosper, it needs to re-invent itself as a 'global city' and overcome the narrative of decline through a material re-ordering of urban space. While, as I have pointed out, Kolkata is not singular in employing such a strategy of becoming 'world class,' that strategy and its underlying ideology have become the most ubiquitous discourse among civic leaders and urban planners. In the context of Kolkata, that strategy is construed as the only antidote to urban decay and crises. In common with other cities in the Global South, those in positions of power in

Kolkata have long sought to utilize its diasporic connections to forge, maintain, and demonstrate its world-class status. In their vision, the new Kolkata will be a city in which diasporic Bengalis will be proud to live, and their presence will in turn change the fortune of its residents as a whole.

References

Atkinson, R. and G. Bridge, Eds. (2005). *Gentrification in a global context: the new urban colonialism.* London, Routledge.

Banerjee, S. (2012). "The march of the mega-city: governance in West Bengal and the wetlands to the east of Kolkata." *South Asia Chronicle* **2**(2012): 93–118.

Bardhan, P. and D. Mookherjee (2012). Political clientelism and capture: theory and evidence from West Bengal, India. *WIDER Working Paper, 2012.* Helsinki, United Nations University (UNU).

Baviskar, A. and R. Ray (2011). *Elite and everyman: the cultural politics of the Indian middle classes.* New Delhi, Routledge.

Bridge, G. (2007). "A global gentrifier class?" *Environment and Planning A* **39**(1): 32–46.

Brosius, C. (2010). *India's middle class: new forms of urban leisure, consumption, and prosperity.* New Delhi, Routledge.

Chattopadhyay, S. (2006). *Representing Calcutta: modernity, nationalism and the colonial uncanny.* London, Routledge.

Dey, I., R. Samaddar and S. K. Sen (2013). *Beyond Kolkata: Rajarhat and the dystopia of urban imagination.* New Delhi, Routledge.

Donner, H. (2014). Of untold riches and unruly homes. *Routledge Handbook of Gender in South Asia.* L. Fernandes. London, Routledge: xii.

Fernandes, L. (2006). *India's new middle class: democratic politics in an era of economic reform.* Minneapolis, University of Minnesota Press.

Ganguly-Scrase, R. and T. J. Scrase (2009). *Globalisation and the middle classes in India: the social and cultural impact of neoliberal reforms.* London, Routledge.

Geniş, Ş. (2007). "Producing elite localities: the rise of gated communities in Istanbul." *Urban Studies* **44**(4): 771–798.

Harvey, D. (2008). *Social justice and the city.* Revised edition. Athens, GA, University of Georgia Press.

Hutnyk, J. (1996). *The rumour of Calcutta: tourism, charity and the poverty of representation.* London, Zed Books.

Maimbo, S. and Kapur, D. (2005). *Remittances: development impacts and future prospects.* Washington, DC, World Bank.

Roy, A. (2003). *City requiem Calcutta: gender and the politics of poverty.* Minneapolis, University of Minnesota Press.

Roy, A. (2009). "The 21st-century metropolis: new geographies of theory." *Regional Studies* **43**(6): 819–830.

Roy, A. (2011a). "Slumdog cities: rethinking subaltern urbanism." *International Journal of Urban and Regional Research* **35**(2): 223–238.

Roy, A. (2011b). The blockade of the world-class city: dialectical images of Indian urbanism. *Worlding Cities: Asian Experiments and the Art of Being Global.* A. Roy and A. Ong. Oxford, Wiley-Blackwell: 259–278.

Samaddar, R. (2009). "Primitive accumulation and some aspects of work and life in India." *Economic and Political Weekly* **44**(18): 33–42.

Searle, L. G. (2013). "Constructing prestige and elaborating the 'professional': elite residential complexes in the National Capital Region, India." *Contributions to Indian Sociology* **47**(2): 271–302.

Searle, L. G. (2014). "Conflict and commensuration: contested market making in India's private real estate development sector." *International Journal of Urban and Regional Research* **38**(1): 60–78.

Suraiya, J. (2007). *Calcutta: a city remembered.* New Delhi, Bennett, Coleman and Co.

Index

For Product Safety Concerns and Information please contact our EU
representative GPSR@taylorandfrancis.com
Taylor & Francis Verlag GmbH, Kaufingerstraße 24, 80331 München, Germany